MAKING
THE
SOCIAL WORLD

MAKING
THE
SOCIAL WORLD

The Structure of Human Civilization

JOHN R. SEARLE

OXFORD
UNIVERSITY PRESS

2010

OXFORD
UNIVERSITY PRESS

Oxford University Press, Inc., publishes works that further
Oxford University's objective of excellence
in research, scholarship, and education.

Oxford   New York
Auckland   Cape Town   Dar es Salaam   Hong Kong   Karachi
Kuala Lumpur   Madrid   Melbourne   Mexico City   Nairobi
New Delhi   Shanghai   Taipei   Toronto

With offices in
Argentina   Austria   Brazil   Chile   Czech Republic   France   Greece
Guatemala   Hungary   Italy   Japan   Poland   Portugal   Singapore
South Korea   Switzerland   Thailand   Turkey   Ukraine   Vietnam

Published by Oxford University Press, Inc.
198 Madison Avenue, New York, NY 10016

www.oup.com

Library of Congress Cataloging-in-Publication Data
Searle, John R.
Making the social world: the structure of human civilization / John R. Searle.
          p.   cm.
ISBN 978–0–19–539617–1
1. Social sciences–Philosophy. 2. Civilization.
3. Social epistemology. I. Title.
H61.S4475 2009
300.1—dc22
2009013179

1 3 5 7 9 8 6 4 2

Printed in the United States of America
on acid-free paper

For Dagmar

CONTENTS

PREFACE

This book attempts to explain the fundamental nature and mode of existence—what philosophers call the essence and the ontology—of human social institutional reality. What is the mode of existence of nation-states, money, corporations, ski clubs, summer vacations, cocktail parties, and football games, to mention just a few? I attempt to explain the exact role of language in the creation, constitution, and maintenance of social reality.

The book continues a line of argument begun in my earlier book, *The Construction of Social Reality.*[1] One way to highlight the puzzling character of social ontology is to point out an apparent paradox in our understanding of social reality. We make statements about social facts that are completely objective—for example, Barack Obama is president of the United States, the piece of paper in my hand is a twenty-dollar bill, I got married in London, England, and so on. And yet, though these are objective statements, the facts corresponding to them are all created by human subjective attitudes. An initial form of the paradox is to ask, How is it possible that we can have factual objective knowledge of a reality that is created by subjective opinions? One of the reasons I find that question so fascinating is that it is part of a much larger question: How can we give an account of ourselves, with our peculiar human traits—as mindful, rational, speech-act performing, free-will having, social, political human beings—in a world that we know independently consists of mindless, meaningless, physical particles? How can we account for our social and mental existence in a realm of brute physical facts? In answering that question, we have to avoid postulating different ontological realms, a mental and a physical, or worse yet, a mental, a physical, and a social. We are just

1. Searle, John R., *The Construction of Social Reality,* New York: Free Press, 1995.

talking about one reality, and we have to explain how the human reality fits into that one reality.

After I have given a general theory of social ontology, I then try to apply the theory to special questions, such as the nature of political power, the status of universal human rights, and the role of rationality in society.

ACKNOWLEDGMENTS

I have had more help with this book than with any of the other books I have published. Two of the reasons for this are: First, the book is a continuation of a line of argument I begin in *The Construction of Social Reality*,[2] and that argument received a great deal of comment not only from philosophers but from economists, sociologists, psychologists, and social scientists generally. Second, I am a member of the Berkeley Social Ontology Group, in which these and related issues are discussed on a weekly basis. I cannot possibly thank all the people who have been helpful to me, but I must at least mention some of them.

I have had wonderful assistants. It does not give an adequate conception of their contribution to my intellectual life to say that they are "research assistants." All of them were in every sense collaborators with me. I am especially grateful to Jennifer Hudin, Asya Passinsky, Romelia Drager, Beatrice Kobow, Matt Wolf, Anders Hedman, Vida Yao, Danielle Vasak, Biskin Lee, and Francesca Lattanzi.

Nearly all of them are members of the Berkeley Social Ontology Group. Other people in the group who have been especially helpful to me are Cyrus Siavoshy, Andrew Moisey, Marga Vega, Klaus Strelau, Maya Kronfeld, Ásta Sveinsdóttir, Dina Gusejnova, Raffaela Giovagnoli, and Andy Wand.

A number of volumes of journals and collections of essays were devoted to the issues in *The Construction of Social Reality*, and I am grateful for these contributions. Specifically, there was a special issue of *The American Journal of Economics and Sociology*[3] edited by David Koepsell and Laurence S. Moss,

2. Searle, John, *The Construction of Social Reality*, New York: The Free Press, 1995.
3. *The American Journal of Economics and Sociology* 62, no. 1 (January, 2003). Also reprinted as a separate volume, Koepsell, David, and Laurence S. Moss (eds.), *John Searle's Ideas about Social Reality: Extensions, Criticisms, and Reconstructions*, Malden, Mass.: Blackwell, 2003.

entitled *John Searle's Ideas about Social Reality: Extensions, Criticisms, and Reconstructions,* with articles by Alex Viskovatoff, Dan Fitzpatrick, Hans Bernhard Schmid, Mariam Thalos, Raimo Tuomelo, W. M. Meijers, Frank A. Hindriks, Leo Zaibert, Ingvar Johansson, Nenad Miscevic, Philip Brey, and Barry Smith. This was subsequently published as a book.

Roy D'Andrade edited a special issue of *Anthropological Theory*[4] entitled *Searle on Institutions,* with articles by D'Andrade, Steven Lukes, Richard A. Schweder, and Neil Gross. Savas Tsohatzidis edited a volume entitled *Intentional Acts and Institutional Facts: Essays on John Searle's Social Ontology*[5] with articles by Tsohatzidis, Margaret Gilbert, Kirk Ludwig, Seumas Miller, Anthonie Meijers, Hannes Rakoczy and Michael Tomasello, Robert A. Wilson, Leo Zaibert and Barry Smith, Ignacio Sánchez-Cuenca, and Steven Lukes.

The Journal of Economic Methodology published a symposium entitled "The Ramifications of John Searle's Social Philosophy of Economics." This contains articles by Stephan Boehm, Jochen Runde, Philip Faulkner, Peter J. Boettke and J. Robert Subrick, Alex Viskovatoff, and Steven Horwitz.[6]

An international conference held on my work in Bielefeld, under the auspices of ZIF, resulted in a volume called *Speech Acts, Mind, and Social Reality: Discussions with John Searle,*[7] edited by Günter Grewendorf and Georg Meggle. Of the various sections of the conference, one was devoted to social reality with papers by Stanley B. Barnes, Georg Meggle, Josef Moural, David Sosa, and Raimo Tuomela.

Barry Smith edited a volume, *John Searle,*[8] which, along with many articles about other aspects of my work, contains discussions of the issues in this book by Smith, Nick Fotion, Leo Zaibert, and George P. Fletcher. Smith also organized three conferences about social ontology, and one of these, in 2003, was about both my work and that of Hernando de Soto. This resulted in *The Mystery of Capital and the Construction of Social Reality,*[9] edited by Barry Smith, Isaac Ehrlich, and David Mark, with articles relevant to my work by Hernando de Soto, Barry Smith, Jeremy Shearmur, Ingvar Johans-

---

4. *Anthropological Theory* 6, no. 1 (2006).
5. Dordrecht: Springer, 2007.
6. Vol. 9, no. 1 (March, 2002), 1–87.
7. Dordrecht: Kluwer, 2002.
8. Cambridge: Cambridge University Press, 2003.
9. Chicago: Open Court, 2008.

son, Josef Moural, Errol Meidinger, Erik Stubkjær, Daniel R. Montello, Dan Fitzpatrick, and Eric Palmer.

In addition to the published volumes discussing my ideas, I have also benefited from opportunities to present my ideas in lectures and lecture series literally around the world. For me, having my ideas examined, assessed, and attacked is an essential part of doing philosophy. Among my precepts are these: if you can't say it clearly you don't understand it yourself, and if you can't defend it successfully in public debates you shouldn't publish it. I will not attempt to list all or even most of these presentations, but some deserve special mention.

One of the most important to me was the conference *Collective Intentionality VI*, held in Berkeley in July 2008, organized by Jennifer Hudin and Beatrice Kobow. Some of the ideas in this book were presented there as a keynote address, and I benefited from other conference sessions. I also lectured at *Collective Intentionality V* in Rotterdam in 2006. In 2007, I presented some of this material in lectures in Beijing as a plenary speaker to the 13th International Congress of Logic, Methodology and Philosophy of Science at Tsinghua University. I also gave lectures at the East China Normal University in Shanghai. I am immensely indebted to my hosts in China, especially Shushan Cai and He Gang. I gave the Puffendorf Lectures at the University of Lund, Sweden, 2005. My hosts were Åsa Andersson and Victoria Höög, both of whom are founding members of the Berkeley Social Ontology Group. Also in 2007, I gave the Messenger Lectures at Cornell University, where my host was Trevor Pinch.

I have been helped by my Italian friends and colleagues, especially in Torino and Palermo, in each of which I have been a visiting professor twice. I thank Francesca di Lorenzo Ajello, Giuseppe Vicari, Ugo Perone, Bruno Bara, Paolo di Lucia, and Giuseppe Lorini.

The Prague connection is also especially important to me. I have on several occasions addressed the Center for Theoretical Studies. Thanks to Ivan Havel, Josef Moural, and Pavla Toráčová.

In 2008 I gave a series of lectures as the annual Meisterklasse at the University of Konstanz, Germany, organized by Bernhard Giesen. Other institutions where I have exposed some of these ideas to critical scrutiny include the University of Vienna, the University of Hawaii, the University of British Columbia, the Mountain States Philosophy Conference in Durango, Colorado, State University of New York at Albany, the University of Freiburg (Germany), the University of Fribourg (Switzerland), the Max

Planck Institute in Leipzig, the University of Chicago, the Catholic University of Lublin, the TARK conference at Stanford University, the University of Venice, the Neurosciences Institute in San Diego, the Inter-University Centre Dubrovnik, and the University of Herdecke.

For their contributions to these encounters, I am especially grateful to Nikolaus Ritt, Jeannie Lum, Richard Sikora, Margaret Schabas, Dugald Owen, Istvan Kecskes, Michael Kober, Michael Tomasello, Martine Nida-Rümelin, Les Beldo, Gerald Edelman, Zdravko Radman, Chris Mantzavinos, and Markus Witte.

Other friends, colleagues, and students who have been helpful and supportive include Brian Berkey, Ben Boudreaux, Michael Bratman, Gustavo Faigenbaum, Mahdi Gad, Mattia Gallotti, Anne Hénault, Geoffrey Hodgson, Danièle Moyal-Sharrock, Ralph Pred, Axel Seeman, Avrum Stroll, and Jim Swindler.

Special thanks to Romelia Drager for extraordinary efforts at the copy-editing stage of this book and to Jennifer Hudin for preparing the index.

I am sure I have left out people I should thank, but this is at least a start. Most of all, I thank my wife, Dagmar Searle, for her continued help and support, now extending more than fifty-two years, and I dedicate this book to her.

MAKING
THE
SOCIAL WORLD

1

THE PURPOSE OF THIS BOOK

I. Society, the Basic Facts, and the Overall Philosophical Project

This book is concerned with the creation and maintenance of the distinctive features of human society and therefore, of human civilization. Because this investigation is part of a much more general philosophical project, I want to situate this work within that larger question, which I regard as the fundamental question in contemporary philosophy: How, if at all, can we reconcile a certain conception of the world as described by physics, chemistry, and the other basic sciences with what we know, or think we know, about ourselves as human beings? How is it possible in a universe consisting entirely of physical particles in fields of force that there can be such things as consciousness, intentionality, free will, language, society, ethics, aesthetics, and political obligations? Though many, perhaps most, contemporary philosophers do not address it directly, I believe that this is the single overriding question in contemporary philosophy. I have devoted most of my professional life to various aspects of it. This book uses my account of intentionality and my theory of speech acts to explain social ontology. How do we get from electrons to elections and from protons to presidents?

There are two conditions of adequacy on any account of the sort I am about to propose, and I need to state them in advance. First, we must not allow ourselves to postulate two worlds or three worlds or anything of the sort. Our task is to give an account of how we live in exactly one world, and how all of these different phenomena, from quarks and gravitational attraction to cocktail parties and governments, are part of that one world. Our rejection of

3

dualism, trialism[1] and other ontological extravagances is not to be taken as an endorsement of "monism," for the use of the term "monism" already accepts the metaphysical ontologizing that we are out to reject and replace. A second condition of adequacy is that the account must respect the basic facts of the structure of the universe. These basic facts are given by physics and chemistry, by evolutionary biology and the other natural sciences. We need to show how all the other parts of reality are dependent on, and in various ways derive from, the basic facts. For our purposes the two most fundamental sets of basic facts are the atomic theory of matter and the evolutionary theory of biology. Our mental life depends on the basic facts. Both conscious and unconscious mental phenomena are caused by neurobiological processes in the brain and are realized in the brain, and the neuronal processes themselves are manifestations of and dependent on even more fundamental processes at the molecular, atomic, and subatomic levels. Our capacity for consciousness and other mental phenomena is the result of long periods of biological evolution. Collective mental phenomena of the sort we get in organized societies are themselves dependent on and derived from the mental phenomena of individuals. This same pattern of dependence continues higher as we see that social institutions such as governments and corporations are dependent on and derived from the mental phenomena and behavior of individual human beings. This is the *basic requirement* of our investigation: the account must be consistent with the basic facts and show how the nonbasic facts are dependent on and derived from the basic facts. The ambiguity in the expression "basic requirement" is deliberate. I want to capture both the fact that the phenomena we discuss—money, universities, cocktail parties, and income tax—are dependent on more *basic phenomena* and that meeting this condition is the fundamental or *basic requirement* of our enterprise. We have to show how everything we say is not only consistent with but in various ways derived from and dependent on the basic facts.

People brought up on contemporary philosophy will note that I have avoided using the notion of "reduction" and other such notions such as "supervenience." I think these notions have been sources of confusion as

1. The expression "trialism" was invented by Sir John Eccles to name the view that reality consists not in one part as is insisted by monists or two parts as is insisted by dualists, but three parts: the physical, the mental, and "culture in all of its manifestations." Eccles, John, "Culture: The Creation of Man and the Creator of Man," in Eccles (ed.), *Mind and Brain: The Many-Faceted Problems*, Washington: Paragon House, 1982, 65–75.

they tend to cover over crucial distinctions we will need to make in the course of the investigation.

II. The Philosophy of Society

The entire enterprise is in part based on, and in part an attempt to justify, the assumption that we need a new branch of philosophy that might be called "The Philosophy of Society." Philosophical disciplines are not eternal. Some of the most important have been created fairly recently. Perhaps without knowing it, Gottlob Frege, along with Bertrand Russell, Ludwig Wittgenstein, and others, invented the philosophy of language in the late nineteenth and early twentieth centuries. But in the sense in which we now regard the philosophy of language as a central part of philosophy, Immanuel Kant did not have and could not have had such an attitude. I am proposing that "The Philosophy of Society" ought to be regarded as a legitimate branch of philosophy along with such disciplines as the philosophy of mind and the philosophy of language. I believe this is already happening, as is evidenced by the recent interest in questions of "social ontology" and "collective intentionality." One might object that there already was a recognized branch of philosophy called "social philosophy," on which there are numerous university courses. But social philosophy courses, as they have traditionally been conceived, tended to be either the philosophy of social science or a continuation of political philosophy, sometimes called "political and social philosophy." Thus in such a course one is likely to study either such topics as C. G. Hempel on deductive nomological explanations or John Rawls on the theory of justice. I am suggesting that there is a line of research that is more fundamental than either the philosophy of social science or social and political philosophy, namely, the study of the nature of human society itself: what is the mode of existence of social entities such as governments, families, cocktail parties, summer vacations, trade unions, baseball games, and passports? I believe it will deepen our understanding of social phenomena generally and help our research in the social sciences if we get a clearer understanding of the nature and the mode of existence of social reality. We need not so much a philosophy *of* the social sciences of the present and the past as we need a philosophy *for* the social sciences of the future and, indeed, for anyone who wants a deeper understanding of social phenomena.

This investigation is historically situated. It is not the sort of thing that could have been undertaken a hundred years ago or even fifty years ago. In earlier eras, from the seventeenth century until the late twentieth century, most philosophers in the Western tradition were preoccupied with epistemic questions. Even questions about language and society were construed as largely epistemic: How do we know what other people mean when they talk? How do we know that the statements we make about social reality are really true? How do we verify them? These are interesting questions, but I regard them as peripheral. One of the agreeable features of writing in the present era is that we have in large part overcome our three-hundred-year obsession with epistemology and skepticism. No doubt many interesting epistemic questions remain, but in this investigation I will mostly ignore them.

It is an odd fact of intellectual history that the great philosophers of the past century had little or nothing to say about social ontology. I am thinking of such figures as Frege, Russell, and Wittgenstein, as well as Quine, Carnap, Strawson, and Austin. But if they did not address the problems that interest me in this book, they did develop techniques of analysis and approaches to language that I intend to use. Standing on their shoulders, as well as on my own earlier work, I am going to try to look at a terrain they did not see. And why is this an appropriate subject for philosophy and not the proper domain of empirical sciences? Because it turns out that society has a logical (conceptual, propositional) structure that admits of, indeed requires, logical analysis.

III. The Conceptual Apparatus

In this section, I will begin by giving a brief summary of most of the basic conceptual apparatus that I will use in this book. No doubt this will all be done too swiftly, and to get a full understanding you will have to read the rest of the book. But I want you to see from the start what I am up to and why I think it is important.

This work proceeds on the basis of a certain methodological assumption: at the very beginning we have to assume that human society, a society that is importantly different from all other animal societies known to me, is based on certain rather simple principles. Indeed, I will argue that its institutional structures are based on exactly one principle. The enormous complexities of human society are different surface manifestations of an underlying commonality. It is typical of domains where we have a secure understanding of the ontology, that there is a single unifying principle of that ontology. In physics it is the atom, in chemistry it is the chemical bond, in biology it is the cell, in genetics it is the DNA molecule, and in geology it is the tectonic plate. I will argue that there is similarly an underlying principle of social ontology, and one of the primary aims of this book is to explain it. In making these analogies to the natural sciences I do not imply that the social sciences are just like the natural sciences. That is not the point. The point rather is that it seems to me implausible to suppose that we would use a series of logically independent mechanisms for creating institutional facts, and I am in search of a single mechanism. I claim we use one formal linguistic mechanism, and we apply it over and over with different contents.

Before explaining this basic principle that creates and maintains human society, I need to explain half a dozen other notions that relate to that principle.

I. STATUS FUNCTIONS

The distinctive feature of human social reality, the way in which it differs from other forms of animal reality known to me,[2] is that humans have the capacity to impose functions on objects and people where the objects and the people cannot perform the functions solely in virtue of their physical structure. The performance of the function requires that there be a collectively recognized status that the person or object has, and it is only in virtue of that status that the person or object can perform the function in question. Examples are pretty much everywhere: a piece of private property, the president of the United States, a twenty-dollar bill, and a professor in a university are all people or objects that are able to perform certain functions in virtue of the fact that they have a collectively recognized status that enables them to perform those functions in a way they could not do without the collective recognition of the status.

---

2. In this book I sometimes contrast humans and other animals. The point is not to make a plea for the superiority of our species but to analyze the logical structure of some distinctive human phenomena. If it should turn out that some other species also have income tax, presidential elections, divorce courts, and other institutional facts, I welcome them to the club. Their existence would not be an objection to the account but a further subject of investigation.

2. COLLECTIVE INTENTIONALITY

How does the system of status functions work? I will have a great deal more to say about this later, but at present, I can say that for the status functions to actually work, there must be collective *acceptance* or *recognition* of the object or person as having that status. In earlier writings, I tended to emphasize acceptance, but several commentators, especially Jennifer Hudin, thought this might imply approval. I did not mean it to imply approval. Acceptance, as I construe it, goes all the way from enthusiastic endorsement to grudging acknowledgment, even the acknowledgment that one is simply helpless to do anything about, or reject, the institutions in which one finds oneself. So in this book, to avoid this misunderstanding, I will use "recognition" or sometimes the disjunction "recognition or acceptance." The point is that status functions can only work to the extent that they are collectively recognized. I want to emphasize again that "recognition" does not imply "approval." Hatred, apathy, and even despair are consistent with the recognition of that which one hates, is apathetic toward, and despairs of changing.

Status functions depend on collective intentionality. In this book I devote a whole chapter to collective intentionality, so I will not tell you about it now, except to say that a remarkable fact about human beings and some animals is that they have the capacity to cooperate. They can cooperate not only in the actions that they perform, but they can even have shared attitudes, shared desires, and shared beliefs. An interesting theoretical question, by no means resolved by animal psychologists,[3] is, To what extent does collective intentionality exist in other species? But one thing is clear. It exists in the human species. It is only in virtue of collective recognition that this piece of paper is a twenty-dollar bill, that Barack Obama is president of the United States, that I am a citizen of the United States, that the Giants beat the Dodgers three to two in eleven innings, and that the car in the driveway is my property.

3. DEONTIC POWERS

So far I have claimed that there are status functions that exist in virtue of collective intentionality. But why are they so important? Without exception, the status functions carry what I call "deontic powers." That is, they carry

---

3. De Waal, Frans, *Our Inner Ape: A Leading Primatologist Explains Why We Are Who We Are*, New York: Riverhead, 2005; and Call, Joseph, and Michael Tomasello, *Primate Cognition*, New York: Oxford University Press, 1997.

rights, duties, obligations, requirements, permissions, authorizations, entitlements, and so on. I introduce the expression "deontic powers" to cover all of these, both the positive deontic powers (e.g., when I have a right) and the negative deontic powers (e.g., when I have an obligation), as well as other logical permutations such as conditional deontic powers and disjunctive deontic powers. An example of a conditional deontic power would be my power to vote in the Democratic primary if I register as a Democrat. I have the power to vote, but only conditional on registration. An example of a disjunctive deontic power would be my power to register either as a Democrat or as a Republican, but not both.

4. DESIRE INDEPENDENT REASONS FOR ACTION

It is because status functions carry deontic powers that they provide the glue that holds human civilization together. And how do they do that? Deontic powers have a unique trait, again, I think, uncommon and perhaps unknown in the animal kingdom: once recognized, they provide us with reasons for acting that are independent of our inclinations and desires. If I recognize an object as "your property," for example, then I recognize that I am under an obligation not to take it or use it without your permission. Even if I am a thief, I recognize that I am violating your *rights* when I appropriate your property. Indeed, the profession of being a thief would be meaningless without the belief in the institution of private property, because what the thief hopes to do is to take somebody else's private property and make it his own, thus reinforcing his commitment and the society's commitment to the institution of private property. So status functions are the glue that holds society together. They are created by collective intentionality and they function by carrying deontic powers. But that raises a very interesting question: how on Earth could human beings create such a marvelous feature and how do they maintain it in existence once it is created? I will put off answering that question until we get to the discussion in the next section, "Status Functions as Created by Declarations."

5. CONSTITUTIVE RULES

It is important to distinguish at least two kinds of rules. Our favorite examples of rules regulate antecedently existing forms of behavior. For example, the rule "Drive on the right-hand side of the road" regulates driving in the United

States, but driving can exist independently of this rule. Some rules, however, do not just regulate, but they also create the possibility of the very behavior that they regulate. So the rules of chess, for example, do not just regulate pushing pieces around on a board, but acting in accordance with a sufficient number of the rules is a logically necessary condition for playing chess, because chess does not exist apart from the rules. Characteristically, regulative rules have the form "Do X," constitutive rules have the form "X counts as Y in context C." Thus, for example, such and such *counts as* a legal knight move in a game of chess, such and such a position *counts as* checkmate. Applied to institutions, because Barack Obama satisfies certain conditions X, he *counts as* the president Y, of the United States C.

One can multiply examples easily. The piece of paper in my hand *counts as* a twenty-dollar bill, thus giving it a status and with that status a function that it cannot perform without collective recognition of that status. A football game, a stock market transaction, a cocktail party, private property, and the adjournment of a meeting are all examples of status functions that are brought into existence by constitutive rules.

The same principle applies to the most fundamental institution of all: language. But it applies in an importantly different way: the meaning of the sentence "Snow is white" by itself determines that its appropriate utterance *counts as* a statement to the effect that snow is white. You do not need a separate act of "counting as." Why not? I will say more about this difference later, both in this chapter and in Chapter 5.

6. INSTITUTIONAL FACTS

Some facts exist independently of any human institution. I call these brute facts. But some facts require human institutions in order to exist at all. An example of a brute fact is that the Earth is 93 million miles from the sun, and an example of an institutional fact is that Barack Obama is president of the United States. Institutional facts are typically objective facts, but oddly enough, they are only facts by human agreement or acceptance. Such facts require institutions for their existence. Typically, institutional facts are facts that exist only within human institutions. And what exactly is a human institution? We have already seen an implicit answer to that, and I now want to make it explicit. An institution is a system of constitutive rules, and such a system automatically creates the possibility of institutional facts. Thus the fact that Obama is president or the fact that I am a licensed driver or the fact that a chess match was won by a certain person and lost by a certain other person are all institutional facts because they exist within systems of constitutive rules.

IV. Status Functions as Created by Declarations

The elements of the apparatus that I have introduced so far were originally presented in earlier writings by me.[4] The main theoretical innovation of this book, and one, though not the only, reason for my writing it is that I want to introduce a very strong theoretical claim. All institutional facts, and therefore all status functions, are created by speech acts of a type that in 1975 I baptized as "Declarations."[5] To explain that notion, I have to say something about how language works and about speech acts (if you do not understand this now, do not worry too much, because I will spend all of Chapter 4 explaining what language is and how it works). Some speech acts, indeed the philosophers' favorites, function by purporting to represent how things are in the world. To take some philosophical favorites, "The cat is on the mat," "Snow is white," and "Socrates is mortal" are statements that purport to represent how things are in the world, and they are assessed as true or false depending on the extent to which they do successfully represent how things are in the world. I think in rather crude, simple-minded metaphors, so I think of these speech acts as hovering over the world and pointing down at it, as fitting or failing to fit the world, as having what I call the word-to-world direction of fit. I represent these with the downward arrow ↓. The simplest test for whether a speech act has the word-to-world direction of fit is, Can you literally say of it that it is true or false? True if the correct fit exists, false if it does not.

But there are lots of speech acts that are not in the business of trying to tell us how things are in the world. They are trying to change the world to match the content of the speech act. So, for example, if I order someone to leave the room or promise to come and visit someone on Wednesday, in those cases I am not trying to tell them how things are in the world, but I am trying to

4. Especially in Searle, John R., *The Construction of Social Reality*, New York: Free Press, 1995.
5. Searle, John R., "A Taxonomy of Illocutionary Acts," in Keith Gunderson (ed.), *Language, Mind and Knowledge*, Minnesota Studies in the Philosophy of Science, Vol. VII, Minneapolis: University of Minnesota Press, 1975.

change the world by producing a speech act, the aim of which is to cause a change. The order is aimed at causing obedience; the promise is aimed at causing fulfillment. In these cases it is not the aim of the speech act to match an independently existing reality. Rather, the aim is to change reality so that it will match the content of the speech act. If I promise to come and see you on Wednesday, the point of the utterance is to bring about a change in reality by creating a reason for me to come and see you on Wednesday and thus getting me to keep the promise. If I order you to leave the room, the aim is to try to get you to leave the room by way of obeying my order, to get your behavior to match the content of the speech act. I say of these cases that they have the world-to-word direction of fit. Their point is to get the world to change to match the content of the speech act. I represent the upward or world-to-word direction of fit with an upward arrow ↑. There are some other speech acts that I won't go into at present, which don't have either of these directions of fit but where the fit is taken for granted, such as when I apologize for stepping on your foot or thank you for giving me a million dollars. But they are not relevant to our present inquiry, so I will put off their discussion until Chapter 4.

There is a fascinating class of speech acts that combine the word-to-world ↓ and the world-to-word ↑ direction of fit, which have both directions of fit simultaneously in a single speech act ↕. These are cases where we change reality to match the propositional content of the speech act and thus achieve world-to-word direction of fit. But, and this is the amazing part, we succeed in so doing because we represent the reality as being so changed. More than three decades ago, I baptized these as "Declarations." They change the world by declaring that a state of affairs exists and thus bringing that state of affairs into existence.

The most famous cases of Declarations are what Austin called "performative utterances."[6] These are the cases where you make something the case by explicitly saying that it is the case. Thus you make it the case that you promise by saying, "I promise." You make it the case that you apologize by saying, "I apologize." Someone makes it the case that he gives an order by saying, "I order" or even "I hereby order." These are the purest cases of the Declaration.

One of the primary theoretical points of this book is to make a very strong claim. With the important exception of language itself, all of institutional reality, and therefore, in a sense, all of human civilization, is created by speech

6. Austin, John L. *How to Do Things with Words*, Cambridge: Harvard University Press, 1962.

acts that have the same logical form as Declarations. Not all of them are, strictly speaking, Declarations, because sometimes we just linguistically treat or describe, or refer to, or talk about, or even think about an object in a way that creates a reality by representing that reality as created. These representations have the same double direction of fit as Declarations, but they are not strictly speaking Declarations because there is no Declarational speech act.

Let us call these cases where we create an institutional reality of status functions by representing them as existing as "Status Function Declarations" (sometimes for short, "SF Declarations") even in cases where there is no explicit speech act of Declaration. *The claim that I will be expounding and defending in this book is that all of human institutional reality is created and maintained in existence by (representations that have the same logical form as) SF Declarations, including the cases that are not speech acts in the explicit form of Declarations.*

If I am right that all institutional reality is created and indeed maintained in its existence by sets of linguistic representations that have the same logical form as Declarations, then we need to explain how constitutive rules fit in. And I will now attempt to do that. The most general form of the creation of an institutional fact is that we (or I) make it the case by Declaration that the status function Y exists. Constitutive rules of the form "X counts as Y in C" are what we might think of as *standing Declarations.* Thus the rule that says such and such a position in check counts as checkmate can be thought of as a standing Declaration, and specific instances will simply be applications of that rule: a position where the king is in check and there is no legal move by which the king can get out of check counts as checkmate. So we are now distinguishing between the constitutive rule and the applications of the rule in particular cases. The rule itself is a standing SF Declaration and it will be applied in individual cases where there need be no separate act of acceptance or recognition because the recognition is already implicit in the acceptance of the rule. Rules of games and constitutions of nations are typical examples where the constitutive rules function as standing Declarations. So for example, the Constitution of the United States makes it the case by Declaration that any presidential candidate who receives the majority of votes in the electoral college counts as the president-elect. Because the constitutional provision functions as a standing Declaration, no further act of acceptance or recognition is necessary to accept that such and such a candidate is now the elected president. The acceptance of the constitutive rule, which is part of the Constitution itself, is sufficient to commit the participants in the institution to accepting that anybody who satisfies such and such a condition is the president-elect.

This discussion so far reinforces a point made in my earlier work, *The Construction of Social Reality*, and that is that <u>all of institutional reality is created by linguistic representation</u>. You do not always need actual words of existing languages, but you need some sorts of symbolic representation for the institutional fact to exist. As I noted before, there is, however, an interesting and crucial class of exceptions: linguistic phenomena themselves. Thus, the <u>existence of a Declaration is itself an institutional fact</u> and thus a status <u>function</u>. But does it itself require a further Declaration to exist? It does not. Indeed, if it did, we would have an infinite regress. But now, what is it about language that makes it a system of status functions that is exempt from the general requirement that all status functions are created by Status Function Declarations? We <u>use semantics to create a reality that goes beyond semantics</u>, and <u>semantics to create powers that go beyond semantic powers</u>. But the linguistic facts, the fact that such and such an utterance counts as a statement or a promise, are not facts where the semantics goes beyond the semantics. On the contrary, semantics is sufficient to account for the existence of the statement or the promise. The semantic content of the speech act by itself cannot make money or private property, but the <u>semantic content of the speech act by itself is sufficient to make statements</u>, promises, requests, and <u>questions</u>. The difference is in the nature of the meanings involved, and I will explain that difference in much further detail in Chapters 4 and 5.

At first sight, it might seem that formulae of the form "X counts as Y in C" function the same for language as they do for other institutional facts. Thus, it is indeed the case that an appropriate utterance of the sentence "Snow is white" counts as the making of the statement that snow is white, as it is the case that because he meets certain conditions, Barack Obama counts as the president of the United States. But in spite of this apparent similarity, there is a huge difference, and it has to do with the nature of meaning. <u>The meaning</u> of the sentence "Snow is white" <u>by itself is sufficient</u> to guarantee that an appropriate utterance will constitute the making of a statement to the effect that snow is white. But the meaning of the sentence "Obama is president" by itself is in no way sufficient to guarantee that Obama is in fact president. In the case of the sentence, formulae of the form "<u>X counts as Y in C</u>" describe the *constitution* of meaning and not a separate linguistic operation that we perform. But in the case of <u>nonlinguistic institutional facts</u>, constitutive rules of the form "X counts as Y in C" describe a *linguistic operation* that we

Not analogous

perform by which we create new institutional facts, facts whose existence involves more than just the meaning of the sentences and utterances used to create them. I will have more to say about this distinction in Chapter 5.

V. How This Book Fits into the Overall Philosophical Project

I work from an overall philosophical vision that I will now summarize so that the reader can see how each individual claim fits into the overall pattern. The mind has a beautiful and symmetrical formal structure. By "formal" I just mean that the structural features of beliefs, desires, perceptions, intentions, and so on can be specified independently of any particular contents. Basic to that formal structure is the distinction between the "cognitive faculties"—perception, memory, and belief—and the "conative and volitional faculties"—desire, prior intention, and intention-in-action. These two sets relate to reality in quite different ways. I have already introduced the notion of direction of fit as a feature of speech acts, but I hope it is obvious that it applies equally well to mental states. Beliefs, like statements, have the downward or mind (or word)-to-world direction of fit ↓. And desires and intentions, like orders and promises, have the upward or world-to-mind (or word) direction of fit ↑. Beliefs and perceptions, like statements, are supposed to represent how things are in the world, and in that sense they are supposed to fit the world; they have mind-to-world direction of fit ↓. The conative-volitional states such as desires, prior intentions, and intentions-in-action, like orders and promises, have the world-to-mind direction of fit ↑. They are not supposed to represent how things are but how we would like them to be or how we intend to make them be. In addition to these two faculties, there is a third, imagination, where the propositional content is not supposed to fit reality in the way that the propositional contents in cognition and volition are supposed to fit, but which nonetheless functions crucially in creating social and institutional reality. Imagination, like fiction, has a propositional content. If, for example, I try to imagine what it would have been like to live in ancient Rome, it is a bit like giving a fictional account of my life in ancient Rome in that in neither case am I actually committed to something having occurred to me in fact. In both imagination and fiction the world-relating commitment is abandoned and we have a propositional content without any commitment that it represent with either direction of fit. These topics form the subject matter of most of the next chapter, and their extension to collective mental processes, processes involving more than one person, collective intentionality, is the subject matter of Chapter 3.

The mind, for present purposes, consists of mental states, processes, and events, including intentional actions. The human mind is able to create systems of symbolic representations. We can use those systems to perform meaningful speech acts. The structure of the speech acts is as beautifully simple and elegant as the structure of the mental states. Once you see how the nature of meaning creates the possibility of speech acts, you can see that the limits set by a language are already limits set by the mind. Because of the nature of meaning itself, there are five and only five possible types of illocutionary speech acts,[7] which I have labeled, respectively, Assertives (which we use to tell how things are, for example, statements and assertions), Directives (which we use to tell people to do things, for example, orders and commands), Commissives (which we use to commit ourselves to doing things, for example, promises and vows), Expressives (which we use to express our feelings and attitudes, for example, apologies and thanks), and Declarations (which we use to make something the case by declaring it to be the case, for example, declaring war and adjourning a meeting).[8] Of these types, the Declaration is peculiar in that it creates the very reality that it represents. As I said in the previous section, all of non-linguistic human institutional reality is created by Declaration. How is such a thing possible? In Chapter 4 I try to explain what language is and in Chapter 5, I explain how it works to create nonlinguistic institutional reality. Once you see the power of the Declaration to create an institutional reality, a reality of governments, universities, marriages, private property, money, and all the rest of it, you can see that social reality has a formal structure as simple and elegant as the structure of the language used to create it.

VI. Some Principles and Distinctions that Guide the Investigation

I want to make some fundamental distinctions and state a few general principles that will form conditions on the arguments that follow. I think all of these are obvious, indeed commonsensical, but all of them have been denied by some thinker or other, so it is important to get them out in the open at the beginning.

7. The term "illocutionary" is due to J. L. Austin, *How to Do Things with Words*.
8. Because they are technical terms, I capitalize the names of the various types of speech acts: Assertives, Directives, Commissives, Expressives, and Declarations.

I. MENTAL, MIND-DEPENDENT AND MIND-INDEPENDENT PHENOMENA, INTENTIONALITY-RELATIVE

Intuitively, lots of phenomena are mental in an obvious sense. These would include not only intentional phenomena such as beliefs, hopes, fears, and desires, but nonintentional phenomena such as pains and states of undirected anxiety. Equally intuitively, there are many phenomena that are totally independent of the mind, such as mountains, molecules, and tectonic plates. In addition to these timeworn categories, we need to introduce a class of phenomena that are not actually located in our minds but are dependent on our attitudes. These would include money, property, government, and marriage. In earlier writings I called these "observer-relative." But that expression, quite reasonably, can be misleading because it seems to imply that it is outside observers, adopting an anthropological standpoint, who assign observer-relative statuses to people and objects. But that is not my intent at all. Money is money because the actual participants in the institution regard it as money. So instead of saying "observer-relative" I am going to use the expression "intentionality-relative." What I want to convey is that people's attitudes are necessary to constitute something as money, government, political parties, or final examinations. So on this account, in addition to the traditional distinction between "mental" and "nonmental," you need to identify a category of entities that are not, so to speak, intrinsically mental in a way that intentions and pains are, but are dependent for their existence on the mental in the sense that they are intentionality-relative, and these would include our favorites such as money, property, marriage, and government. Actual intentional states are not themselves intentionality-relative because they exist regardless of what anybody outside thinks about them.

All of these phenomena we will be investigating are intentionality-relative. Institutional facts are thus relative, but they do not thereby become epistemically subjective, and that leads to a further distinction we need to make.

VII. Epistemic Objectivity and Subjectivity versus Ontological Objectivity and Subjectivity

One way to put the paradox that drives the investigation is to say that we are investigating a class of entities that are objective, such as money and nation-states. It is not just a matter of my opinion, for example, that this piece of paper is a twenty-dollar bill; it is a matter of objective fact. But at the same time, these institutional facts exist only because of our subjective attitudes. How can one and the same thing be both subjective and objective? The answer is that this distinction is profoundly ambiguous. There are at least two different senses of the objective/subjective distinction: an epistemic sense and an ontological sense. The epistemic sense has to do with knowledge. The ontological sense has to do with existence. Pains, tickles, and itches are ontologically subjective in the sense that they exist only as experienced by human or animal subjects. In this sense they differ from mountains and volcanoes, which are ontologically objective, in the sense that their existence does not depend on anybody's subjective experiences. But in addition to that, there is an epistemic sense of the distinction. Some propositions can be known to be true independently of anybody's feelings or attitudes. For example, the statement that Vincent van Gogh died in France is epistemically objective, because its truth or falsity can be ascertained independently of the attitudes and opinions of observers. But the statement "Van Gogh was a better painter than Manet" is, as they say, a matter of subjective opinion. It is epistemically subjective. It is not a matter of epistemically objective fact. Ontological objectivity and subjectivity have to do with the mode of existence of *entities*. Epistemic objectivity and subjectivity have to do with epistemic status of *claims*. We can now put our apparent paradox in a way that removes at least some of the appearance of paradox. The question is not, How can there be an objective reality which is subjective? But rather, *How can there be an epistemically objective set of statements about a reality which is ontologically subjective?* In large part, that is what this book is about.

APPENDIX: COMPARISON BETWEEN THE GENERAL THEORY OF THIS BOOK AND THE SPECIAL THEORY OF THE CONSTRUCTION OF SOCIAL REALITY

This book is part of an ongoing research project and is a continuation of the line of investigation in my earlier work, *The Construction of Social Reality*. In this Appendix, I want to make explicit the similarities and differences. I now think of the theory of *The Construction* as stating a *special* theory that is an implementation of the more *general* theory expounded in this book. The main difference between the present work and my earlier work is that at that time I did not see the centrality of Status Function Declarations in both creating and maintaining institutional facts. I saw that language was essential to the creation and the maintenance of institutional reality, but I thought that the constitutive rule "X counts as Y in C" was sufficient to explain the phenomena. I now see that though "X counts as Y in C" is one form of Status Function Declaration, there are also other forms.

One way to clarify the differences is to consider objections made by myself and by other authors to the account of the *The Construction*.

I. *The Ad Hoc Cases*

One problem is that there are some institutional facts that do not seem to require an institution. Indeed, it seems that in order to create institutions in the first place, you have to be able to count certain things as having a status without there being a preexisting institution. In *The Construction* I imagine a tribe that comes to treat a line of stones as a boundary without having a general constitutive rule. Furthermore, such a tribe might simply count a certain person as their leader, giving the leader the usual apparatus of deontic powers and status functions, though there is no existing institution, no set of general constitutive rules, for the selection of a leader. When I wrote *The Construction* I discussed such cases and others, but I did not see them as posing a problem for my account, because they exemplify the same logical structure as the constitutive rules of institutions. Thus, on an ad hoc basis the members of the tribe count this X as this Y in this C, this man as this leader in this time and place—and that is already a step on the way to adopting a general rule of the form "X counts as Y in context C." The tribe does not have an institution for selecting leaders, but it is only one step away from it. If, for example, they decide, as many tribes did indeed decide, that the oldest living son of the deceased leader would be the succeeding leader, they have adopted a constitutive rule.

2. *Freestanding Y Terms*

Another interesting case arises when it turns out, in very sophisticated societies, that there are forms of the imposition of status functions, forms of deontic powers, that do not even require an object or person on whom the status function is imposed. Thus, what Barry Smith calls "freestanding Y terms"[9] exist when a status function is created without there being an existing person or object who is counted as the bearer of the status function. The most obvious case of this is the creation of corporations. And indeed, the whole idea of the limited liability corporation is that there need not be any person or group of persons who is the corporation because those persons would have to accept the liability of the corporation if they were indeed identical with or constituted the corporation. But as they are not identical with the corporation, the corporation can exist, and continue to exist, even if it has no physical reality. Another case is the case of electronic money, where what exists are electronic *representations* of money; for example, magnetic traces on computer disks in banks. There need be no physical realization of the money in the form of currency or specie; all that exists *physically* is the magnetic traces on the computer disk. But these traces are *representations* of money, not money. Another obvious example is blindfold chess. The players have the powers of having the queen or the bishop or the rook, all of them deontic

9. Smith, Barry, "John Searle: From Speech Acts to Social Reality," in *John Searle*, Barry Smith (ed.), Cambridge: Cambridge University Press, 2003, 1–33. A similar objection was made by Amie Thomasson, "Foundations for a Social Ontology," *Protosociology: An International Journal of Interdisciplinary Research* 18–19 (2002): 269–90.

powers, but there is no physical object which is the queen or the bishop or the rook, only the *representation* of these in the standard chess notation.

3. Institutional Facts that Do Not Require Collective Recognition

A third objection, posed by some philosophers and social scientists[10] to the account given in *The Construction*, is that there do seem to be institutional facts that are not matters of collective agreement, acceptance or recognition, but which can be discovered, for example, by social scientists. Thus, for example, the existence of a recession in the economy can be an epistemically objective fact even though it is unknown to the participants in the economic transactions. Indeed, the concept of a recession did not come into existence until the twentieth century, though there were many recessions prior to that time. In short, such institutional facts as the existence of a recession do not seem to require collective recognition.

So we have at least three classes of objections to the account given in *The Construction of Social Reality*: the ad hoc cases, the freestanding Y terms, and the institutional facts that do not require collective acceptance. What should we say about these cases? Actually, I think they can all be rather easily dealt with within the framework provided by *The Construction*, and I have in fact published answers to all three, which I will summarize briefly here. The ad hoc cases exemplify the same form, X counts as Y in C. They are therefore steps on the way to having constitutive rules. A tribe that selects a leader on an ad hoc basis has already imposed a status function with an operation that has the same logical structure as a constitutive rule, and in that sense it has taken a step toward codification in the form of rules. The ad hoc cases are not counter-examples to the account, but rather pre-institutional examples of the same logical form.

The objection about freestanding Y terms can similarly be answered within the framework of *The Construction*. The freestanding Y terms do not bottom out in concrete objects, but they do bottom out in actual people who have the deontic powers in question. So there is no object or person who is the

---

10. Thomasson, ibid.; and Friedman, Jonathan, "Comment on Searle's 'Social Ontology': The Reality of the Imagination and the Cunning of the Non-Intentional," in *Anthropological Theory*, Roy D'Andrade (ed.), 6, no. 1 (March 2006): 70–80.

corporation, but there are the president, the board of directors, the stock-holders, and others, and the deontic powers accrue to them. A corporation is just a placeholder for a set of actual power relationships among actual people. The same holds for electronic money and blindfold chess. The owner of the money and the possessor of the queen have the relevant powers.

The third objection, about institutional facts that are discovered, can also be answered within the analytical framework of *The Construction*. Such facts are facts about systematic fallouts or consequences of ground-floor institutional facts. The ground-floor facts about the economy are the buying and selling and other economic activities and attitudes of participants. These will have certain macro consequences such as, for example, the trade cycle. But the systematic fallouts are macro facts that are all constituted by the ground-floor or lower-level institutional facts. I introduced the expression "systematic fallouts."[11] Åsa Andersson in her book calls these "macro institutional facts."[12] In general, one can say that ground-floor economic institutional facts are studied by microeconomics, systematic fallouts by macroeconomics.

So the principal objections to *The Construction* seem to me answerable within the general framework of the theory. However, reflection on all these issues has led me to extend the original theory, and one of the primary aims of this book is to spell out that extension.

The apparent cases where we are on the road to having institutions, where on an ad hoc basis we simply count X as Y, we count so and so as the king, such and such a line of stones as the boundary, again exemplify the form of Status Function Declarations. In these cases, we are counting an X as a Y without a preexisting institutional structure, but counting an X as a Y is a case of making an X into a Y by representing it as being a Y. That is precisely the form of the Status Function Declaration. The special feature of these cases is that we do it on an ad hoc basis. The problem with the freestanding Y terms is also easily dealt with. These are cases where we create a status function—for example, we create electronic money, or we create a corporation—by Declaration. And indeed as we will see in Chapter 5, the statutory law for creating corporations is itself a Declaration that declares that certain other Declarations will create corporations. The individual creations of corporations are then specific Declarations within an institution of standing Declarations.

11. Searle, John R., "Reality and Social Construction: Reply to Friedman," in *Anthropological Theory*, Roy D'Andrade (ed.), 6, no. 1 (March 2006): 81–88, esp. 84.
12. Andersson, Åsa, *Power and Social Ontology*, Malmö: Bokbox Publications, 2007.

Our third class of objections to the account in *The Construction* can also be easily dealt with. Indeed, we do not need to change our earlier answer. Just as there are ground-floor institutional facts that require collective recognition, so there are macro or systematic fallouts of institutional facts that do not require collective recognition in order to exist but simply are consequences of the ground-floor institutional facts. This forces a change in the terminology that I will remark on later. Strictly speaking, these cases are not cases of institutional facts.

Changes in the Terminology

The new account gives us a rather simple set of equivalences and logical implications: institutional facts = status functions → deontic powers → desire-independent reasons for action. In plain English, all and only institutional facts are status functions; status functions imply deontic powers, and deontic powers always provide desire-independent reasons for action.

Implicit in this summary, however, are three changes from the terminology I used in *The Construction*. One of these is purely notational; the others are substantive. In *The Construction* I said that all institutional facts exist within institutions. But once we agree that some status functions can exist outside established institutions we are faced with a choice: we either have to say that there are some institutional facts that exist outside institutions or we have to say that not all status functions are institutional facts. I find it more useful to treat the concept of an institutional fact and the concept of the status function as coextensive. So I change the terminology accordingly. All status functions are institutional facts, but not all institutional facts exist within preexisting institutions consisting of constitutive rules.

Furthermore, as I suggested briefly above, because they do not carry deontic powers, the systematic consequences of institutional facts are not themselves institutional facts. That is, the fact that the economy is currently in a recession is a fact about a whole lot of other institutions, but it is not itself an institutional fact because it carries no deontic powers. If, for example, Congress passed a law requiring that the Federal Reserve Board lower interest rates during periods of recession, then being a recession would become an institutional fact because it would carry a deontic power. It would have the typical form of institutional facts whereby something at one level, the level of being a recession, carries a deontology at a higher level, placing the Federal Reserve Board under an obligation.

A third change is also implicit. In *The Construction* I said that in general, institutional facts carry deontic powers but that there were some exceptions, most notably the honorific cases. If someone gets an honorary degree from a university or someone is awarded the title of Miss Alameda County, they acquire a new institutional status, but they have no new powers. No power is carried by purely honorific statuses. But I now think it is more useful to treat honor as a kind of deontic power. A limiting case, perhaps, but still a kind of power—honor is supposed to be accorded respect, for example. So I now say that all status functions create deontic powers. To summarize, there are three changes in the terminology. First, some institutional facts can exist outside of any established institutions. Second, some facts that do require existence within institutions are not themselves institutional facts because they carry no deontologies. And third, all institutional facts by definition carry a deontology, however limited or weak it may be.

2

INTENTIONALITY

Our aim is to explain human social ontology. Because that ontology is created by the mind, we have to begin with that property of the mind that creates the reality we are trying to analyze. We have to begin with intentionality.

This direction of analysis also satisfies our basic requirement of showing how the higher level phenomena of mind and society are dependent on lower level phenomena of physics and biology: Biology depends on physics. Neurobiology is a branch of biology. Consciousness and intentionality are caused by and realized in neurobiology. Collective intentionality is a type of intentionality, and society is created by collective intentionality.

I. Intentionality: The Fundamentals

"Intentionality" is a fancy philosopher's term for that capacity of the mind by which it is directed at, or about, objects and states of affairs in the world, typically independent of itself. So if I believe that it is raining, fear a rise in interest rates, want to go to the movies, or prefer cabernet sauvignon to pinot noir, I am in each case in an intentional state. Intentional states are always *about*, or *refer to*, something. Intending, in the ordinary sense in which I intend to go to the movies, is just one type of intentional state among many others such as belief, desire, hope, and fear.[1]

---

1. If intending is just one kind of intentionality among many, then why use a word that makes it sound as if there is some special connection between intentionality and intending? The answer is that we got the word from German-speaking philosophers (who got it from medieval Latin *intensio*). In German, "Intentionalität" does not sound at all like "Absicht," the German word for intention.

We have to start with intentionality because to understand society, you have to understand collective human behavior. Collective human behavior is a manifestation of collective intentionality, and to understand this you have to understand individual intentionality. Indeed, to understand any of this you have to understand consciousness, and of course a deep understanding of consciousness would require an understanding of how consciousness is caused by, and realized in, brain structures. Right now nobody knows the answers to these questions: how is consciousness caused by brain processes and how is it realized in the brain? I think we understand a fair amount about the philosophical aspects of consciousness, but I will not deal with them here except insofar as they bear on my main concern, which is intentionality. In this chapter I am going to give you the bare bones of a theory of intentionality which will form the essential prerequisite for understanding social ontology. The main task is to explain a handful of fundamental notions, and I will do that in a rather flat-footed set-piece fashion. Here goes.[2]

INTENTIONALITY AND CONSCIOUSNESS

I said that intentionality is a name for the directedness or aboutness of mental states. Not all mental states are intentional. I can be in a state of anxiety or nervousness where I do not know what I am anxious or nervous about and may not be anxious or nervous *about* anything. At any given moment in my waking life some of my intentional states are conscious. Right now I am conscious of being hungry, for example, but many of my mental states are unconscious most of the time. I believe that George Washington was the first U.S. president even when I am not thinking about it, indeed, even when I am asleep. So the distinction between consciousness and unconsciousness and the distinction between intentional and nonintentional cut across each other in such a way as to give us four logically possible forms: conscious intentional states, unconscious intentional states, conscious nonintentional states, and unconscious nonintentional states. There are clearly cases of the first three. I am not at all sure there are any examples of the fourth, unconscious nonintentional mental states. Perhaps unconscious undirected anxiety would

2. The account that follows is in large part derived from Searle, John R., *Intentionality: An Essay in the Philosophy of Mind,* Cambridge: Cambridge University Press, 1983. Two points made here that were not present in that earlier account are the discussion of free will and the discussion of the imagination.

be an example of such a state. I am not sure there are any such examples, but at least the taxonomy allows for the possibility of their existence.

THE STRUCTURE OF INTENTIONAL STATES

Each intentional state divides into two components: the type of state it is and its content, typically a propositional content. We can represent the distinction between intentional type and propositional content with the notation "S(p)." For example, I can believe that it is raining, fear that it is raining, or desire that it be raining. In each of these cases I have the same propositional content, p, that it is raining, but I have them in different intentional types, that is, different psychological modes: belief, fear, desire, and so on, represented by the 'S.' Many intentional states come in whole propositions, and for that reason those that do are often described by philosophers as "propositional attitudes." This is a bad terminology because it suggests that my intentional state is an attitude to a proposition. In general, beliefs, desires, and so on are not attitudes to propositions. If I believe that Washington was the first president, my attitude is to Washington and not to the proposition. Very few of our intentional states are directed at propositions. Most are directed at objects and states of affairs in the world independent of any proposition. Sometimes an intentional state might be directed at a proposition. If, for example, I believe that Bernoulli's principle is trivial, then the object of my belief is a proposition, namely, Bernoulli's principle. In the sentence "John believes that Washington was the first president," it looks like the proposition that Washington was the first president is the object of the belief. But that is a grammatical illusion. The proposition is the *content* of the belief, not the *object* of the belief. In this case, the object of the belief is Washington. It is impossible to exaggerate the damage done to philosophy and cognitive science by the mistaken view that "believe" and other intentional verbs name relations between believers and propositions.

Some intentional states do not have a whole proposition as content. So, for example, one can be in love with Sally or hate Bill or admire Thomas Jefferson, where the intentional state does not contain a whole propositional content but contains a representation of an object. We can represent this as S(n), as in "Love (Sally)," "Hate (Bill)" or "Admire (Jefferson)."

As we saw in the previous chapter, speech acts represent reality with different *directions of fit*, and the same concept of direction of fit also applies to intentional states. Thus the aim of a belief is to be true, and it fails if it is false. Insofar as it is true, we can say that the belief matches, or fits, or accurately represents, the world. It has the mind-to-world direction of fit ↓. Desires and intentions, on the other hand, are not supposed to represent how the world is but how we would like it to be (in the case of desires) or how we intend to make it be (in the case of intentions). We can say in such cases that the intention and the desire have the *world-to-mind* direction of fit ↑. Perhaps a better term than "direction" would be "responsibility" for fitting. The belief is supposed to be true, and thus its *responsibility* is to match the world. It has the mind-to-world direction of fit. If the belief succeeds in achieving that fit, it is true; otherwise it is false. But if the desire or the intention fails, it is not the desire or intention that is at fault but the world which is, so to speak, at fault. And for this reason we can say that desires and intentions have the world-to-mind direction of fit or responsibility for fitting. I hope the distinction is intuitively obvious. A good clue is this: if you can literally say of the mental state that it can be true or false, then it is likely to have the mind-to-world direction of fit because truth and falsity are the standard terms for assessing success or failure in achieving the mind-to-world direction of fit. Beliefs can be true or false, but desires and intentions cannot. (Tiresomely, in English we do sometimes say, "My wish came true." All the same, wishes are not literally true or false.) Desires and intentions can be satisfied or frustrated, carried out or not carried out; these are marks of the fact that they do not have the mind-to-world but the world-to-mind direction of fit.

It is an important fact, remarked on in Chapter 1, and whose importance will emerge in Chapter 4, that the same distinctions carry over to language. Just as in intentional states we can make a distinction between the type of state that it is, marked by "S," and the content of the state, marked by "p," so in the theory of language we can make a distinction between the type of speech act it is, what Austin called the "illocutionary force,"[3] marked by "F," and the propositional content, marked by "p." Thus just as I can believe that you will leave the room or hope that you will leave the room, so I can predict that you will leave the room or order you to leave the room. In each case, we have the same propositional content with different psychological mode in the case of the intentional states, and different illocutionary force or type in the case of the speech acts. Furthermore, just as my beliefs can be true or false and thus have the mind-to-world direction of fit, so my statements can be true or false and thus have the word-to-world direction of fit. And just as my desires and

3. Austin, John L. *How to Do Things with Words*, Cambridge, Mass.: Harvard University Press, 1962.

intentions cannot be true or false but can be in various ways satisfied or unsatisfied, so my orders and promises cannot be true or false but can be in various ways satisfied or unsatisfied, by being obeyed or not obeyed in the case of an order, or by being kept or not kept in the case of a promise. So far this gives us a very simple bare bones account of intentionality and implies an important result: we can think of intentional states that have a whole proposition as content, and a direction of fit, as representations of what must be the case in the world if the fit is to come about. I introduce a name for the conditions in the world which must be satisfied if the intentional state is to be satisfied: *conditions of satisfaction*. We can think of all of the intentional states that have a whole propositional content and a direction of fit as representations of their conditions of satisfaction. A belief represents its truth conditions, a desire represents its fulfillment conditions, an intention represents its carrying out conditions. The key to understanding intentionality, at least for these simple cases, is "representation" in a very specific sense. The intentional state represents its conditions of satisfaction.

So far our account is rather limited, as we will see. Some intentional states with whole propositional contents do not seem to have a direction of fit. Thus if I am proud that I have a big nose or I am ashamed that I have a big nose, in both cases the fact that I have a big nose is simply taken for granted. That is, it is not the aim of the intentional state to represent the fact that I have a big nose (mind-to-world ↓), nor is it its aim to bring it about that I have a big nose (world-to-mind ↑). In these states we simply *presuppose* that I have a big nose. In earlier writings I have said that such states have the *null direction of fit*, because the fit is simply presupposed. I think that terminology may be misleading if it suggests that there is no fit at all. On the contrary, a fit is *presupposed* and the emotion of pride or shame would be inappropriate or misdirected if I did not have a big nose. Because in these cases the existence of the fit is presupposed, I propose to change the notation from "null," or "Ø," to "Presup Fit," or simply "Presup" for short. So instead of saying, as I said in earlier writings,[4] that the emotions, such as pride and shame, have the Ø direction of fit, I will now say they have Presup fit. It is an ugly expression, but at least it is not misleading.

Furthermore, we have not yet accounted for those intentional states that do not have a whole proposition as content, such as being in love with Sally or

4. Searle, John R., *Intentionality: An Essay in the Philosophy of Mind,* Cambridge: Cambridge University Press, 1983.

admiring Jefferson. I will come back to them after I have made a few more distinctions.

It is important to see that none of this account of intentionality is necessarily intended to describe how things seem to us or how they feel to us on the spot. As we move through the affairs of life we seldom give a thought to these matters. It is important to emphasize that I am not trying to describe how things seem to us. There is a movement in philosophy called "Phenomenology," some of whose practitioners think that a decisive consideration in the study of intentionality is how things seem to us. "Phenomenology," indeed, is often used as another name for the philosophical study of consciousness. I want you to understand that I am not claiming that there is always an immediate phenomenological reality to the processes of having—and operating with—beliefs, desires, intentions, and other intentional states. It takes a great deal of reflection to see that all of one's beliefs and desires are representations of their conditions of satisfaction with a direction of fit. That is not immediately obvious phenomenologically. Just as there needs to be no immediate phenomenological reality to intentionality, so there need be no phenomenological reality to intentional representations. The notion of representation is sometimes challenged because people erroneously suppose that every mental representation must be consciously thought as a mental representation. But the notion of a representation as I am using it is a functional and not an ontological notion. Anything that has conditions of satisfaction, that can succeed or fail in a way that is characteristic of intentionality, is by definition a representation of its conditions of satisfaction.

So far I have been concerned to lay out certain fundamental distinctions. The one important theoretical claim that I have made is to say that intentional states in general are representations of their conditions of satisfaction; but remember that I have also pointed to a number of apparent counterexamples. We will need to account for those intentional states that do not seem to have a direction of fit, cases where the fit is presupposed: intentional states like the emotions of love and hate, pride and shame. Furthermore, we will need to account for those cases that do not have a whole propositional content but where the intentional state is just directed at an object. So far, to summarize, I want you to be familiar with the following notions: propositional content, psychological mode, direction of fit (of which there are four varieties: ↓, ↑, Presup, and ↕), and conditions of satisfaction.

II. The Network and the Background

Two other notions we need in our bare bones theory of intentionality are the notion of the Network and the notion of the Background. My intentional states do not come to me as isolated units. I cannot intend to go to the movies unless I have a whole lot of other beliefs and desires. I have to believe that movies are forms of public entertainment, that often one sees a movie by going to a movie theater in which the movie is being shown, that one enters after paying the price of admission, that one sits in the theater and watches the movie on a large screen, and so on with a whole lot of other intentional states.

But in addition to this Network of intentional states, you also need the notion of a set of presuppositions for the application of intentionality, including a set of abilities. If you follow out the threads in the Network you will realize that a typical intentional state requires a complex set of other interrelated intentional states in order to function. So, for example, I now intend to drive to my office on the university campus. What must I believe, desire, and so on in order to have the intention to drive to the office? It turns out that it is a rather long list, and I will not even attempt to state all or most of it. I have to believe that I have a car and that I am able to drive a car. I have to believe that such and such is the route to the campus, and I have to believe that cars are means of transportation and that they operate on streets and are driven by drivers of which I am one. I will let you continue with this list, but there is one thing I want you to notice, and that is, if you follow out the list, some of the things on it do not look like typical intentional states. For example, I do indeed have to believe that the campus is within driving distance. But how about my ability to drive itself? I take that ability for granted, and the ability does not consist in a set of intentional states. Similarly, I take it for granted that I will be traveling on the surface of the Earth. Much of what I take for granted, as well as my abilities, do not seem to be appropriately thought of as just more intentional states. We need a set of abilities, capacities, and so on for applying those intentional states. This set of abilities and capacities I will call the Background. The Background consists of all of those abilities, capacities, dispositions, ways of doing things, and general know-how that enable us to carry out our intentions and apply our intentional states generally.

There is a category difference between the Network, construed as a set of intentional states most of which are unconscious at any moment, and the

Background, construed as a set of abilities, dispositions, and capacities. But in practice there is no sharp dividing line if only because the unconscious elements of the Network when they are unconscious consist in the Background ability to bring them to consciousness. There are many disputes in contemporary philosophy about these issues, but for the purposes of the present book I am not going to enter into these debates. What I need for this discussion is the idea that whenever we deal with the world either in thought or action or perception we have to take a great deal for granted. What I take for granted, when I form the intention, for example, to drive my car to the office, is both a set of beliefs and desires (the Network) and a set of abilities (the Background).

With the notions of the Network and the Background, we can now address the question that seems to trouble our account of intentionality. Namely, how do the notions of conditions of satisfaction and direction of fit apply to those intentional states that do not have a whole propositional content, as is typical with love and hate, and those cases where the propositional content has a Presup fit, but without an upward↑ or downward↓ direction of fit, as in pride and shame? I think these problems can be easily dealt with once we recognize the existence of a Network. It is true that I do not have to have a whole propositional content if, for example, I am in love with Sally. But there is no way that one can be in love with another person without having a whole lot of beliefs and desires about that person. That is, the loving relationship only exists within a Network of other intentional states. The beliefs and desires within the Network are in large part constitutive of the loving relationship. And those elements of the Network do have directions of fit with conditions of satisfaction.

Furthermore, if we think of those intentional states where the fit is presupposed, there is no way that one can have those intentional states without having beliefs and desires. Thus if one is proud to have won the race, then one must believe that one won the race and one must want to have won the race. That is, "X is proud that p" implies "X believes that p" and "X desires that p." Both have a direction of fit with conditions of satisfaction.

So the account of intentionality in terms of conditions of satisfaction is more general than it might seem at first glance. It is going to turn out that the key to understanding intentionality is conditions of satisfaction and that we can analyze the structure of the intentionality of social phenomena by analyzing their conditions of satisfaction.

III. Intentions and Actions

Let us now turn our attention to the problem of intentions in the ordinary sense of "intention," the sense in which, for example, I intend to vote in the next election, and when I raised my arm a few moments ago, I did so intentionally. What shall we say about the relations of intentions to their conditions of satisfaction? Two special features make intentions quite different from beliefs and desires. First, intentions come in two quite distinct logical categories. We need to make a clear distinction between the intentions that one has *prior* to the performance of an action as when, for example, I now intend to raise my arm in thirty seconds, and the intentions that one has *during* the performance of the action itself, as when I raise my arm intentionally and thus have an intention which is part of the action itself. To have a terminology, I will call these, respectively, the "prior intention," that is, the intention that one forms prior to the performance of an intentional action, and the "intention-in-action," where the intention-in-action is a component of the action itself. So in this very simple case where I form a prior intention to raise my arm, if I then raise my arm, the prior intention will result in an intentional action. The intentional action has two components: the intention-in-action and the bodily movement of my arm going up. Another name in English for prior intentions is "plans" and the word that typically names the formation of a prior intention is "decision." If I have decided now to do something later, I have formed a prior intention. If I plan on doing it, I have a prior intention. All actions require intentions-in-action, but not all actions require prior intentions, because sometimes one may do something intentionally, but quite spontaneously, without forming any plan or making any prior decision to do it. In such cases the only decision is the onset of the action itself. For example, when I am sitting in a chair and thinking about a philosophical problem, I sometimes quite spontaneously jump up and start pacing about. In such cases there is no prior intention. I just get up and pace. More strikingly, most of the time, in conversation, people do not plan their next utterance. They just spontaneously respond to their interlocutor.

Ontologically speaking, a prior intention, like a belief or a desire, is a state in the mind, whereas an intention-in-action is an actual event: it is the psychological event that accompanies the bodily movement when I successfully perform an intentional action involving a bodily movement. For example, if I intentionally raise my arm, there are two components to the intentional action: there is an intention-in-action and a bodily movement. If the action is successfully performed, the intention-in-action causes the bodily movement. The closest English word to intention-in-action is "trying." If I want to do something and try but fail to do it, all the same I did have an intention-in-action. If I had the intention-in-action, then I tried. Whereas one can order someone to do something, one cannot give someone an order to have a prior intention. It makes no sense to say "Intend to go to the movies." I might tell them: "Try to form the intention to go to the movies," in which case I am ordering them to try (i.e., have an intention-in-action) to form the prior intention. Another clue to the distinction between prior intentions as states and intentions-in-action as acts of trying is that "intend" in English does not take the present continuous tense, whereas "try" does. Thus in answer to the question, "What are you doing right now?" I cannot say, "I am intending to write an article," but I can say, "I am trying to write an article." I will say more about these relations when we talk about the structure of human action in a few moments.

A second remarkable feature of intentions is that both intentions-in-action and prior intentions, in order to be satisfied, must function causally in the achievement of the conditions of satisfaction. So, for example, if I intend to raise my arm in fifteen seconds but then forget all about that intention and raise my arm for some totally independent reason, my original intention is not in fact carried out or satisfied. *In order to be satisfied, the intention itself must function causally in the production of the action.* Similar considerations hold for intentions-in-action. When I am trying to raise my arm, then if I succeed in the trying, that is to say, if the intention-in-action is satisfied, then the trying itself must cause the movement that I am trying to achieve. Unless the intention-in-action functions causally in producing the bodily movement, the intention-in-action is not satisfied.

In our representation of the conditions of satisfaction of intentions, both prior intentions and intentions-in-action, we have to have a somewhat different notation from what we had for beliefs and desires because the content of the intention makes reference to the very intention of which it is a content. Thus we can say that these intentions are causally self-referential,[5] since the

---

5. The fact that intentions are causally self-referential has been remarked on by a number of authors. For example, Kant points it out at the beginning of his *Critique of Judgment* (Kant, Immanuel, *Critique of Judgment*, Indianapolis: Hacket Publishing, 1987). The term "causal self-referentiality," as far as I know, was first invented by Gilbert Harman (Harman, Gilbert, "Practical Reasoning," *Review of Metaphysics* 29 (1976): 431–63).

form in which the content sets a condition of satisfaction is a causal one that refers to the intentional state itself. Thus to spell it all out for a simple case, suppose I have a prior intention to raise my arm and I carry out the prior intention by intentionally raising my arm. The picture of the prior intentions, intentions-in-action and bodily movements looks like this (using "pi" for prior intention, "BM" for bodily movement and "ia" for intention-in-action):

> pi (I perform the action of raising my arm and this pi causes that
>   I perform the action of raising my arm)
> ia (my arm goes up and this ia causes that my arm goes up)

In each case, because the causal clause implies the clause that precedes it, we can leave out the preceding clause. And because the action just consists in the intention-in-action plus the bodily movement (where the bodily movement is caused by the intention-in-action), we get a rather simple, and indeed elegant, picture of these relations:

> pi (this pi causes action)
> ia (this ia causes BM)
> action = event of ia causing BM

And the set of causal relations can be represented with equal simplicity, using an arrow to represent the causal relation:

$$\text{(Action)}$$
$$\text{pi} \rightarrow (\text{ia} \rightarrow \text{BM})$$

IV. Complex Intentions and Actions

To summarize, there are two things that I have so far claimed about the intentionality of ordinary intentions and both are essential to the account of social actions and social ontology. First, we need a distinction between prior intentions and intentions-in-action; and second, both prior intentions and intentions-in-action are causally self-referential. The crucial proof that we need a distinction between prior intentions and intentions-in-action is that the conditions of satisfaction in the two cases are strikingly different. Take a simple example. If I now intend to raise my arm in thirty seconds, I have a prior intention, and its conditions of satisfaction require the occurrence of a whole action. But if I do raise my arm, then the actual occurrence of a conscious event while I am raising my arm, my conscious experience of effort, is an intention-in-action and its conditions of satisfaction require not a whole action, but a bodily movement of my arm going up as caused by the intention-in-action itself.

The crucial argument that both are causally self-referential is that, unlike beliefs and desires, where it does not matter to the satisfaction of the intentional state how that satisfaction comes about, in the case of intentions it is crucial to the functioning of the intention that the intention itself should figure causally in achieving the conditions of satisfaction. Thus if I want to be rich, then that desire will be satisfied if and only if I get rich. It does not matter how I get rich. But if I now have a prior intention to earn enough money to make myself rich, then my intention to earn a lot of money must function causally in achieving the state of affairs of my being rich. Otherwise, the intention is not carried out, even if I get rich in some other way. And if I am now trying to open the door, then my trying, my intention-in-action, will be satisfied only if the trying itself causes the door to open. If something else causes the door to open, someone else opens it for me, for example, then my intention-in-action is not satisfied.

The next step is to explain the structure of complex actions where one does something by means of, or by way of, doing something else. So, for example, if the chairman says, "All those in favor of the motion raise your right hand," and I raise my right hand, I am not only raising my right hand but also voting for the motion. These are not two separate actions—raising my right hand and voting; rather, they are one action with two levels of description of the two different features of the action. Raising my right hand in that circumstance *constitutes* voting. I vote *by way of* raising my hand.

Another type of a complex action is where one intentionally does something that causes something else to occur. For example, I fire a gun *by means of* pulling the trigger. Here again there are not two actions—pulling the trigger and firing the gun—but only one action with two different levels of description. At the bottom level I intentionally pull the trigger. My pulling the trigger causes the gun to fire. My pulling the trigger does not cause me to fire the gun; in that context it just is firing the gun. But firing the gun is a complex act, where I intentionally achieve the effect that the gun fires by the causal "by means of" relation, whereby my bottom-level intentional movement causes the higher level effect, and the combination is the total action.

So we have at least two sources of complexity in the structure of complex actions. We have different levels of description where one level is constituted by the behavior at the lower level: voting is constituted, in that context, by raising my arm. But in addition to the *constitutive by way of relation* we also have the *causal by means of relation*: pulling the trigger causes the gun to fire. And thus I fire the gun by means of pulling the trigger.

These internal structures of the intention-in-action can become very complicated. Thus, for example, we might say, Jones fired the gun by means of pulling the trigger, and he shot his political enemy by means of firing the gun, and he assassinated the enemy by means of shooting him, and he achieved his desire for vengeance by way of assassinating his political enemy. This complex structure whereby one can expand or contract the description of the action— pulling the trigger, firing the gun, shooting the victim, assassinating the victim, achieving revenge—is called "the accordion effect"[6] because one can expand or contract the description like expanding or contracting an accordion. It is sometimes said that the accordion effect goes on indefinitely. But if we are talking about the accordion of intentional action, then the boundaries of the accordion are set by the conditions of satisfaction of the complex intention-in-action. There are all sorts of further side effects or long-term effects that are not part of the content of the intention-in-action and thus not part of its conditions of satisfaction. Furthermore, the initial act that one performs, where one does not do anything by way of or by means of which one does it, is called a basic action.[7] Anything that you can do intentionally, where you do not need to do anything else intentionally by way of which or by means of which you do the first thing, is a basic action. In our example of firing the gun by means of pulling the trigger, and killing the enemy by means of firing the gun, we may think of pulling the trigger as a basic action. We assume that the agent does not need to intentionally do anything else by way of which or by means of which he pulls the trigger. He just pulls it.

I hope it is clear from this account that what is basic for one person may not be basic for another. Basicness depends on Background abilities. For example, a good pianist may be able to play an entire arpeggio as a basic

6. The term "accordion effect" was invented by Feinberg, J., *Doing and Deserving: Essays in the Theory of Responsibility*, Princeton: Princeton University Press, 1970, 34.

7. The term "basic action" was invented by Arthur Danto (Danto, "Basic Actions," in A. R. White (ed.), *The Philosophy of Action*, Oxford: Oxford University Press, 1968, 43–58.

action. She just does it. There isn't any question, How did she do it? Or by what means did she do it? But for a beginning pianist, to play a piece of any complexity requires a set of subsidiary intentions-in-actions—for example, hit this key with the left thumb—by way of which he intends to play the whole piece.

V. The General Structure of Intentionality

So far, I have said very little about memory and perception because this book will be mostly concerned with actions rather than these more strictly cognitive phenomena. However, for the sake of completeness, let me point out that perception and memory, like prior intentions and intentions-in-action, are causally self-referential. You see the object only if the presence of the object caused your visual experience of it. You remember the picnic only if the fact that you experienced the picnic causes your present memory of the picnic. But the direction of fit and direction of causation of memory and perception are the mirror image of prior intentions and intentions-in-action. The memory and the perception have the downward or mind-to-world direction of fit, but unlike prior intentions and intentions-in-action, they have upward or world-to-mind direction of causation. The causal self-referentiality of the visual experience and the memory experience is such that they are satisfied only if the state itself is caused by the state of affairs represented in the content of the state. The result is that we get a rather elegant set of formal relationships between the types of intentionality that I have so far described. I show them in the accompanying chart. I use the somewhat old-fashioned terms "cognition" and "volition" to name basic types of intentional states. (The expression "N/A" means not applicable. Because beliefs and desires do not have a causally self-referential condition in their intentional content, the question of the direction of causation does not arise.)

TABLE 2.1 Intentionality

	Cognition			Volition		
	Perception	Memory	Belief	Intention-in-action	Prior intention	Desire
Direction of fit	↓	↓	↓	↑	↑	↑
Direction of causation	↑	↑	N/A	↓	↓	N/A
Causally self-referential?	yes	yes	no	yes	yes	no

The formal relations among the various components of intentionality are so elegant, and indeed so beautiful, that I have to at least remark on the implications of the symmetries. It is absolutely fundamental to our conception of our relations to the real world through the primary forms of cognition—that is, perception and memory—that we think we achieve satisfaction in the form of the downward direction of fit only if the state of affairs that constitutes the conditions of satisfaction causes the very perception or memory that has that state of affairs as its condition of satisfaction. With volition we get exactly the mirror image of this. It is equally fundamental to our conception of succeeding in our tryings and our plans, our intentions-in-action and our prior intentions, that we succeed in achieving the world-to-mind or upward direction of fit only if our very plans and tryings cause that success; only if the intentional phenomena, the mental phenomena, cause the states of affairs in the world that they represent. We achieve world-to-mind direction of fit only in virtue of mind-to-world direction of causation.

In sum: for perception and memory, we represent how things really are and thus achieve mind-to-world direction of fit only in virtue of world-to-mind direction of causation. For prior intentions and intentions-in-action, we get a match between how we intend things to be and how they actually are, and thus achieve world-to-mind direction of fit, only in virtue of mind-to-world direction of causation.

Many philosophers think that the primary forms of intentionality are belief and desire. But we should see these as derivative and etiolated forms of the more biologically basic forms of intentionality in action and perception. In belief and desire these causal relations have been bleached out. Beliefs and desires are much more flexible for that very reason, because they do not have a causally self-referential component. But the biologically more basic forms of relating to reality are in our plans (prior intentions), our tryings (intentions-in-action), our perceivings, and our rememberings. In these we have both the causal and the representational component, and they are joined in precisely the way I have described.

One faculty that is left out of the chart, because it does not have a direction of fit, is imagination. The distinction between type of state S and content p applies to imagination. Just as I can believe, or wish, that it is raining, so I can imagine that it is raining. But unlike belief, which has the downward direction of fit, or desire, which has the upward direction of fit, my imagining something commits me neither to believing that what I imagine is the case, nor to wanting it to be the case. Sometimes one fantasizes what one would like to occur, but it is not an essential feature of fantasy or imagination that they are forms of desire. One can fantasize what one fears or hates, as well as what one believes might happen, and indeed what one believes could not possibly happen. There is no responsibility for fitting with imagination. Another feature peculiar to imagining is that it is, or can be, a free voluntary action. I can imagine anything I want in a way that I cannot believe, desire, or intend at will. "Imagine" comfortably takes the imperative mood in a way that the other verbs do not. "Imagine living in Venice," by which I mean, "Imagine what it would be like to live in Venice" is okay. "Believe you live in Venice," "Desire to live in Venice" or "Intend to live in Venice" are all bad English. Imagination will have a role in our account of social ontology, because the creation of a reality that exists only because we think it exists requires a certain level of imagination.

There is a natural progression in this account of intentionality from the more basic to the less basic. The most primitive forms of intentionality are perception and intentional action. In these cases, the animal is in direct contact with the environment, with the environment causing something in the animal (perception) or the animal causing some change in the environment (intention-in-action). Less basic than these are the representations that have these as their conditions of satisfaction. These are prior intentions and perceptual memories. In these cases, we still have the causal component, but we lose the direct causal connection with the conditions of satisfaction. Memories represent the past; prior intentions represent the future. Then the next stage is belief and desire, where we eliminate the requirement of a causal component. You can believe something and the belief can be satisfied even if the thing you believe didn't cause your belief and you can desire something and your desire can be satisfied even if your desire didn't cause the satisfaction of the desire. In imagination you lose the internal connection with the conditions of satisfaction.

There is one last addition to our account of intentionality that is essential both to understanding human behavior and to understanding human social behavior and social reality, as I will later demonstrate. There is an asymmetry between cognition and volition that is not represented in the chart. In the case of our voluntary actions, we characteristically experience a causal gap between our reflection on our beliefs and desires and the formation of a prior intention, the formation of a decision. There is a causal gap in the sense that typically those beliefs and desires, though they are the reasons for the decision and hence for the formation of the prior intention, are not by themselves causally sufficient to force the decision. Furthermore, we typically experience a causal gap between the prior intention and the actual initiation of the action in the form of the intention-in-action. After I have made up my mind to do something, I still have to haul off and do it. And typically, the prior intention is not causally sufficient to force the onset of the action. I have to make an effort. Furthermore, where we have an extended action or series of actions such as writing a book or swimming the English Channel, the intentionality at any given stage, the mere existence of the intention-in-action, is not by itself sufficient to continue the process to completion. One has to make a continuous effort. So there are at least three gaps, or rather three parts of a continuous gap in intentional action between the intentional phenomena at any stage and the continuation to the next stage: the gap between reasons and decision (the formation of the prior intention), the gap between the decision and the onset of the action (the intention-in-action), and, for complex actions, the gap between the onset of the action and the continuation to its completion. In philosophy, there is a traditional name for this gap: it is called the "freedom of the will." Whether we like it or not, in our dealings with the world we are forced to presuppose freedom of the will. The chart below illustrates the positions of the manifestations of the gap. The gap of voluntary action is continuous, but it has three special places where it manifests itself, as is shown by the chart.

Reasons for Action (Beliefs, desires, obligations, needs, etc.) →
(Gap) Decision → (Gap) Onset of Action → (Gap) Continuation to Completion

I have tried to emphasize that we have the *experience* of freedom in the sense that we do not typically experience our reasons as determining the decision, or the decision as determining the action, or the onset of the action as determining its continuation to completion. But I have to emphasize that the fact that we have these experiences does not guarantee that we actually have free will. It still remains an open question whether or not the experiences are illusory.

I apologize for the brevity and swiftness of this chapter. I am trying to convey an apparatus that will be essential in the chapters that follow.

3

COLLECTIVE INTENTIONALITY AND THE ASSIGNMENT OF FUNCTION

Remember that our project is not just to explain the nature of human society but to show how its features are both consistent with, and are natural developments from, the basic facts. The basic facts are given by physics, chemistry, evolutionary biology, and the other so-called hard sciences. So far, I have given an account that tries to show how we can think of intentionality as a natural biological phenomenon that has interesting logical properties. It is important to keep reminding ourselves that natural brain processes, at a certain level of description, have logical semantic properties. They have conditions of satisfaction, such as truth conditions, and other logical relations; and these logical properties are as much a part of our natural biology as is the secretion of neurotransmitters into synaptic clefts. Yes, you can have brain processes that are logically inconsistent with other brain processes. Right now, as you read these words, there is an electro-chemical process going on in your brain that has the semantic contents of which you are now aware. In our dualist tradition we are not used to thinking of natural biological phenomena as intrinsically having logical properties. Logical properties are supposed to exist in an abstract realm apart from squishy biology. Frege even postulated a third realm, something in addition to mind and body, where they could dwell timelessly. I am trying to bring them down to earth. I am insisting that, as you read this sentence, the thoughts going through your mind are also neurobiological processes in the brain, and those processes have logical properties, exactly the same logical properties as those of the thoughts, because they are simply the neurobiological realization of the thoughts. Every so often in philosophy someone tries to "naturalize" intentionality. By naturalizing intentionality they usually mean denying that it really exists, or asserting that it is really something else. My answer to this is that intentionality really does exist and is not something else.

Intentionality is already naturalized because, for example, thinking is as natural as digesting.

I. Analyzing Collective Intentionality

I have tried to describe some of those logical properties in the last chapter. In this chapter, I am going to continue to describe the logical structure of intentionality, but I will focus on what I believe is the fundamental building block of all human social ontology and human society in general: human beings, along with a lot of other social animals, have the capacity for collective intentionality. So far, we have considered only individual intentionality which would be expressed in sentences in the first-person singular such as "I believe" or "I want." But in this chapter, we will consider first-person plural forms of intentionality as in sentences of the form "We are doing such and such," "We intend to do such and such," "We believe such and such." I call all of these sorts of cases "collective intentionality," but for the purposes of this book, the most important form of collective intentionality is collective intentions in planning and acting, that is, collective prior intentions and collective intentions-in-action. But there are also forms of collective intentionality in such things as believing and desiring. I might, for example, as a member of a religious faith, believe something only as part of our believing it, as part of our faith. I might, as part of a political movement, desire something as a part of our desiring it. Such cases are indeed cases of collective intentionality, but in this chapter I will mostly be concerned with collectively intending in the sense in which we might collectively intend to go on a picnic together or collectively try to push a car together. One of my main aims in this chapter is to say what exactly constitutes collective intentionality in cooperative planning and acting.

Furthermore, an important application of collective intentionality is the collective assignment of function to people and objects. Functions are always intentionality-relative and an important class of functions, one which is essential to the explanatory apparatus of this book, is the class in which the functions are imposed by collective intentionality. I will conclude this chapter with a discussion of those functions.

One might think that the way to deal with collective intentionality is just to take the account that I gave in the last chapter of individual intentionality and preface all intentional representations with a "we" instead of an "I." So instead of "I am going to the store," we simply say "We are going to the store," and do the exact analysis of intentionality that I provided for the "I" case. There are several problems with this approach, some of them serious. The first is that as long as we respect the basic facts we have to acknowledge that all human intentionality exists only in individual human brains. And if we are going to substitute a "we" for an "I" in the analysis of intentionality, we need to say in exactly whose individual brain or brains the we-intentionality exists. There isn't any other place for intentionality to be except in human brains. A second difficulty is that my personal individual intentionality can only range over actions that I can personally cause; and typically in cooperative behavior, there is an intentionality that is beyond the range of my causation. A third difficulty is that there are many forms of collective behavior in which in order for us to cooperate in an action, the content of what I am doing must be different from the content of what you are doing in order to achieve what we are both trying to do together. This is illustrated by such cases as when we are playing as members of a team in a game such as baseball where different members of the team have to perform different actions. Another example is when one plays a musical instrument as part of a musical group. A simple case is when we are playing a duet in which I play the piano part and you play the violin part. In all such cases there is genuine cooperative behavior but the content of each individual's intention differs from the content of the others' intentions even though they share a common overall goal of playing the game or playing a piece of music. In what follows, we are going to try to solve these problems. There are several conditions of adequacy that any account of collective intentionality has to meet. And just so we know what these are, I will list them now:

1. We must have a clear distinction between prior intentions and intentions-in-action. This is as important for collective acts and intentions as it is for individual acts and intentions.

2. We need to make it absolutely clear that the conditions of satisfaction of both prior intentions and intentions-in-action are causally self-referential.

3. All intentionality, whether collective or individual, has to exist inside individuals' heads.

4. In cases of collective intentionality, we have to distinguish what I can individually cause, that which can be part of the condition of satisfaction of my intentional content, and that which I take for granted as contributed by my collaborators in the collective intentionality. If we

are playing in a symphony, all that I can actually cause is my individual performance. But I make that performance as my contribution to the total collective performance.

5. In the specification of the conditions of satisfaction, we must be clear what can go in the propositional content and what cannot. The propositional content can only represent the condition of satisfaction of the intention. The general point is that the propositional content of an intentional state always specifies the conditions of satisfaction as distinct from the type of state that it is, which is specified outside the propositional content. Because both prior intentions and intentions-in-action are causally self-referential, the propositional content can only represent elements that the agent can (or thinks he can) causally influence.

6. In collective intentionality, it cannot be required of each individual's intentionality that he know what the intentionality on the part of others is. In complex forms of teamwork or collective behavior, one typically does not know what the others are doing in detail. All one needs to believe is that they share one's collective goal and intend to do their part in achieving the goal.

II. Current Accounts of Collective Intentionality

Collective intentionality has recently become something of a cottage industry in analytic philosophy. There is even a biennial conference with the title "Collective Intentionality," and several important works have been published on the subject. There is, as one might guess, a great deal of controversy within the subject, and there certainly is no generally accepted account of collective intentionality

If this book was intended as a historical survey of the field, I would have to devote several chapters to the important books and articles by such pioneers as Margaret Gilbert[1] and Raimo Tuomela.[2] Important authors who would

1. Gilbert, Margaret, *On Social Facts*, London: Routledge, 1989. See also "Walking Together: A Paradigmatic Social Phenomenon," *Midwest Studies in Philosophy* 15 (1990): 1–14.
2. Tuomela, Raimo, "We Will Do It: An Analysis of Group-Intentions," *Philosophy and Phenomenological Research* 51 (1991): 249–77. See also Tuomela, Raimo, and Kaarlo Miller, "We-intentions," *Philosophical Studies* 53 (1988): 367–89. See also Tuomela, Raimo, *The Philosophy of Sociality: The Shared Point of View*, New York: Oxford University Press, 2007.

have to be covered in detail are Michael Bratman,[3] Seumas Miller,[4] David Velleman,[5] and others. In an earlier draft of this chapter I did include discussions of most of these authors. However, it now seems to me that to do a thorough and adequate job would require another book, or at least a major digression from my main objectives. So instead of discussing other authors with the detailed attention that they deserve, I will simply state some general features in which my account differs from others I have seen.

The general project is to analyze sentences of the prior intention form "We intend that we perform act A" and intention-in-action sentences of the form, "We are now (intentionally) performing A." The most common attempts are to eliminate the "We" by reducing "we" sentences to sets of "I" sentences. Most of the accounts that I have seen deal only with prior intentions, and it is not clear to me if the authors recognize the distinction between prior intentions and intentions-in-action. So a typical analysis might begin:

> X and Y intend to clean the yard together if and only if
> X intends to do his part of cleaning the yard, and Y intends to do his part
> and each has mutual belief about the other's intentions.

Mutual (common) knowledge (or belief) about intention occurs between two people, when each intends, and each knows that the other intends and each knows that the other knows that, and each knows that each knows that other knows that, and so on indefinitely.

I think what motivates this pattern of analysis is respect for the basic facts. In this case the basic fact is that all intentionality has to exist in individual brains. But if "we" intentionality exists only in individual brains then it seems that all "we intend" statements made by any three people A, B, and C must reduce to " I, as A, intend" plus "I, as B, intend" plus "I, as C, intend" plus mutual beliefs among A, B, and C.

Against this pattern of analysis I argue two things: first, that respect for the basic facts does not require that "We intend" statements be reducible to "I intend" statements, and second, that the proposed reductions fail.

3. Bratman, Michael E., *Faces of Intention,* Cambridge: Cambridge University Press, 1999.
4. Miller, Seumas, *Social Action: A Teleological Account,* New York: Cambridge University Press, 2001.
5. Velleman, David J., *Practical Reflection,* Princeton, N.J.: Princeton University Press, 1989.

In other writings, I have argued that respect for the basic facts, in this case the fact that all intentionality has to exist in the heads of individuals, does not require that we-intentionality be reducible to I-intentionality.[6] There is no reason why we cannot have an irreducible we-intention in each of our heads when we are engaging in some cooperative activity. Of course, that we-intention has to be systematically related to certain I-intentions if the we-intention is to be able to move each body. And I will discuss those relations later in this chapter. But the general requirements of what is sometimes called "methodological individualism" do not require that we-intentions be reducible to I-intentions, because the requirement that all intentionality exist in individual brains does not imply that the content that exists in the individual brains cannot exist in a plural grammatical form. If we are cleaning the yard together, then in my head I have the thought, "We are cleaning the yard" and in your head you have the thought, "We are cleaning the yard."

An Argument against Reducing We-Intentionality to I-Intentionality

I have earlier offered a general counterexample[7] that I think works against all of the attempts I have seen to reduce collective intentionality, we-intentionality, to individual intentionality, I-intentionality. Here is how it goes:

BUSINESS SCHOOL CASE I

Imagine a group of Harvard Business School graduates who were taught and come to believe Adam Smith's theory of the invisible hand. After graduation day, each goes out in the world to try to benefit humanity by being as selfish as

---

6. Searle, John R., "Collective Intentions and Actions," in P. Cohen, J. Morgan, and M. E. Pollack (eds.), *Intentions in Communications*, Cambridge, Mass.: MIT Press/Bradford Books, 1990, reprinted in Searle, *Consciousness and Language*, Cambridge: Cambridge University Press, 2002.

7. Ibid. With this example I intend no disrespect to either Adam Smith or the Harvard Business School. It is quite possible that the historical Adam Smith did not believe the views that are commonly attributed to him and it is quite possible that the Harvard Business School does not have the conception of business that is commonly attributed to it. If so, I apologize to both for continuing this misconception. My point here is simply to give a clear example.

each of them possibly can and by trying to become as individually rich as they can. Each does this in the mutual knowledge that the others are doing it. Thus there is a goal that each has, and each knows that all the others know that each has it and that they know that each knows that each has it. All the same, there is no cooperation. There is even an ideology that there should be no cooperation. This is a case where the people have an end, and people have common knowledge that other people have that end, but there is no collective intentionality in my sense.

BUSINESS SCHOOL CASE 2

There is a second possible case where we imagine they all get together on graduation day and make a solemn pact that they will each go out and try to help humanity by becoming as rich as they can and by acting as selfishly as they can. All this will be done in order to help humanity. In this case there is genuine cooperation and genuine collective intentionality even though it is a higher level of cooperation to the effect that there should be no lower level cooperation. I want to say that the first case is not a case of collective intentionality and the second case is a case of collective intentionality.

But one might object, What difference does it make? After all, we supposed that the behavior is exactly the same in the two cases. In each case, each individual tries to help humanity by becoming as rich as he or she can. There is a tremendous difference in the two cases because in the second case there is an obligation assumed by each individual member. In the first case, the individuals have no pact or promise to act in this way. If someone changes his or her mind, that person is free to drop out at any point and go to work for the Peace Corps. But in the second case, there is a solemn promise made by each to all of the others.

III. Different Conceptions of Collective Intentionality

Much of the apparent irresolubility of the disputes about collective intentionality derives from two sources of misunderstanding. First, people have different conceptions of the notion to be analyzed. In the case of collective intentionality, there is no commonly accepted commonsense ordinary usage of this term to which we can appeal. Typically in philosophy with a concept like *truth* or *knowledge* there are commonsense ordinary uses of "true" and "know" and analyses have to answer to at least some of ordinary usage. Sometimes, as in the case of Tarski's famous definition of truth,[8] one may self-consciously depart from some of the aspects of the ordinary use of the term, but there is still a common core concept to which one is appealing. But when it comes to "collective intentionality," there is no commonly used notion corresponding to this expression. There are a whole lot of different notions. Let me list several of these. First, it is just a feature of ordinary English that if I am doing something and you are doing the same thing, then there is at least a sense in which we are both doing it. For example, if I am driving to San Francisco and you are driving to San Francisco, then it is true to say that we are both driving to San Francisco. But this is not necessarily collective intentionality, for you may be driving and I may know that you are doing it, and I may be doing the same thing, and you may know that I am doing it. There may even be mutual knowledge, but in no sense are we cooperating. Furthermore, there are even cases when we are trying to achieve a shared common *goal* without any cooperation. As it happens, right now I do various things to try to improve the environment. I try, for example, to minimize air pollution, whenever I can. But I am not in any sense cooperating with anybody when I do it, even though I know that a large number of other people do the same things with the same goal. Just having the same goal, even having the same goal in the knowledge that other people share that goal and even in the knowledge that they know that I share that goal with them, is not by itself enough for cooperation in my sense. When I talk about this form of collective intentionality, I am talking about the capacity of humans and other animals to actually *cooperate* in their activities. Cooperation *implies* the existence of common knowledge or common belief, but the common knowledge or belief, together with individual intentions to achieve a common goal is not by itself sufficient for cooperation.

A second common feature in accounts I have read is that the authors tend to assume that the collective intentionality they are analyzing arises among language-using adults. That is of course a reasonable assumption for most theoretical purposes, but for me it cannot be the fundamental concept in analyzing human society, because it already presupposes language, and if you have a language, for reasons I will spell out in the next chapter, you already

8. Tarski, A. "The Semantic Conception of Truth and the Foundations of Semantics," *Philosophy and Phenomenological Research* 4 (1944): 341–76.

have a human society. If you assume that collective intentionality results in commitments undertaken through conversation, then you have to presuppose collective intentionality even to begin to have the conversation that results in the commitment. There is a ground-floor form of collective intentionality, one that exists prior to the exercise of language and which makes the use of language possible at all. It is a crucial human Background capacity, essential to what we think of as the functioning of society, that in cultures known to me, one can approach any stranger and engage in certain sorts of conversation. One can ask a question such as, "Excuse me, how do I get to Dwinelle Hall?" If the stranger responds in any way, even by saying, for example, "I don't know," or "Don't ask stupid questions," or even "I don't speak English," collective intentionality is well under way. You do not need a promise in order to have collective intentionality: indeed, the very conversation in which the promise is made, and is accepted or rejected, is already a form of collective intentionality. The conversation presupposes a Background capacity to engage in conversation, and the Background capacity depends on having a more fundamental prelinguistic form of collective intentionality. The initiation of the conversation is itself a high level of collective intentionality. So from my point of view, creating a commitment by making a promise is already two floors up in the building of collective intentionality. You have to have a prelinguistic form of collective intentionality on which the linguistic forms are built, and you have to have the collective intentionality of the conversation in order to make the commitment.

IV. How Can We-Intentionality Move Individual Bodies?

There are some further problems about collective intentionality once we have accepted the fact that not all occurrences of "we intend," "we believe," and "we desire," can be reduced to "I intend," "I believe," "I desire," and so on, plus mutual belief. The deep question is, How can it be the case that We-intentionality can move individual bodies if the content of the "We" is not the same as the content of the "I," which constitutes doing one's part of the collective effort? If we are playing a piano-violin duet, I might be doing my part by playing the piano and you might be doing your part by playing the violin. How could *our* collective intentionality move *my* body? How do we get from "We are playing the duet" to "I am playing the piano part" said by me and "I am playing the violin part" said by you?

As I have said repeatedly, intentions divide into two kinds: prior intentions, which begin prior to the onset of an action, and intentions-in-action, which are the intentional components of actions. Both prior intentions and intentions-in-action are causally self-referential.

If we consider a simple example such as raising my arm, then we can represent these facts in the following notation, where the part inside the parentheses represents the propositional content of the intention and the part before the parentheses represents the type of intentional state it is.

Prior intention (this prior intention causes that I perform the action of raising my arm)
Intention-in-action (this intention-in-action causes that my arm goes up)

Using obvious abbreviations, "pi" for prior intention, "ia" for intention-in-action, "BM" for bodily movement, and "a" for action, we can say (and here I am repeating the analysis of Chapter 2) that the general form of these relations is given by the following schemata.

pi (this pi causes a)
ia (this ia causes BM)
a = ia + BM, where ia causes BM

Human actions also have some very special features deriving from the fact that typically I do not just perform a simple action like raising my arm, but I do something *by way of* or *by means of* doing something else. These relations give rise to the accordion effect, described in Chapter 2. So, for example, I fire the gun *by means of* pulling the trigger and I vote in the committee meeting *by way of* raising my arm. Pulling the trigger causes the gun to fire, but raising my arm does not cause the vote to take place; it just constitutes voting. I call these two types of inner structure of action *the casual by-means-of relation* and *the constitutive by-way-of relation*. We can represent these relations in the following notation:

ia B by means of A (this ia causes A, which causes B)
ia B by way of A (this ia causes A, which constitutes B)

Now the question for our present discussion is, How does all this apparatus carry over to collective intentions and actions? If we are cooperating in some group endeavor, where our individual contribution causes some further effect, then we have the causal by-means-of relation. And if we are cooperating in an endeavor where our individual efforts constitute the desired effect, then we have the constitutive by-way-of relation.[9]

We can work out these cases by considering examples of collective intentions-in-action involving both the causal relation and the constitutive relation. Consider an example of the causal relation where you and I are both trying to start a car engine by means of me pushing the car and you sitting in the driver's seat and letting the clutch out after the car has attained a certain amount of speed. Causally speaking, *we* are starting the engine *by means of me pushing* and *you releasing the clutch* while the ignition is on. Another case, considered in my earlier writings, is where we make Bearnaise sauce together by me pouring and you stirring. Causally speaking, we are making the sauce *by means of* me pouring and you stirring.

Compare those with the case in which we are performing a duet where I play the piano part and you play the violin part. Here our playing does not *cause* the duet to be performed. My playing and your playing simply *constitute* the performance of the duet. So from my point of view, I have a collective intention-in-action that *we* play the duet by way of *me* playing the piano, *in a context where I take it for granted that you are playing the violin.*

Part of what it means to say that the intentionality is collective is that each agent has to assume that the other members of the collective are doing their parts. And what does that mean exactly? It means each has to assume that the others also have an intention-in-action which has the same goal, the same "collective B" where the singular A can be different because each person can only perform his own action A.

How can we represent all of that in our canonical notation for representing the structure of intentionality? Here is the causal case:

ia collective B by means of singular A (this ia causes: A car moves, causes: B engine starts)

In English, this is to be read as: I have a collective intention-in-action B, in which I do my part by performing my singular act A, and the content of the intention is that, in that context, this intention-in-action causes it to be the case, as A, that the car moves which, in that context, causes it to be the case that B, the engine starts. Notice furthermore that the free variables "B" and

---

9. What follows is a continuation of the discussion in John R. Searle, "Collective Intentions and Actions."

"A" are bound inside the bracket by the verb phrases "car moves" and "engine starts," that follow the respective letters.

Notice that the assumption behind my collective intentionality is that if I make my contribution on the assumption that you make your contribution, together we will be trying to cause the car to start. Notice also that there is no reference to your intentionality or your behavior inside the propositional content of my intention-in-action, because they are phenomena that I am *not* in a position to influence causally. In collective intentionality I have to presuppose that others are cooperating with me, but the fact of their cooperation is not part of the propositional content of my part of the collective intentionality; rather, it is specified in the form of the collective intentionality, outside the brackets. The expression "collective B" implicitly expresses the presupposition that in performing act A I am not acting alone but as part of a collective and that the goal of achieving B is shared by the other members of the collective. This point has been misunderstood by some of my critics.[10] The simplest way to block the misunderstanding is to add an explicit representation of the belief that others are cooperating.

Bel (my partner in the collective also has intentions-in-action of the form (ia collective B by means of singular A (this ia causes: A clutch releases, causes: B engine starts))).

In ordinary English, this extra clause reads as follows: I have a belief to the effect that my partner in the collective also has intentions-in-action of the same form as mine, namely, to achieve a collective B by means of a singular A, in his case to release the clutch, as A, which in that context causes it to be the case that the engine starts, as B.

Two things about this additional clause should be emphasized. First, it is a *belief* implicit in the idea of collective behavior, but it is not a part of the content of my intention-in-action. The content of my intention-in-action can only make reference to things I can cause (or at least believe I can cause). In order to engage in collective behavior I have to believe (or assume or presuppose) that others are cooperating with me. And their cooperation will consist in their having intentions-in-action that specify the same goal as I have but need not specify the same means to the goal. I have to believe they are

---

10. For a discussion, see Bardsley, Nicholas, "On Collective Intentions: Collective Action in Economics and Philosophy," *Synthese* 157 (2007): 141–59.

cooperating, but except for unusual cases, it is not part of the content of my own intention-in-action to cause that cooperation.

The second feature is that I need not know what their contribution is. I need not know the value of "A" in the form of their intention-in-action. In the particular example under consideration, I do know the value of "A" but for complex acts of large groups no one knows what everybody else is doing.

Now we turn to consider the case of the constitutive by-way-of relation where I am playing the piano part and you are playing the violin part in the performance of the duet. I can only cause my piano playing; I have to presuppose your violin playing. Thus for my intentional content we have

> ia collective B by way of singular A (this ia causes: A piano plays, constitutes: B duet is performed)

And the corresponding belief, parallel to the causal case, is

> Bel (my partner in the collective has an intention in action of the form (ia collective B by way of singular A (this ia causes: violin plays, constitutes: B duet is performed)))

In ordinary English again, these can be read as, I have a collective intention-in-action to achieve B by way of contributing my part, the singular A. The content of that intention is, this intention-in-action causes it to be the case, as A, that the piano plays, which, in that context, constitutes its being the case, as B, that the duet is performed. The extra clause about belief reads as follows: I have a belief to the effect that my partner in the collective also has intentions-in-action of the same form as mine, namely, to achieve a collective B by way of a singular A, in this case to play the violin, as A, which in that context constitutes its being the case, as B, that the duet is played.

A crucial feature is worth repeating: the content of my singular intentionality in both cases does not make essential reference to the content of your singular intentionality. I simply take it for granted, in that context, that if I do my part we will be trying to achieve the goal, because I am operating on the assumption that you will do your part, and you are operating on the assumption that I will do my part. There is an epistemic basis for this: often one does not know what the individual intentionality in the minds of the other members of the collective is. I might have collective intentionality to achieve a certain goal, and I have that on the assumption that you are working toward the same goal as I am. But it need not be the case that I actually know the content of your intentionality. In a football game, the offensive lineman blocking on a pass play does not necessarily need to know what routes are being followed by the wide receivers or how many steps backward the quarterback is taking before throwing the pass. All he has to know is what he is supposed to do ("his assignment" in the jargon of football coaches), and this notation is an attempt to capture the condition of satisfaction of his intention.

If I am successful in this analysis then I will have succeeded in showing how it can be the case that collective intentionality can exist in the minds of individuals and at the same time that collective intentionality, though irreducibly collective, can nonetheless cause the movements of individual bodies. The action does not get performed if my body does not move, and this has to be reflected in the collective intentional content, even though the collective intentional content exists entirely in my brain and your brain and the brains of the other members of the collective.

V. The Intuitive Motivation for the Analysis

The analysis presented may seem complex, and I want briefly, perhaps at the cost of some repetition, to explain its intuitive motivation. The way to analyze the structure of collective intentionality is to ask yourself, What exactly is the collective trying to do? Remember that "trying" is the ordinary English name for the intention-in-action. And remember also that though trying is always trying to succeed, there is a difference between trying and succeeding. All that is in the intention-in-action is the trying.

The only intentionality that can exist is in the heads of individuals. There is no collective intentionality beyond what is in the head of each member of the collective. So the next step is to ask, Well, what is each individual of the collective trying to achieve? And if you think of the causal by-means-of cases, then each member is trying to achieve the common goal by means of making his or her individual contribution. But that individual contribution is only made on the assumption that others are making their contribution. That is what is meant by saying that one is acting as part of a collective. One may be mistaken that others are making their contribution, but that is an essential belief or presupposition that goes with the individual effort, where the individual effort is made as part of a collective effort. So we need at least two elements in our analysis of collective intentionality. We need a representation of the intention itself, where the intention can only refer to things that the agent can achieve (or thinks he can achieve) and cannot involve references to other agents' actions, and then we need a representation of a belief, and the belief is a belief about what the other agents are doing.

There are cases where an individual's intentionality can make reference to the intentionality of other members of the collective. This is the case, for example, when the commander of the military unit issues a command; it is designed to create intentionality in the other members of the collective. Another case is where the quarterback of the football team calls a play in the huddle and creates an intention in each member of the team to carry out his assignment in the execution of the play. But in normal cases where you and I are doing something together, when, for example, we are mixing the sauce by means of you pouring and me stirring, my intentionality cannot cover your pouring. That you are pouring is just a belief that I have. It is not part of the intentional content of my intention-in-action. The thing that bothered some critics in my earlier statement of the analysis was that it looks as if the agent must be having his intention cover the behavior of other people. But of course that is not a part of, nor is it implied by, the analysis. It is only given the contributions of the other members of the collective that the agent can achieve what he does, but nonetheless, his intention is to try to achieve the common goal. If I vote for a political candidate, I am trying to get that candidate elected, even though I know that my vote is only one vote among millions.

VI. The Distinction between Cooperation and Collective Recognition

So far I have been concerned primarily to explain the structure of full-blown cooperation as manifested in collective prior intentions and collective intentions-in-action. However, there is a much weaker form of collective attitudes, which will also be important for our analysis of society. And that is what I call "collective recognition." For example, in an actual transaction when I buy something from somebody and put money in their hands, which they accept, we have full-blown cooperation. But in addition to this intentionality, we have prior to the transaction and continuing after the transaction an attitude toward the pieces of paper of the type that I am placing in the hands of the seller, that we both recognize or accept the pieces of paper as money, and indeed, we accept the general institution of money as well as the institution of commerce. As a general point, institutional structures require *collective recognition* by the participants in the institution in order to function, but particular transactions within the institution require *cooperation* of the sort that I have been describing. So the couple who are planning marriage accept the institution of marriage prior to actually getting married. This is not a case of cooperating in a form of behavior but simply going along with an institution. But the actual marriage ceremony is an example of cooperation. Full-blown cooperative collective intentionality of the sort that I have described is often necessary for the creation of the institution. Think of the creation of the United States at the time of the Declaration of Independence, for example. In this chapter I have been analyzing cooperation, but I want to emphasize that in order for cooperation to take place within an institutional structure, there has to be a general collective recognition or acceptance of the institution, and that does not necessarily involve active cooperation.

What exactly is involved in the structure of collective recognition or acceptance? In earlier writings I just used the notion of acceptance, but to many people that implied some degree of approval, and I do not want to imply that. One can recognize and act within institutions even in cases where one thinks the institution is a bad thing. I sometimes use the hybrid notion of "collective recognition or acceptance,"[11] and I want to make it clear that it marks a continuum that goes all the way from enthusiastic endorsement to just going along with the structure. At the time of the Nazi regime, for example, members of the Nazi Party enthusiastically endorsed the institutional structure of the Third Reich. But there were lots of people in Germany at the time, who, while not endorsing the institutional structure, went along with it as a matter of nationalism, indifference, prudence, or even just apathy. Cooperation also exists on a continuum, but this continuum cuts across the continuum of collective recognition or acceptance. I have argued that in the case of cooperation, collective intentionality cannot in general be reduced to individual intentionality plus mutual belief. But what about cases of collective recognition? Can the collective recognition be reduced to individual recognition plus mutual belief among the recognizers? Here the prospects seem much brighter, because no active cooperation is required. In the case of active cooperation, merely having individual intentions together with mutual belief about the others' intentions is not sufficient, as the Harvard Business School case illustrated. Can we construct a similar counterexample to the case of collective recognition? In the Business School case there

11. The term collective recognition was originally suggested by Jennifer Hudin.

was no cooperation, but in the case of collective recognition, even if the participants are opposed to collective recognition, all the same if they each individually recognize the phenomenon, and there is mutual knowledge that they so recognize it, then it looks like we have collective recognition. What is the difference in the two cases? Cooperation requires the collective intention to cooperate. But collective recognition need not be a form of cooperation and thus does not require a collective intention to cooperate.

Consider the Harvard Business School cases discussed earlier. In both the case of cooperation and in the case where there is no cooperation, the participants in the business school scene take the existence and validity of money for granted. They simply recognize it. Of what does the collective recognition consist? It does not seem to me that it requires *cooperation*. Rather, what it requires is that each participant accepts the existence and validity of money in the belief that there is mutual acceptance on the part of the others. So we have an interesting result; namely, that the existence of an institution does not require cooperation but simply collective acceptance or recognition. Particular acts within the institution such as buying or selling or getting married or participating in an election require cooperation. This is an important point, because it shows that there are some forms of collective intentionality which are reducible to I-intentionality plus mutual belief. If you have collective recognition of something as money, that collective recognition can be constituted by the fact that each person recognizes money and there is mutual knowledge among the participants that they all recognize money.[12]

VII. The Imposition of Function

Human beings, along with certain other species, have the capacity to impose functions on objects, where the imposition of function creates an intentionality-relative phenomenon, the function. Typically an object will have a function imposed on it when the object is used for a certain purpose. I call these "agentive functions."[13] Humans create agentive functions to a rather spectacular extent with all of their tools. But even nonhuman animals can have objects that perform certain functions where the function is intended by

---

12. I am indebted to Jennifer Hudin and Asya Passinsky for discussion of the issues in this section. For further discussion see Hudin's "Can Status Functions Be Discovered?" (forthcoming in *The Journal for the Theory of Social Behaviour*).
13. The term was originally suggested to me by Jennifer Hudin.

the users of the object: think of birds' nests, beaver dams, and primates using a stick to dig food out of the ground. For our present purposes, it is important to point out that *functions are always intentionality-relative.* This is disguised from us by the fact that in biology we often *discover* functions in nature. We discover, for example, that the function of the heart is to pump blood (something that was unknown until the seventeenth century), or that the function of the vestibular ocular reflex is to stabilize the retinal image. But when we discover functions in nature, what we are doing is discovering how certain causes operate to serve certain purposes, where the notion of purpose is not intrinsic to mind-independent nature, but is relative to our sets of values. So we can discover that the heart pumps blood, but when we say that the function of the heart is to pump blood, we take it for granted that life, survival, and reproduction are positive values, and that the functioning of biological organs serves these values. But where do the values come from? The clue that there is a normative component to the notion of function is that once we have described something in terms of function we can introduce a normative vocabulary. We can say things like, "This is a better heart than that heart," "This heart is malfunctioning," "This heart is suffering from disease." We cannot do any of these things for stones: stones do not suffer from stone malfunction or stone disease; but if we assign a function to a stone—such as being a paperweight or projectile—we could make evaluative appraisals. To put the point succinctly, if perhaps too crudely, *a function is a cause that serves a purpose.* And the purposes have to come from somewhere; in this case, they come from human beings. In this sense, functions are intentionality-relative and therefore mind dependent.

This book will be largely concerned with a special class of functions that I have baptized "status functions." Like all functions, status functions are intentionality-relative. But unlike many other functions, they have two special features. First, in the cases important for our investigation, they require collective intentionality, both for their initial creation and for their continued existence. And second, they are functions that a person or other entity has, not in virtue of physical structure, or at any rate not solely in virtue of physical structure, but in virtue of collective imposition and recognition of a status. The entity has a certain status, and collective recognition of that status enables the entity to perform the status function. In the creation of human institutional ontology, collective intentionality and the assignment of function go hand in hand, because the crucial functions in question require collective intentionality. It is possible for an individual to construct a "private" institution and "private" institutional facts for his or her own usage. For example, an individual might invent a game that only he plays. But the cases important for our investigation, for making the social world, cases such as money and government, require collective intentionality.

VIII. Conclusion

This chapter has three main aims. First and most important has been to describe the structure of collective intentionality in a way that will show how it is consistent with the basic facts. We do not have to postulate some mysterious type of thought processes existing outside of individual minds. All intentionality, collective or individual, exists in individual minds. But at the same time, we can grant that the strong forms of collective intentionality, those involving cooperation, are irreducible to I-intentionality. Furthermore, and this was the most important aim of the chapter, we can show how we can assimilate collective intentionality to the general account of intentionality that I gave in Chapter 2. Second, I made a distinction between cooperation and collective recognition or acceptance. Both are forms of collective intentionality, but cooperation is a much stronger form because it involves more than the participants just having certain attitudes together with mutual belief. Third, we have shown how the imposition of function relates to collective intentionality. I have argued that functions are always intentionality-relative, and I have tried to show how the imposition of function relates to collective intentionality. We have now assembled most of, though not all, the materials necessary to construct an account of social and institutional reality.

4

LANGUAGE AS BIOLOGICAL AND SOCIAL

I have two main aims in this chapter. First, I want to give an account of language that is thoroughly naturalistic. It is naturalistic in the sense that it treats language as an extension of biologically basic, prelinguistic forms of intentionality, and thus meets our basic requirement of showing how the human reality is a natural outgrowth of more fundamental—physical, chemical, and biological—phenomena. Second, I want to explain the special features of language that enable it to provide the foundation for all institutional ontology. The progression of the book is from intentionality to language and then from language to social institutions. This is the bridge chapter between mind and society.

Corresponding to these two aims are two more argumentative claims that I will be making against the philosophical tradition. First, in spite of its enormous achievements, it seems to me that analytic philosophy has been remiss in not treating language as a natural, biological phenomenon. Language is typically not seen as an extension of prelinguistic forms of intentionality. On the contrary, language is often seen as the primary form of intentionality, and some philosophers (for example, Donald Davidson and Michael Dummett)[1] claim that without language, there can be no thought at all. I believe that this view is more than a philosophical error; it is bad biology, and I will say more about it later. Second, the tradition of discussing the foundations of society has not, in general, faced up to the fact that without

1. Davidson, Donald, "Rational Animals," *Dialectica* 36, no. 4 (1982): 317–27; Dummett, Michael, *Origins of Analytical Philosophy*, Cambridge, Mass.: Harvard University Press, 1994.

an account of language, it is impossible to give an adequate account of social ontology.

In giving an account of language, I will try to overcome the curse of all social (and political) theorizing from Aristotle through Durkheim, Weber, and Simmel to Habermas, Bourdieu, and Foucault. All of the philosophers of politics and society that I know of take language for granted. They all assume that we are language-speaking animals and then they are off and running with an account of society, social facts, ideal types, political obligation, the social contract, communicative action, validity claims, discursive formations, the habitus, bio-power, and all the rest of it.[2] It may seem odd that I claim that Habermas, Bourdieu, and Foucault take language for granted, because they all have a great deal to say about it and they recognize its importance for their philosophical/sociological researches. But the problem with all of them is that they do not tell us what language is. They take it for granted that we already know what language is and go on from there. The worst offenders in this regard are the Social Contract theorists. They assume the existence of us as language-speaking creatures, and then they speculate how we might have got together in "a state of nature" to form a social contract. The point I will be making, over and over, is that once you have a shared language you already have a social contract; indeed, you already have society. If by "state of nature" is meant a state in which there are no human institutions, *then for language-speaking animals, there is no such thing as a state of nature.*

In order that you can begin to explain the nature of society, or the role of language in society, you first have to answer the question, What is language? In this chapter I want to answer (at least part of) that question in a way that will enable us to see how language is different from other social institutions, different in such a way as to make the existence of all the others dependent on language. You can have a society that has language but does not have governments, private property, or money. But you cannot have a society that has government, private property, and money, but does not have a language. I think everyone would agree to this, but the philosophically important task is to say exactly why it is true. All human social institutions are brought into existence and continue in their existence by a single logico-linguistic operation that can be applied over and over again.

---

2. I realize that Locke has a whole section on language in his famous *Essay*. But the account is inadequate even as an account of language, and he gives no evidence of seeing that any account of language could show how language underlies society.

I will explain in this chapter and in the next one in what sense language is constitutive of institutional reality, and consequently in what sense all human institutions are essentially linguistic.

There is a top-down connection between language and institutional facts: you cannot have institutional facts without language. And once you have a shared language you can create institutional facts at will. We could, right now, decide to form a club of people interested in the issues discussed in this book. But there is also a bottom-up connection, because once you have language, it is, I believe, inevitable that you will get nonlinguistic institutional facts. Given a language you can, so to speak, create institutional facts at will (that is the top-down part); but when you have a language, other social institutions will inevitably grow up out of language (this is the bottom-up part).

I. Language as Phonology, Syntax, and Semantics

Standard textbook accounts list three components of natural human languages: the phonological component, which determines how the words and sentences are pronounced; the syntactical component that determines how the elements are arranged in sentences; and the semantic component that determines the meanings of words and morphemes. More sophisticated accounts add a fourth component, pragmatics, which is not specific to particular languages but sets general constraints on the *use* of language. For our purposes, we can ignore phonology because it is not essential to our account that language be spoken. In fact, there are forms of human linguistic communication that do not require speech—for instance, sign languages—and it is easy to imagine a language that exists only in written form.

Syntax, however, is crucial. It involves three distinct features: discreteness, compositionality, and generativity. These three features of syntax organize semantics, in a way that I will now explain.

DISCRETENESS

It is a feature of sentences that though they are composed of words and morphemes (hereafter, "words" for short), the words maintain their identity in the recombinations. This is unlike, for example, the way a cake is composed of its ingredients, where the ingredients do not retain their identity. You can have an apple pie with three apples or two apples or two and a half apples. You can have a sentence of eight words or ten words, but you cannot have a sentence of eight and a half words. Any pie ingredients such as apples, flour, butter, sugar, and cinnamon can merge and lose their identity, whereas in language, the words retain their identity under recombination. Sentences maintain the discreteness of their components, in a way that apple pies do not.

COMPOSITIONALITY

Compositionality is a matter both of how the sentence is composed syntactically and how the meanings are arranged syntactically. So certain formulations constitute English sentences, while others do not. But, and this is a crucial point for our present investigation, if the sentence contains meaningful words, then the syntactical arrangement of words in the sentence will affect the meaning of the sentence. Thus we understand the sentence "John loves Mary" differently from the sentence "Mary loves John" because we understand in each case that though the words with their meanings are the same, the different arrangement determines a different meaning to the sentence.

GENERATIVITY

The third feature is generativity, by which I mean the infinite generative capacity of natural languages. Once you have certain sorts of rules, such as the rule for forming relative clauses or the rule for inserting conjunctions, then you can have, strictly speaking, an infinite number of sentences. There is no limit to the new sentences that can be produced. The possibility of an infinite number of new sentences creates the possibility of expressing an infinite number of new thoughts, of new semantic contents. So the three features—discreteness, compositionality, and generativity—are not just features of the syntax; they are the principles by which the syntax organizes the semantics. The semantic units retain their identity under syntactical transformation. The meaning of the sentence is a compositional function of the meaning of the components and of their syntactical arrangement in the sentence. The possibility of generating an infinite number of sentences carries with it the possibility of generating an infinite number of new sentential meanings.

I said that this was the standard textbook account of language. What is wrong with it? I think it is OK as far as it goes, but it leaves unanswered the crucial question, What is semantics (meaning)? And when we answer that question we will see that the standard textbook account leaves out the crucial deontological elements that come with the use of language. And that will lead us to some results that fall outside the traditional conceptions of the relations of semantics and pragmatics. We will find that we use meaning (semantics) to create a reality that goes beyond meaning.

II. What Features Are Common to Language and Prelinguistic Mentality?

One way to see the structure of the argument I am about to present is to imagine it as an account of how language could have evolved. I am not, for these purposes, interested in making actual speculations about how it did evolve, but I want to make some conceptual points about the different elements that go into language. Assume we have a race of hominids that have no language but have the full range of human prelinguistic intentional capacities. They have perception, intentional action, at least short-term memory, beliefs, desires, and so on that I have already described, in Chapters 2 and 3. By "hominid" I mean to include prelinguistic humans. We are imagining a race of early humans possessing the biological forms of intentionality, both individual and collective, but lacking language. We imagine that they are capable of cooperative behavior and that they have the full range of perception, memory, belief, desire, prior intentions, and intentions-in-action. What do they acquire when they acquire language? This is not a science fiction fantasy, because as far as we know there were early humans more or less like ourselves walking on the face of the earth without language, and later they got language. What did they get?

We can also think of our question as an engineering question: you are an engineer designing a language for people who are like us but happen to be without language. What do they have already, and what must you give them to build a full-blown human language?

I have to reemphasize that in structuring the question this way I am not engaging in speculative evolutionary biology. There is a legitimate branch of evolutionary biology that is concerned with the evolution of human languages.[3]

---

3. For some recent work on the evolution of communication, see Hauser, Marc, Noam Chomsky, and Tecumseh Fitch, "The Faculty of Language: What Is It, Who Has It, and How Did It Evolve?" *Science* 298 (Nov. 22, 2002): 1569–79. Tomasello, Michael, *The Origins of Human Communication.* Cambridge, Mass.: MIT Press, 2008.

It is a difficult enterprise because we have very little fossil evidence that bears directly on the evolution of language. I am emphatically not engaging in that enterprise. My question is conceptual. Subtract language from a species like us and what do you have? Now add language. What are you adding?

The whole investigation proceeds on the assumption that mental states exist in people intrinsically in a non-intentionality-relative fashion. I have my intentional states of hunger and thirst, for example, regardless of what anybody else thinks. But the intentionality of language, of words and sentences, called "meanings," is intentionality-dependent. The intentionality of language is created by the intrinsic, or mind-independent, intentionality of human beings.

There are four questions we need to answer. I will use the word "consciousness" as a shorthand for "consciousness and intentionality."

1. What features of language are already present in prelinguistic consciousness?
2. What features of language are lacking in prelinguistic consciousness?
3. What features of consciousness are lacking in language?
4. What functions do we need language to perform, given that we already have prelinguistic consciousness?

Our first question is, What are the features common to prelinguistic consciousness and to language? Well, we have already answered most of that question in previous chapters. Both speech acts and intentional states have propositional contents, conditions of satisfaction, and directions of fit. I have not yet discussed the relation between the various types of psychological mode, such as beliefs and desires, and the various types of speech acts, such as statements and promises. We will get to that question later in this chapter, but we already have an apparatus that includes intentional states of the form

$$S\ (p)$$

where "S" marks the psychological mode, and "p" marks the propositional content. We need to explain how animals get from such structures to speech acts that have the parallel form

$$F\ (p)$$

where "F" marks the type of speech act, its illocutionary force, and "p" marks the propositional content.

In addition to the structure of propositional content in a psychological mode, prelinguistic consciousness already carries two essential elements that go along with that structure, both of which I describe briefly in Chapters 1 and 2. The first element is direction of fit. The cognitive intentional states such as belief and perception, like Assertive speech acts, have the downward or mind-to-world direction of fit ↓. The volitive and conative states such as desire and intention, like Directive and Commissive speech acts, have the upward or world-to-mind direction of fit ↑. The second element is that all of the states that have these directions of fit have conditions of satisfaction determined by the propositional content. So the formal structures of intentional states and speech acts are surprisingly similar, and I will show how to build on these similarities.

Another feature common to prelinguistic forms of consciousness and to language is that in the possession of prelinguistic forms of consciousness, the animal is already able to operate with a rather large number of traditional philosophical (e.g., Kantian and Aristotelian) categories. An animal that is consciously able to cope with the environment already has the category of object, or thing, because it can discriminate the things that it encounters from each other. For example, it distinguishes a tree or another animal from other features of the environment. It has the categories of space and time because it observes objects as located in space, and it experiences changes through time. For example, it observes an animal walking over there and another animal sitting here, and about itself, it experiences that first it foraged and then it ate. It also has the category of agency because it can experience making things happen as opposed to things simply happening to it. For example, it experiences the distinction between digging in the ground with its own effort, and objects falling on it. With the category of object it already has the categories of identity and individuation, because, for at least some objects, it can see that this object is the same object as the object it saw before, and it can see that this object is distinct from that object. Once it has objects, with identity and individuation, it is already in possession of properties and relations. For example, it can see that this object over there is brown and that it is bigger than this green object nearer here. It can see that that object over there stands in a spatial relation to this object over here. I will not continue this list because my aim now is just to get you to see that the intentionalistic apparatus prior to language is heavily endowed with categories. I must emphasize that I am using the word "category" rather than "concept" because I am not claiming that in dealing with the environment the prelinguistic animal has anything that we would think of as concepts in the full sense. What I am claiming is that the prelinguistic conscious experiences of animals such as ourselves, and those similarly biologically endowed, are already *structured* by metaphysical categories such as space, time, individuation, object, causation, agency, and so on.

III. What Features Does Language Have that Prelinguistic Consciousness Lacks?

I said earlier that language contains sentences composed of syntactical elements. But in language these syntactical elements can be manipulated freely, whereas nonlinguistic intentional states have no such manipulable components. The dog might think that someone is approaching the door. But he cannot think the false thought, the door is approaching someone, and he cannot even distinguish the thought that someone is approaching the door from the thought that the door is being approached by someone. Once in possession of a language structured into sentences, where the sentences are composed of words (together with sentence boundaries, intonation contour, and all the rest of it), the animal can manipulate semantically loaded syntactical elements at will. It turns out that this is going to be crucial for the construction of human civilization.

Related to the fact that the sentence contains manipulable elements is the fact that language itself structures experiences into discrete segments. Nonlinguistic consciousness is, or at least can be, a continuous flow, broken only by dreamless sleep or other forms of unconsciousness. But language is essentially segmented. Each sentence must be discrete, and indeed even a fragment of a sentence, if uttered as a complete speech act, must be discrete. Suppose I now have the thought, "Because it is getting cold in here, I must turn on the heater." That thought occurs in time because it occurred to me in an English sentence that went through my brain in a temporal sequence. But it still has a kind of discreteness that prelinguistic thoughts do not always have. If I am skiing or walking or dancing, the stream of my conscious experiences can be in a continuous unsegmented flow.

Another feature that language has that prelinguistic thoughts lack is representations that have the double direction of fit characteristic of speech acts of Declaration, which I described in Chapter 1. The most famous examples are such performative utterances as "I pronounce you husband and wife" and "I promise to come and see you." In such cases language enables us to create a reality by representing that reality as existing. At one level this will seem a very mysterious capacity of language, but when we understand it fully we will see that it is the device that enables us to create a social and institutional reality out of language and collective intentionality. We will see that the creation of human institutional facts always has the same underlying logical structure as the performative utterance.

There are five, and only five, possible types of speech acts, five types of illocutionary acts.[4] These are (1) Assertives (statements, descriptions, assertions, etc.) whose point is to represent how things are and which therefore have the downhill or word-to-world direction of fit ↓; (2) Directives (orders, commands, requests, etc.) whose point is to try to get other people to do things, and which have the uphill or world-to-word direction of fit ↑; (3) Commissives (promises, vows, pledges, etc.) whose point is to commit the speaker to some course of action, and which, like directives, have the uphill or world-to-word direction of fit ↑; (4) Expressives, (apologies, thanks, congratulations, etc.) whose point is to express the speaker's feelings and attitudes about a state of affairs that is in most cases presupposed to exist already; and (5) Declarations, which, remarkably, have both directions of fit at once. In a Declaration we make something the case by declaring it to be the case. The first four types of speech acts have exact analogues in intentional states: corresponding to Assertives are beliefs↓, corresponding to Directives are desires↑, corresponding to Commissives are intentions↑, and corresponding to Expressives is the whole range of emotions and other intentional states where the Presup fit is taken for granted. *But there is no prelinguistic analogue for the Declarations. Prelinguistic intentional states cannot create facts in the world by representing those facts as already existing. This remarkable feat requires a language.*[5]

IV. Special Features of Consciousness that Language Lacks

There is a traditional problem in the philosophy of language that simply does not arise for prelinguistic consciousness. In the philosophy of language it is

---

4. I have argued at some length for this claim elsewhere. See especially *Intentionality: An Essay in the Philosophy of Mind.* Basically, the form of the argument is to show that meaning itself restricts the possibilities of what one can do with language. I won't repeat the argument here.
5. There are some odd apparent exceptions to this. Descartes' thinking that he is thinking can create the fact that he is thinking. I was reminded of this by Ernest Sosa.

sometimes called the problem of the "unity of the proposition" or, syntactically, "the unity of the sentence." The question is, Given that sentences contain these discrete elements, words and morphemes, how is it possible that a sentence can be a unified entity? What is the difference between a sentence and a mere jumble of words? And to put the question as one about propositions, How is it that the proposition, which after all contains discrete elements, turns out always to be a unified whole? Thus for example, we all understand the sentence, "There are two white fence posts on the left," as expressing a coherent proposition and as being a grammatically coherent sentence. But the sequence of words "white left posts there fence two on are the," does not in that way express any coherent thought. This is an interesting problem for the philosophy of language but consciousness solves it immediately. There is no problem of how I can put the elements of my experience together to form a unity in the way that there is a problem about how I can put discrete words together to form a unified sentence. This is because, pathologies apart, conscious experiences come with a unity already built into them. In conscious visual perceptions, hunger, thirst, and so on, the determination of the conditions of satisfaction is already fixed by the character of the experience itself.

A second feature of conscious experience that seems somehow at odds with the unity of the conscious experience is the fact that in perceptions, objects are salient; they stick out. If I look around the room now, I see discrete objects and not just the colored surfaces. Right now I see a computer screen in front of me. There is no way that I can see *the screen* in front of me without seeing *that there is a screen* in front of me. That is, the conditions of satisfaction come in whole states of affairs and not just objects; but all the same, when I do see that there is a screen in front of me, I do see the screen. I see both the object and the whole state of affairs, and they are internally related in the sense that I cannot do one without the other. Reports in the "see that" form typically require that the seer possesses the appropriate concept. My dog, for example, can see a burglar, but he cannot see that there is a burglar there because he lacks the appropriate concept. All the same, he does see that something is there.

Now the fact that conscious experience already segments objects and features will provide a basis for corresponding elements of language. True, different languages segment experiences differently. Famously, not all languages have a color vocabulary that matches that of the standard European languages. But there are limits to how many different ways we can reasonably segment experiences in language. We could easily imagine a language that does not have words for material objects. But though such a language is imaginable, it runs counter to our perceptual experience, which makes the material object salient. In normal perception, as shown by the Gestalt psychologists, the perception is typically of an object with its features against a background.

V. The Functions of Language: Meaning, Communication, Representation, and Expression

We now turn to the last of our four questions: what primary function, or functions, are performed by language? By primary function, I mean one such that a language could not be a language at all if it did not perform that function.

The first primary function is this: we need language to provide a mechanism by which our hominids can communicate with each other. What does "communicate" mean? And what gets communicated? The standard answer to the second question is that in speaking we communicate information. But "information" is one of the most confused and ill-defined notions in contemporary intellectual life. So I am wary of using it except incidentally. I will just state flatly that what typically gets communicated in speech acts are intentional states, and because intentional states represent the world, what gets communicated by way of intentional states is typically information *about the world*. If I communicate to you my belief that it is raining, the point is typically *not* to tell you about me and my beliefs, but about the weather. But there is no way I can intentionally tell you something about the weather except by way of using my mental representations of the weather, my weather-directed intentional states, such as my beliefs.

Our prelinguistic hominids already have perception, intentional action, and prelinguistic thought processes. All of these are intentional states with full propositional contents. And when one such creature intentionally communicates to another, it tries to reproduce its own intentional content in the head of the other person. When it communicates, for example, "There is danger here," it has the belief that there is danger here and it acts in such a way as to convey this belief to another animal.

The simplest type of communication would be the cases in which one animal communicates information about the world by communicating an unstructured proposition to another animal. By unstructured I mean that the propositional content has no internal syntax. There is nothing there corresponding to the words of natural languages. This type of communication is apparently very common among animals. Think of warning cries, for example. Such examples are cases of what Peter Strawson[6] once called "feature placing." We simply communicate the presence of a feature in the environment. In actual languages these feature-placing utterances can often be done with one word: "Danger!" "Rain!" "Fire!" And when we expand one of these into a whole sentence, the other parts of the sentence are sometimes semantically empty, as when we say "It is raining" though there is nothing referred to by "it." Such simple cases of intentional communication do indeed transfer an intentional content from one animal to another, but they are a very small step on the road to real language because they are so limited. All sorts of animals have this kind of communication, but it is not yet linguistic in the full sense of natural human languages.

VI. The Distinction between Expression and Representation

To show how we can go beyond the limitations of such simple one-word communications, I first have to explain some important distinctions and concepts. First, we need to distinguish expression from representation. That is, we need to distinguish between those communicative acts that involve intentionally representing a state of affairs in the world and those that simply express (in the original sense of pressing out, of giving vent to) an animal's internal state, where that expression may convey information about the world but it does not do so by representing that something is the case, or by representing other sorts of conditions of satisfaction. Thus if I say "Rain!" I represent the weather even if the representation is unstructured. But if I say "Ouch!" as a spontaneous expression of pain, I convey information but I do not represent anything. Let us now make a generalization that will make our task clearer: simple expressive speech acts, even when performed intentionally, are not "linguistic" in the sense we are trying to make explicit, and the corresponding words of actual languages are not "words" in our sense. Ouch! Damn! Yuck! Wow! are all used to express mental states, both intentional and nonintentional, but they are not the kind of linguistic phenomena

---

6. Strawson, P. F., *Individuals: An Essay in Descriptive Metaphysics*, London: Methuen, 1959, 202ff–14ff.

we are trying to explain here. Why not? Because, though in the way that I am imagining them used, they give vent to intentional or other states of the speaker, they do not represent. What we want to understand is how our early humans could have evolved linguistic *representation*.

What is the difference exactly between representing and expressing? If I say "Rain!" with the intention of describing the state of the weather, my utterance can be literally true or false, because it represents the current state of the weather. I can, for example, lie when I make this utterance. But if I say "Ouch!" though I do convey information about myself, I say nothing that is literally true or false. If I say "Ouch" when I am not in pain I may mislead and misinform, but I do not strictly speaking lie.[7] In our investigation, we will be concentrating on representation, not on expression.

VII. Speaker Meaning as the Imposition of Conditions of Satisfaction on Conditions of Satisfaction

The next notion we need to explain is the notion of speaker meaning. It is customary, and I think correct, to distinguish between the standing conventional meaning of a sentence, or sentence meaning for short, and the speaker's meaning that the speaker has on the particular occasion of a particular utterance. We will explain speaker meaning before we explain conventional sentence meaning, because speaker meaning is logically prior, in the sense that the conventional meaning of a sentence is, so to speak, a standard or communicable or fungible form of speaker meaning. Conventional meaning is what enables speakers to utter sentences and mean something by them in a way that will be understood. Sentences are to talk with.

In the case of our early humans, suppose that one early human wishes to convey some information to another, such as that there is danger or fire or food here, and he makes an utterance with the intention of communicating that information. What fact about that utterance makes it meaningful? The distinction between just intentionally producing an utterance and producing an utterance and meaning something by it is a matter of the difference in the

---

7. We can construct examples where what is normally a purely expressive speech act can be performed representatively. If my dentist tells me to say "Ouch" if it hurts too much, then in saying "Ouch" I am making a statement to the effect that it hurts too much.

intentional content in the two cases. In both cases, the speaker has the intention to make an utterance, but if the utterance is meaningful, then the speaker intends that the utterance itself has further conditions of satisfaction. We can say, then, that the essence of speaker meaning, when a speaker says something and means something by it, is that the speaker intentionally imposes conditions of satisfaction on conditions of satisfaction.

I can best illustrate this point by showing how it works for existing languages. Suppose I am standing in the shower practicing French pronunciation. I say over and over "Il pleut." The conditions of satisfaction of my intention in action are that I should correctly produce the French sounds. If somebody shouts at me "It's not raining, you idiot. You are simply standing in the shower," he will have misunderstood what I was trying to do. I did not *mean* that it's raining. But now suppose that later we go outside and I discover that it's raining. This time I say "Il pleut," and I mean it. What is the difference between the two cases? In both cases I intend to produce the French sounds, and the correct production of the sounds is a condition of satisfaction of both utterances. But in the second case I intend that the production of the sounds should itself have further conditions of satisfaction, namely, that it is raining. Speaker meaning, to repeat, is the imposition of conditions of satisfaction on conditions of satisfaction.

The capacity to do this is a crucial element of human cognitive capacities. It requires the ability to think on two levels at once, in a way that is essential for the use of language. At one level the speaker intentionally produces a physical utterance, but at another level the utterance represents something. And the same duality infects the symbol itself. At one level it is a physical object like any other. At another level it has a meaning; it represents a type of a state of affairs.

So far I have insisted on a distinction between expression and representation, and I have said that the uses of language that we need to concentrate on are the representative cases because those are genuinely semantic. They are semantically evaluable because they can be, for example, literally true or false. I further insisted that speaker meaning is a matter of the intentional imposition of conditions of satisfaction on conditions of satisfaction. The next notion to explain is communication. If the speaker says something and means something by it, and furthermore intends to communicate that meaning to the hearer, he must further intend that the hearer should recognize his meaning intention. That is, if he makes an utterance and he intends, for example, to represent the state of affairs that it is raining, if he intends to communicate this information to the hearer, then he must intend that the hearer recognize his meaning intention and indeed recognize that he is intended to recognize it. This is the standard speech act situation. The speaker makes a meaningful utterance. He intends to represent a state of affairs in one of the possible illocutionary modes. He intends to communicate that representation to the hearer, and his intention to communicate is the intention that the hearer should recognize his meaning intention and recognize that he is intended to so recognize it.[8]

VIII. Linguistic Conventions and Word and Sentence Meaning

The last notion I need to explain is the notion of a convention. I have described how speakers may communicate to hearers by creating meaningful utterances, but if they are to succeed on anything like a regular basis, there has to be some socially recognized device, some repeatable device, the production of which can regularly be intended by speakers to convey the message. With the introduction of repeatable devices that can be used to convey speaker meaning on a regular and repeatable basis, we have introduced the notion of a linguistic convention and with it the notion of a standing word or sentence meaning. The conventional device for conveying speaker meaning now has a permanent sentence meaning of its own. In describing this we have invoked the distinction between types and tokens. The convention already involves a kind of generality because it involves the possibility of repeating the same thing over and over on different occasions. The conventional meaning attaches to the type, word or sentence, and thus enables different token occurrences of that type to convey that meaning.

8. Grice, Paul, "Meaning," *Philosophical Review* 66 (1957), 377–88. This account of communication derives from Grice's analysis of meaning but differs importantly from that account. I have claimed in other writings that Grice confuses meaning and communication. The distinctive feature of Grice's account was that he introduced a self-referential class of intentions, and he claimed that the meaning intention was the intention to produce a perlocutionary effect on the hearer by getting the hearer to recognize the intention to produce that effect. I have a number of objections to this account, but among them I claim that this is an analysis of communication but not of meaning. In order that there be communication, there must be a meaning that gets communicated.

There are two separate aspects to what I have said so far about meaning. First, speaker meaning consists in the double level of intentionality I have tried to describe. The speaker intentionally produces an utterance, and he intends that the utterance should itself have conditions of satisfaction—for example, truth conditions. But, and this is the next crucial point, if he is to succeed on a regular basis, then there has to be some *socially recognized conventional device*, some repeatable device, the production of which can be regularly and conventionally taken by his interlocutors to convey the message. Now we are getting much closer to language, because the first phenomenon is essential to the performance of speech acts, and the second phenomenon, the repeatable devices, consists typically of words and sentences of a language.

We have then taken considerable steps on the road to actual human languages if we imagine that our hominids have the capacity to create meaningful utterances and communicate these meanings by invoking existing conventions of a language. And in the case of the meaningful utterances in question, they are representations and not merely expressions of their internal intentional states. However, so far, they have nothing by way of syntactical complexity. All that we have imagined so far is that they have something roughly equivalent to our one-word sentences. The next step is to give internal syntactical structure to the sentences.

IX. Syntactical Compositionality

A further step on the road to language (and remember, the metaphor of "steps" implies nothing historical—I am speaking of logical components; I have no idea what the actual history was) is the introduction of simple syntactical devices that can be combined with other syntactical devices to produce complex syntactical devices, and each one of the complex devices will be used to communicate an entire intentional state. That is another way of saying that the hominids need to evolve elements that correspond to our words and morphemes, and they need ways of combining these into sentences in a compositional manner, in a way that enables the participants to figure out the meaning of the sentences from the meanings of the elements and their arrangement in the sentence. For us the minimal unit of communication, the minimal unit of the speech act, is the whole sentence. It ought, by the way, to strike us as amazing that all languages have sentences and a very large number (possibly all) also have noun phrases and verb phrases. The obvious explanation of the fact that all languages have sentences is that the sentence is the minimal unit for performing a complete speech act and thus for expressing an entire intentional state. The principle that guides the selection of the syntactical devices within the sentence is that they perform a semantic function. There must be repeatable devices each of which can function as a possible communication unit (sentence), and these must be composed of elements (words) which are such that the communicative content of the whole is determined by the elements and by the principles of their combination in the sentence.

How do we introduce these features—words and sentences—where the sentences are systematically built out of the words? We have to build on the resources that the animal already has, and these are in fact quite rich. Because our beasts already have the capacity to identify and re-identify objects, we can introduce *names* of objects, and because they have the capacity to recognize different tokens of the same type, we can introduce such *general names* as "dog," "cat," "man," and so on, and because the objects have features, we can introduce something corresponding to *adjectives* and *verbs*. But notice the crucial constraints on these. We are not assuming that reference and predication, the speech acts corresponding to noun phrases and verb phrases, are in any way simple independent elements, but rather that once we have the total speech act we can abstract these as component elements. Following Frege, we think of the noun phrases and verb phrases as derived from the total sentence and not of the total sentence as arrived at by combining noun phrases and verb phrases.

What does that mean? Our animals already have unstructured propositional contents. But corresponding to these are structured features of the real world and the animals have the capacity to recognize these structures *and their elements*. So we are not begging any questions when we give the hominid a sentential structure that corresponds to the conditions of satisfaction that it already has. The semantic function comes for free because we have already introduced meaning. Here is the basic idea: the animal has perceptual and belief contents that lack syntactic structure. It can see, and therefore believe, something that we can report (but the animal cannot report) as "It is coming toward me." Now if the animal has the capacity to produce semantically meaningful events, that is, speech acts, then it can represent this state of affairs with the double-level intentionality that I described earlier. From the animal's point of view the representation might be of the form: "Coming-toward-me-thing-now," where we are to think of this so far as if it were one word, without repeatable elements.

The animal has feature placing, but not yet reference and predication. To get reference and predication it needs symbolic devices that break up the propositional content into components. But it already has the material to construct those components from its prelinguistic intentionality. It can see something coming toward it now and thus believe that something is coming toward it now. And that is enough to give us the possibility of introducing devices that can perform the functions of reference and predication, devices that are forms of noun phrases and verb phrases. We will add rules or procedures for arranging those devices (words) into the complex resultant structures (sentences). It does not much matter how we construct these subsentential elements or how we combine them as long as they break up the sentence into repeatable components, and as long as the components match the components of the prelinguistic intentional contents. I have been assuming that they are broken up in a style similar to the European languages I know, but that is not a necessary assumption. I have been assuming that the presyntactical *coming-toward-me-thing-now* breaks up into a device that refers to a contextually specific object, such as a man, and the predication of coming toward me now, as here:

A man is coming toward me now.

It is not logically necessary that it be done this way, but doing it this way fits our prelinguistic phenomenology better than some ways we can imagine. We could imagine a language in which what we think of as objects are treated as recurring and repeatable processes, so it would come out as

It is manning now towards me comingly.

on analogy with

It is raining now on me heavily.

But such a language would not reflect the object salience of our perceptual phenomenology.

How do we explain the pervasiveness of noun phrases and verb phrases in human languages, and how do we explain that, typically, sentences contain both noun phrases and verb phrases? If we look at the phenomenological structure of our experiences, particularly conscious, perceptual experiences, we will see that *objects and their features* are salient. Though the conditions of satisfaction of our visual experiences require whole states of affairs, so that we never just see an object, but, for example, we see that an object with such and such features is over there; all the same, phenomenologically, we are aware of seeing objects and seeing that they have such and such features. So the propositional unity expressed by the complete sentence is already provided by prelinguistic intentionality, and the internal subject-predicate structure is provided by the way our phenomenology presents the propositional content to us.

So far, then, we have taken three steps on the road to language: First the creation of speaker meaning, that is, the imposition of conditions of satisfaction on conditions of satisfaction. Second, the creation of conventional devices for performing acts of speaker meaning, which gives us something approaching sentence meaning, where sentence meaning is the standing possibility of speaker meaning. Sentence meaning is conventional. Speaker meaning is typically the employment or use of those conventions in the performance of the speech act. Third, we have added internal structure to the speech act in the form of discriminable syntactic elements that have meanings, semantic content, but cannot stand on their own in utterances. They are parts of sentences and thus correspond to words, but they are not yet whole sentences. We also need rules for combining these devices into whole sentences and distinguishing between grammatical and ungrammatical strings. Both of these are crucial to any account of language. The first gives us meaningful units big enough to function in communication; the second gives us compositionality. The sentence is composed of meaningful elements, and those meaningful elements, together with their rules of combination, enable us to generate new sentences and to figure out the meanings of sentences and utterances that we have never heard before.

We do not yet have generativity, that is, the capacity of speakers to produce and understand a potentially infinite number of new sentences; but it is easy to add generativity to compositionality by simply adding some recursive rules, rules that apply over and over endlessly. Examples of ways of providing generativity are such expressions as "It is possible that" or "Sally believes that" or rules for forming relative clauses such as in "Sally saw the man who lives next door." What about sentence connectives? They do not seem hard to add either. Indeed, we already have an implicit sentence connective when we conjoin two sentences in the speech act. If I say "It is raining. I am hungry," I have already said something equivalent to "It is raining and I am hungry." We can add explicit connectives to do these jobs, connectives corresponding to the English "and," "or," "if . . . then," and "not."

Notice that with the addition of linguistic syntax to animal intentionality we enable speakers to do something no nonlinguistic animal can do. The speaker can intentionally construct many different representations of actual, possible, and even impossible states of affairs in the world. We break the connection between the representation and the perceptual stimulus so the speaker can use tenses and modalities. The speaker can now think and say not only "The man is coming toward me now," but "The man will come toward me next week," or "The mountain will come toward me," and so on endlessly.

With the apparatus so far developed, the hominids can extend the vocabulary to enable them to think thoughts and perform speech acts that are literally unthinkable without language. Given numerals, initially introduced to match the fingers, the hominid can count indefinitely and have thoughts with numerical components that he cannot have without numerals. Without language he might think, "There are three dogs in the field," but with language he can think, "I wish there were a thousand dogs in the field."

X. The Next Step: Deontology

So, with meaning conventions plus compositionality and generativity, we are well on the road to language.

Why is that not enough? Why are we just on the road and not already there? I think there is a sense in which we are already there if we understand the implications of the account that I have given in a certain very specific way. It is essential to see that in the account I have given so far it is implicit that the speaker employing the conventional device in a social setting for the purpose, for example, of conveying some truth about the world to the hearer, is thereby *committed* to that truth. That is, we will not understand an essential feature of language if we do not see that it necessarily involves social commitments, and that the necessity of these social commitments derives from the social character of the communication situation, the conventional character of the devices used, and the intentionality of speaker meaning. It is this feature that enables language to form the foundation of human society in general. If a speaker intentionally conveys information to a hearer using socially accepted conventions for the purpose of producing a belief in the hearer about a state of affairs in the world, then the speaker is committed to the truth of his utterance. I will now try to explain this point.

We saw earlier that the formal structure of the intentional state, S(p), looks a lot like the formal structure of the corresponding speech act, F(p). But "F(p)" represents an intentional act, and in the cases we are considering it represents an act deliberately performed in accordance with the conventions of a socially accepted language. Recall that the essence of speaker meaning is the intentional imposition of conditions of satisfaction onto utterances, the imposition of the same conditions of satisfaction as those of the intentional state expressed in the utterance. Thus, if I believe that it is raining and I want to say that it is raining, I express my belief by making an utterance that I intend to have the same conditions of satisfaction as the original belief. The utterance inherits the direction of fit of the belief and thus, like the belief, the utterance can be true or false. When I say "It is raining," my utterance has the word-to-world direction of fit and will be true or false depending on whether the propositional content is satisfied. And so on through the other cases.

But now an interesting problem arises concerning the relation between the speech act and the corresponding intentional state. The speech act involves a commitment that goes far beyond the commitments of the intentional state expressed. This is most obvious in the case of statements and promises, but it is also true of other sorts of speech acts such as orders and apologies. When I make a statement I not only express a belief, but I also commit myself to its truth. When I make a promise I not only express an intention, but I also commit myself to carrying it out. But what exactly is a commitment and where do these commitments come from? The belief and the intention have nothing like the commitments of the statement or the promise. If we are trying to explain the logical, conceptual evolution of a language that has statements and promises, it is not enough that we explain how a speaker can convey his belief and his intention to the hearer. We need to know how the speaker adds these special deontologies to the speech act. It is tempting, and indeed true, to say that the constitutive rules of the institutions of statement making and promising make every statement into a commitment to truth and every promise into an obligation to do something. The rules typically have the form "X counts as Y in C." (For example, making such and such an utterance X in this context C counts as making a promise Y). The question is, What is a commitment and how do we get rules, the invocation and use of which commit us?

There are two components to the notion of a commitment.[9] Roughly speaking these are, first, the notion of an undertaking that is hard to reverse

9. For a good discussion of commitment see Miller, Seumas, "Joint Action: The Individual Strikes Back," in Savas Tsohatzidis (ed.), *Intentional Acts and Institutional Facts: Essays on John Searle's Social Ontology*, Dordrecht: Springer, 2007, 73–92.

and, second, the notion of an obligation. These typically combine, for example, in the notion of promising. When I make a promise I make an undertaking that is not easily reversible. But at the same time, I create an obligation. These two features of irreversibility and obligation combine in speech acts performed according to rules. The animal has the intention both to impose conditions of satisfaction on conditions of satisfaction (and thus to create meaning) and to communicate those conditions of satisfaction (and thus, that meaning) to other animals. It does this according to conventional procedures. Those collectively accepted conventional procedures enable the hominids to create a type of commitment that is internal to the procedures but is not present without the conventional procedures. There is no way I can say to someone, publicly, intentionally, explicitly, "There is an animal coming toward us," without being publicly committed to the truth of the proposition that there is an animal coming toward us, and that commitment is much stronger than the commitment to truth of the corresponding belief by itself. Both the belief and the corresponding statement involve commitments. But the commitment of the statement is much stronger. If the privately held belief turns out to be false I need only revise it. But in the case of the statement, I am committed not only to revision in the case of falsehood, but I am committed to being able to provide reasons for the original statement, I am committed to sincerity in making it, and I can be held publicly responsible if it turns out to be false.

So once we have an explicit language in which explicit speech acts can be performed according to the conventions of the language, we already have a deontology. We already have commitments, in the full public sense that combines irreversibility and obligation. Language is the basic form of public deontology, and I am claiming that in the full sense that involves the public assumption of irreversible obligations, there is no such deontology without language. I am now arguing that once you have language, it is inevitable that you will have deontology because there is no way you can make explicit speech acts performed according to the conventions of a language without creating commitments. This is true not just for statements but for all speech acts. Orders commit me to wanting the hearer to obey the order, to the view that it is possible for the hearer to obey the order, and to the view that the objects referred to in the order exist. I cannot order you to leave the room without being committed to the truth of the proposition that you are able to leave the room, that I want you to leave the room, and that there are such things as you and a room, and that you stand in a relation to the room that makes it possible for you to leave the room. All types of speech acts contain an element of commitment. Most utterances are not literally promises; but the type of commitment, including both irreversibility and obligation, for which promising is the paradigm, affects all other sorts of speech acts: orders, thanks, apologies, and so on.

My claim that the deontology in the form of commitment is internal to the performance of the speech act runs counter to the widely held view in philosophy that the deontic requirements are somehow external to the type of speech act, the view that first we have statement making and then we have a rule that enjoins us to making only true ones; first we have promise making and then we have a rule that obligates us to keep the promises. This view of the relation of statements to truth is held by philosophers as diverse as Bernard Williams,[10] Paul Grice,[11] and David Lewis.[12] But it is not correct. You cannot explain what a statement, or a promise, is without explaining that a statement commits the maker of the statement to its truth and the promise commits the maker of the promise to carrying it out. In both cases the commitment is *internal* to the type of speech act being performed, where by "internal" I mean it could not be the type of speech act it is, it could not be that very kind of speech act, if it did not have that commitment. But, to repeat the question, How do we evolve the deontic power out of the act of meaning something by an utterance? Does the act of representing the same conditions of satisfaction as those of a belief somehow essentially involve a commitment that goes beyond the commitment of the belief? Does the action of representing the same conditions of satisfaction as an intention necessarily involve a commitment that goes beyond the commitment of the intention? Or are these other commitments just add-ons? Are they further accretions that come with the historical development of the linguistic institutions? I think they are internal.

To see why, we have to see that the speech act is more than just the expression of an intention or the expression of a belief. *It is above all a public performance.* I am telling something to someone else. But I am not just telling him that I have a belief or that I have an intention; I am telling him something

---

10. Williams, Bernard, *Truth and Truthfulness: An Essay in Genealogy,* Princeton, N.J.: Princeton University Press, 2002.
11. Grice, Paul, "Logic and Conversation," in Peter Cole and Jerry L. Morgan (eds.), *Syntax and Semantics 3: Speech Acts,* New York: Academic Press, 1975, 41–58.
12. Lewis, David, "General Semantics," in G. Harman and D. Davidson (eds.), *Semantics of Natural Language,* 2nd ed., Dordrecht: D. Reidel, 1972, 169–218.

about the world represented by those beliefs and intentions. By committing myself to the conditions of satisfaction of the belief (in making a statement), I am telling him that this is how the world is; by telling him about the conditions of satisfaction of my intention (in making a promise), I am telling him what I am actually going to do. (The self-referentiality of promises comes in here. I do not just promise to do something, but I promise to *do* it *because I promised* to do it. In ordinary parlance, I give my word.)

We can summarize this part of our discussion as follows. In creating a language we found that we needed speaker meaning, conventions, and internal syntactic structure. But if you understand these as relating in a certain way to human intentionality, you can see the different types of illocutionary acts and in so doing, you already get the commitments that typically go with those types of illocutionary acts. Nothing further is necessary to guarantee that speakers will be committed by their utterances. In following the common-sense idea that language could have evolved, and may in fact have evolved, out of prelinguistic forms of intentionality, we found that language so evolved provides something not present in prelinguistic intentionality: the public assumption of conventionally encoded commitments.

So now our primates have language and they are capable of undertaking commitments. Then it seems to me that the next step is to see how they will inevitably evolve other sorts of institutional facts besides just speech acts.

XI. The Extension of Deontology to Social Reality: How Language Enables Us to Create Social Institutions

The argument given so far is that intentional acts of meaning—that is, the intentional imposition of conditions of satisfaction on conditions of satisfaction, performed according to accepted conventions—necessarily involve a deontology. Now, once that deontology is collectively created by these intentional actions, then it is very easy—indeed, I believe, inevitable—that it should be extended to social reality generally. I am not claiming that the extension is logically entailed but that it is empirically inevitable. Once you have the capacity to represent, you already have the capacity to create a reality by those representations, a reality that consists in part of representations. Let me give some examples of this. If you have the capacity to say "He is our leader," "He is my man," "She is my woman," "This is my house," then you have the capacity to do something more than represent preexisting states of affairs. You have the capacity to create states of affairs with a new deontology; you have the capacity to create rights, duties, and obligations by performing and getting other people to accept certain sorts of speech acts. Once you and others recognize someone as a leader, and an object as someone's property, and a man or a woman as someone with whom you have a special bond, then you have already created a public deontology. You have already created public reasons for action that are desire-independent. But notice how the language that we use to describe these phenomena functions. It creates them. The language constitutes them in an important way. Why? Because the phenomena in question are what they are in virtue of being represented as what they are. The representations, which are partly constitutive of institutional reality, the reality of government, private property, and marriage as well as money, universities, and cocktail parties, is essentially linguistic. Language doesn't just describe; it creates, and partly constitutes, what it both describes and creates. The maneuver I am describing has the logical form of a Declaration, as I claimed in Chapter 1. We make something the case by representing it as being the case. So when I say "That woman is my wife" or "He is our leader" or "That is my hut," these categorizations contain two levels of meaning. At one level there is simply a preexisting relationship; but when I describe that relationship in a certain way, when I say that the person or object now "counts as" something more than the existing physical facts, I am adding a deontology to the person or object—and that deontology extends into the future. That deontology is created by a Status Function Declaration.

Compositionality figures essentially in the creation of social and institutional reality. Given compositionality, the animal can do much more than just represent existing states of affairs; it can represent states of affairs that do not exist but which can be brought into existence by getting a community to accept a certain class of speech acts. So, for example, the man who says, "This is my property," or the woman who says, "This is my husband" may be doing more than just reporting an antecedently existing state of affairs; he or she may be creating a state of affairs by Declaration. A person who can get other people to accept this Declaration will succeed in creating an institutional reality that did not exist prior to that Declaration.

We do not yet have performatives, because they require specific performative verbs or other performative expressions; but we do have Declarations with their double direction of fit. If I declare, "This is my house," then I represent myself as having a right to the house (word-to-world direction of fit) and, if I get others to accept my representation, then I create that right because the right only exists by collective acceptance (world-to-word direction of fit). And they are not independent: I create a right by representing myself as having it.

This basic move underlies all of institutional reality. It is not easy to see this point but I think it is essential to understanding society. The utterances can create desire-independent reasons for action if the status functions that they attempt to create are recognized by other members of the community. That same move, that same X-counts-as-Y-in-context-C move, by which you create desire-independent reasons for action in the case of the individual speech act, is now generalizable. So what we think of as private property, for example, involves a kind of standing speech act. It is a kind of permanent speech act affixed to an object. It says that the owner of this object has certain rights and duties, and other people, not owners of this object, do not have those rights or duties. Think of money as a kind of standing permanent speech act. (Sometimes the speech act is spelled out. On American paper currency it says: "This note is legal tender for all debts public and private.")

Throughout this chapter I have been drawing attention to several remarkable features of human language. None is more remarkable than this: in human languages we have the capacity not only to represent reality, both how it is and how we want to make it be, but we also have the capacity to create a new reality by representing that reality as existing. We create private property, money, government, marriage, and a thousand other phenomena by representing them as existing.

The three points I am making here can be summarized as follows. First, language is inevitably deontic because there is no way you can have speech acts according to conventionally established rules without commitments. Second, once you have linguistic commitments, it is inevitable that you will have the extension of those to the forms of institutional realities that are the extensions of the biologically primitive forms, such as family, marriage, property, and status hierarchies. And third, the logical structure of the creation of institutional facts is exactly the same as that of the Declaration: the representations have the double direction of fit because they make something the case by representing it as being the case. I will explain this in more detail in the next chapter.

XII. Summary of the Argument So Far

Much of this chapter has been devoted to trying to explain the conceptual relationships between linguistic structures and prelinguistic intentionality, and that led to a second part of the argument: I tried to show how language both introduces deontology into social relations and how it creates an institutional reality with a deontic structure. The basic intellectual motivation that drives this second part of my argument is the following: there is something left out of the standard textbook accounts of language as consisting of syntax, semantics, and phonology with an extra-linguistic pragmatics thrown in. Basically what is left out is the essential element of commitment involved in having a set of conventional devices that encode the imposition of conditions of satisfaction on conditions of satisfaction. The final part of the argument is about the creation of a social and institutional ontology by linguistically representing certain facts as existing, thus creating the facts. When we understand this third point we will get a deeper insight into the constitutive role of language in the construction of society and of social institutions. Let me review the steps of the argument so that it is as clear as I can make it.

Step 1. We imagine a race of hominids who have consciousness and prelinguistic intentionality and who are endowed with a capacity for free action and collective intentionality. They can cooperate and they have free will.

Step 2. We have to assume that they are capable of evolving procedures for representing states of affairs where the representations have speaker meaning, as I have defined it. They can represent states of affairs that they believe exist, states of affairs they desire to exist, states of affairs they intend to bring about, and so on.

Step 3. These procedures, or at least some of them, become conventionalized, become generally accepted. What does that mean exactly? It means that given collective intentionality, if anyone intentionally engages in one of these procedures, then other members of the group have a right to expect that the procedures are being followed correctly. This, I take it, is the essential thing about conventions. Conventions are arbitrary, but once they are settled they give the participants a right to specific expectations. They are normative.

Step 4. We can also imagine that they break up the representations into repeatable and manipulable components that perform the functions of reference and predication.

Step 5. The central idea in the argument is this: just having a belief or a desire or an intention does not so far commit a person in any public way. Of course, a belief is a commitment to truth and a desire is a commitment to satisfaction and an intention is a commitment to action, but none of these so far are *public* undertakings. There is no social deontology involved, no publicly recognized obligation. But once you freely commit yourself to the conditions of satisfaction of these corresponding intentional states and you do this in a public way by imposing conditions of satisfaction on conditions of satisfaction, and you do it according to the normative conventions of a language, then you are creating obligations and other sorts of deontic commitments. Notice that the commitment is to states of affairs in the world and not just to the corresponding intentional states. Thus if I make a statement, I commit myself to the existence of a fact; if I make a promise, I commit myself to the performance of a future action, and so on.

Step 6. The same basic linguistic move that enables speech acts to carry a deontology of rights, duties, commitments, and so on can be extended to create a social and institutional reality of money, government, marriage, private property, and so on. And each of these is a system of deontologies. Once we introduce the elements of compositionality and generativity into language there is literally no limit to the institutional realities we can create just by agreeing, in language, that we are creating them. We create universities, cocktail parties, and summer vacations, for example. The limits on institutional power are the limits on deontology itself. Deontic powers are powers that exist only because they are recognized and accepted as existing. Sometimes we back them with physical force—in the case of the criminal law, for example—but police forces and armies are also systems of deontologies.

7. The logical form of the creation of institutional reality is that of a Declaration and is therefore the same as that of the performative utterance. We make something the case by representing it as being the case. In the case of institutional reality, all of these are Status Function Declarations because they create Status Functions by declaring them to exist.

XIII. The Nonmysteriousness of Status Function Declarations

I want to conclude this chapter by demystifying status functions. I have been talking about Status Function Declarations in a way that gives them extraordinary powers. However, it must seem mysterious that we can create all these powers just by making noises through our mouths. So I want to bring the whole issue down to a more humble and realistic level. Let us suppose in a pub that I get up from the table and go to the bar and order three beers. I then carry the beers back to the table and set them down. I say, "This one is Sally's; this one is Marianne's; and this one is mine." Now this would not appear to be a very remarkable metaphysical effort, but in fact it has remarkable properties. By making these utterances, I have in fact created new rights. Indeed, they were more than statements; they were deontic commitments of a very special kind. I created a reality according to which, for example, Sally has certain rights that Marianne does not have and Marianne has rights that Sally does not have. This would come out in the fact that if Marianne tried to drink Sally's beer, Sally would have a legitimate complaint. Indeed I need not *say* anything. Just pushing the beer in the direction of their new owners can be a speech act. If the metaphysics of Status Function Declarations can function effectively in a bar, then it should not be too mysterious how they can function at all.

Now how does all of this work? We have a capacity to create a reality by representing it as existing. The only reality that we can so create is a reality of deontology. It is a reality that confers rights, responsibilities, and so on. However, this is not a trivial achievement because these rights, responsibilities, and so on are the glue that holds human society together.

5

THE GENERAL THEORY OF
INSTITUTIONS AND INSTITUTIONAL
FACTS: LANGUAGE AND SOCIAL REALITY

I. The Sea of Institutional Reality

We live in a sea of human institutional facts. Much of this is invisible to us. Just as it is hard for the fish to see the water in which they swim, so it is hard for us to see the institutionality in which we swim. Institutional facts are without exception constituted by language, but the functioning of language is especially hard to see. This might seem an odd thing to say because we are often conscious of language when we engage in a conversation, receive a telephone call, pay our bills, answer our e-mail, and so on. What I mean is that we are not conscious of the role of language in constituting social reality. We are aware of such things as the actual conscious speech acts we perform, and we are often aware of such unimportant things as the accents with which other people speak, but the constitutive role of language in the power relations in which we are immersed is, for the most part, invisible to us.

One of the advantages of living in other cultures is that one can become more acutely conscious of the different and unfamiliar institutional structures. But at home one is less aware of the sea of institutionality. I get up in the morning in a house jointly *owned* by me and my *wife*. I drive to do my *job* on the *campus* in a car that is *registered* to both of us, and I can drive *legally* only because I am the holder of a *valid California driver's license*. On the way, I *illegally* answer a cell phone call from an old *friend*. Once I am in my *office* the weight of institutional reality increases. I am in the *Philosophy Department* of the *University of California* in *Berkeley*. I am surrounded by *students, colleagues,* and *university employees.* I teach *university courses* and make various *assignments* to my *students*. The *university pays* me, but I never see any *cash* because my *pay* is *deposited* automatically into my *bank account*. After my lecture I go to a *restaurant*, and I use my *credit card* to pay the *bill*. When I get back to campus, I telephone my *insurance agent* about my *homeowner's policy*, and I also call my *travel agent* to arrange *airline tickets* for an *invited lecture* at a *professional society*. I *accept* an *invitation* to a *dinner party*. At every stage I am performing *speech acts*. They are the basis of all the institutional realities I have italicized. I will let the reader continue this list with his or her own inventory of institutional entanglements.

All of the italicized expressions in the previous paragraph refer to institutional reality in its various aspects. Institutional facts range all the way from the informality of friendship to the extreme legal complexities of international corporations. The simplest test for whether a phenomenon or fact is genuinely institutional is to ask, Does its existence imply deontic powers, powers such as those of rights, duties, obligations, requirements, and authorizations? There are (uncodified) rights and obligations of friendship and dinner parties, just as there are (codified) rights and obligations of citizenship and employment. There are deontologies without institutional facts (I am, for example, under a moral obligation to help people who are in desperate need of immediate help and whom I am able to help), but there are no institutional facts without some form of deontology. These institutional deontic powers have a common logical structure that I aim to reveal in this chapter.

Here are some typical institutions and types of (nonlinguistic) institutional reality:

Governmental institutions: legislature, executive, judiciary, military, police.

Sports institutions: the National Football League, amateur baseball teams, local sporting clubs.

Special-purpose institutions: hospitals, schools, universities, trade unions, restaurants, theaters, churches.

Economic institutions: industrial corporations, brokerage houses, real estate agencies, businesses, partnerships.

General-purpose structural institutions: money, private property, marriage, government.

Unstructured informal (mostly) uncodified institutions: friendship, family, love affairs, parties.

General forms of human activity that are not themselves institutions
but which contain institutions: science, religion, recreation, literature,
sex, eating.

Professional activities that are not institutions but contain institutions:
law, medicine, academia, theater, carpentry, retail trade.

I said that the test for whether a noun names an institution is whether under
that description the object named has deontic powers. On this test, the Catholic
Church is an institution; religion is not. The National Science Foundation is an
institution; science is not. Private property is an institution; a car is not.

Any one of these institutions will generate institutional facts in ways that
will be clear to people familiar with the operation of the institution: the
legislature passes a bill, the baseball player gets a base hit, Bill spends five
dollars for a bus ticket. Furthermore, there are institutions within institutions.
For example, the U.S. government, one institution, contains Congress, another institution, and Congress sets up government departments, more institutions. Business corporations set up subsidiary businesses. This usage treats
"institution" as a technical term, because there are some things that we
would ordinarily call institutions that would not qualify as institutions on
my definition. For example, the Christian calendar would ordinarily be
thought of as an institution—it was, after all, instituted—but on my definition it is not, because there is no separate deontology that can be created
simply by invoking the calendar. Like the color words, the calendar provides a
vocabulary for situating certain brute facts and institutional facts, but situating
those facts does not create a deontology. For example, in my culture, being the
17th of January is not an institutional fact because no special powers accrue.
Being Christmas Day, on the other hand, is an institutional fact, because,
among other deontologies, it entitles people to a day off.

In my culture, being a bore, an alcoholic, or an intellectual are not
institutional facts. Why not? Because no special collectively recognized deontology is implied by these descriptions. I might feel personally that I have
special obligations as an intellectual, but in my society at large, there is no
special deontology attached to people under the description "intellectual."
And in this respect, being an intellectual differs from being a professor, a car
owner, or a convicted criminal. All of these institutional facts imply a
deontology. In the United States, by the way, we seem to be evolving the
institution of "public intellectuals," which would be a status function, if
generally accepted.

II. The General Theory of Institutions and Institutional Facts

In this chapter I want to use the materials that we have assembled in the preceding chapters to construct a general theory of human nonlinguistic social institutions and institutional facts within those institutions. I have tried, in Chapter 4, to account for language, and now I want to use that account to explain nonlinguistic institutional facts such as money, property, government, and marriage.

There is an awkwardness in terminology that I need to clarify. I want to contrast "linguistic" institutional facts such as the fact that someone stated that it is raining from "nonlinguistic" institutional facts such as the fact that Obama is president. But on my own account all institutional facts are linguistically created and linguistically constituted and maintained. So it can be misleading to describe some of them as "nonlinguistic." What I mean by that is that the facts in question go beyond facts about meanings. The powers of the presidency are created by semantics, but the powers in question go beyond the powers of semantics. Intuitively there is an obvious distinction between facts such as that someone made a statement or asked a question and such facts as that someone is president or has $1,000 in his bank account. I name the former class "linguistic" and the latter class "nonlinguistic," but I do not mean to imply that the nonlinguistic are not linguistically created and maintained. A main aim of this chapter is to explain exactly how.

From now on, when I say "institutional fact" I mean "nonlinguistic institutional fact" unless otherwise noted. I want to answer the following questions: What are the procedures by which we create institutional reality? What is the distinction between institutions and institutional facts within those institutions? What is the distinction between the initial creation and the subsequent continuation of existence of institutional facts? How is it possible to create institutional facts without a preexisting institution?

CREATING INSTITUTIONAL FACTS

I said in Chapter 1 that all institutional facts are created by the same logical operation: the creation of a reality by representing it as existing. The general form for the creation of status functions is this:

We (or I) make it the case by Declaration that the Y status function exists.

This general form is then implemented in a variety of different ways, which I will now explain. To do this I will use the same strategy I used in discussing language. I will give a conceptual evolutionary account. I want to show how we can proceed from simpler to more complex forms. The point, as with language, is not to speculate about the actual evolutionary history of human institutions (though we know a good deal more about the history of institutions than we do about the origins of language) but to explain the increase in conceptual complexity as we move from the simplest cases to the more complicated forms of deontic power.

Type 1: The Creation of an Institutional Fact without an Institution: Wall into Boundary

In earlier writings[1] I described how institutional facts might evolve out of noninstitutional physical facts. I imagined a tribe that builds a wall around its cluster of huts, where the wall performs the function of restricting access in virtue of its physical structure because it is too high to climb over easily. We then imagine that the wall decays until nothing is left but a line of stones. But let us suppose that the inhabitants, as well as outsiders, continue to recognize the line of stones as having a certain status: a status that we could describe by saying it is a boundary. And they continue to *recognize* that they are *not supposed to cross* the boundary unless *authorized.* I want that to sound very innocent, but in fact it is momentous in its implications. In this case we began with an object that performs its function in virtue of its physical structure. But it evolves into an object that performs its function, not in virtue of its physical structure, but in virtue of the fact that there is a collective recognition or acceptance by the people involved, both inside and outside the line of stones, that the line has a certain status and performs its function only in virtue of the collective recognition or acceptance of that status. This is an example of a "status function." I will define a status function as a function that is performed by an object(s), person(s), or other sort of entity(ies) and which can only be performed in virtue of the fact that the community in which the function is performed assigns a certain status to the object, person, or entity in question, and the function is performed in virtue of the collective acceptance or recognition of the object, person, or entity as having that status. I have to mention other sorts of entities besides just objects and people because we will

---

1. Searle, John R., *The Construction of Social Reality*, New York: Free Press, 1995.

have to allow for the attachment of status functions to abstract entities such as the status functions of a limited liability corporation.[2]

The case of the wall as having the status function boundary requires no written language and no general rule. In this case, the people involved impose a status function Y on an object X in a context C.

This case, like all institutional facts, necessarily involves language, or at least some form of symbolism. To understand that, we need to distinguish a simple *disposition* not to cross the line from the case where one recognizes that one is under an *obligation* not to cross it. I might train my dog not to go outside my yard simply by punishing him when he does and rewarding him when he stays inside the boundary. I have changed his disposition so that he will stay inside the yard. But so far there is no question of obligation or duty involved. For humans there will no doubt be a gradual transition between dispositions to behave and recognitions of obligations. But I want us to think of the line of stones as imposing an obligation on those who recognize it as a boundary. The obligation derives from the fact that there is a collectively recognized status assigned to the line of stones. The line of *stones*, X, now has the status *boundary*, Y, but that status can exist only if the participants in the institution have a language rich enough to represent it. That is, I am making a distinction between simple dispositions to behavior, which do not require language, from cases where there is an institutional deontology. *Such a deontology can exist only if it is represented as existing.* This distinction, between deontologies and dispositions, is also exemplified by the difference between a human tribe having a recognized leader and a pack of wolves having an alpha male. The leader has a continuing deontic status, an *authority* represented by and created by language. The alpha male wolf is treated with fear and respect because of his physical strength, but he has no publicly recognized deontology. Such a deontology requires language. Why? Because without a language you have only prelinguistic intentional states such as desires and beliefs together with dispositions. To get to the point that you can recognize an obligation as an obligation, you have to have the concept of an obligation, because you have to be able to represent something as an obligation, that is,

---

2. The notion of a status function involves an extension of the ordinary use of the word "function," because not all status functions would ordinarily be thought of as functions. So, for example, it will turn out that human rights are status functions and we do not normally think of one of our "functions" as exercising freedom of speech. But I will argue that it is sufficiently like ordinary functions assigned in virtue of status that it is legitimate to assimilate it under the general category of status functions.

something that gives you a reason for action independent of your inclinations and desires. You need not have the actual word "obligation" or some synonym, but you must have a conceptual apparatus rich enough to represent deontology.

I want to emphasize that the logical form of the transition from being a line of stones to being a boundary is that of a Status Function Declaration. There need not be any specific moment at which there is a speech act of Declaring, but there must be some speech act or set of speech acts and other sorts of representations that constitute representing the line of stones as a boundary in a way that makes it into a boundary. When the representations are collectively recognized or accepted, the line of stones acquires a new status: it now is a boundary. And such representations exemplify precisely the logical form of the Status Function Declaration.

Type 2: Constitutive Rules of the Form "X Counts as Y in C"

The same tribe that created the status function of boundary might also create the status function of the leader of the tribe by simply assigning that status to a particular person. But as the generations pass they may well evolve a standard procedure for selecting the king. We will suppose that the royal status is inherited through the male line, in a society that is largely illiterate. For centuries, this was the case in Europe, where the status function was awarded to the oldest son of the deceased king. In this case, unlike the boundary case, there actually is a rule: for all x, if x is the oldest living son of the deceased king, then x counts as the king. Not much of a rule, perhaps, but nonetheless a rule that one can codify.[3] The creation and continued existence of the status function does not require a written form of documentation, though typically, a community will use other status indicators such as a special headdress, a crown, or a specific garment. Even in a preliterate society these function as symbols, and though they are not necessary for the creation of a status function, they are useful in its maintenance because they readily identify the holder of the status function in question and they symbolize his or her royal status. Literate societies use lots of nonverbal status indicators such as uniforms and wedding rings.

What is the meaning (logical form, semantic content) of the constitutive rule "X counts as Y in C"—in this case, the rule that the oldest living

---

3. As already remarked, I use small letters "x," "y" as variables of quantification and large letters "X," "Y" as free variables that may be bound by a neighboring noun phrase.

son X of the deceased king counts as the new king Y? We can best understand constitutive rules if we contrast them with regulative rules. The *regulative* rule, "Drive on the right hand side of the road," for example, is a standing Directive. Its function is to bring about a certain form of behavior, and it is satisfied if the behavior matches the content of the rule. The rule has upward, or world-to-word ↑ direction of fit. By contrast, the *constitutive* rule, "The oldest surviving son counts as the new king," is a standing Declaration. Its function is to make it the case that a certain person becomes the new king on the death of the old king. No one has to do anything to satisfy it except to accept its consequences, to count the oldest surviving son as the new king. It has both directions of fit, word-to-world and world-to-word ↕, simultaneously. It makes something the case by representing it as being the case. I call it a standing Status Function Declaration because it makes it the case into the indefinite future that anyone who satisfies the condition of being the oldest surviving son of a deceased king is the new king. It makes something the case, but it applies to an indefinite number of such somethings.

Type 3. A Complex Case: Creating a Corporation

Let us contrast these cases with a much more complicated case that requires explicit rules, a complex legal structure, and a written language: the creation of a limited liability corporation. In the State of California, as in many jurisdictions, explicit laws enable the creation of a corporation by a speech act of Declaration.

The California Code regarding corporations specifies it this way:

> Section 200A: "One or more natural persons, partnerships, associations or corporations, domestic or foreign, may *form a corporation* under this division by *executing and filing articles of incorporation.*"
>
> Section C: "*The corporate existence begins upon the filing of the articles and continues perpetually,* unless otherwise expressly provided by law or in the articles." (italics added)

These two sections, taken together, form a very powerful constitutive rule. The actual texts are standing Declarations. They make it the case by Declaration that any entity that satisfies certain conditions may form a corporation by performing another Declaration, and the corporation will then exist "perpetually" unless certain other conditions occur. So there is a double Declaration involved in the creation of a corporation. The law is itself a (set of) Declaration(s). What it Declares is that anyone who makes a Declaration of a certain sort will have formed a corporation.

Such constitutive rules are Declarations that specify the conditions under which certain institutional facts will be created. Sometimes, as in this case, the conditions involve the performance of another Declaration. Sometimes, as in the case of getting a base hit in baseball or committing first-degree murder, the act, which constitutes the institutional fact, is not itself a speech act. One of our puzzles is, If all institutional facts are created by Declaration, then how do we account for the fact that such events as getting a base hit or committing first-degree murder are not speech acts? The answer is that the physical events in question constitute the institutional facts of getting a base hit or committing first-degree murder only because there is a standing Declaration that assigns status functions to these physical events. The rule declares that satisfying such and such conditions counts as a certain sort of institutional fact.

Notice that in the case of the corporation there was no preexisting object that was turned into a corporation, as there was in the other cases—the line of stones was turned into a recognized boundary and the oldest son was turned into a king. The law does not say that some preexisting X becomes a corporation; rather, it says that a corporation *may be formed*. It says that the performance of these written speech acts—"executing and filing articles of incorporation"—*counts as* the creation of a corporation—"the corporate existence begins upon the filing of the articles and continues perpetually . . . "

In this case we seem to have created a remarkably potent object, a limited liability corporation, so to speak out of thin air. No preexisting object was operated on to turn it into a corporation. Rather, we simply made it the case by fiat, by Declaration, that the corporation exists. Notice also that the whole point of doing this is to create a rather elaborate set of power relationships between actual people; indeed, the corporation consists of such relationships. When one creates a corporation one thereby creates an entity that can do business and that has such positions as the president of the corporation, the board of directors, and the stockholders. When a corporation is created, its status functions accrue to actually existing people, even though the corporation can retain its identity through changes in the people who occupy the various positions of status function within it.

The creation of a boundary out of the line of stones produces a very simple deontology. The creation of a corporation produces an immensely complex deontology involving interrelationships of many people. It is logically possible that there could be a race of beings that could do this without writing, but for human beings of our sort, it is impossible to create and maintain corporations in existence, engaging in all their activities, without an elaborate set of written constitutive rules, two of which I have cited above, and an elaborate written record of the activities of the corporation.

These three types of cases seem to exhibit three distinct logical forms. Is there a common structure exemplified by all three? The basic form of the operator that creates status functions is this:

> We make it the case by Declaration that the Y status function exists in context C.

The different ways this principle is implemented now fall out naturally. The simplest implementation is where you simply impose a status function on a person or object, for example, making a line of stones into a boundary. So if we spell it out, it would come out as this:

> We make it the case by Declaration that object X now has the status function Y in C.

And we can spell that out to make it fully explicit, so it looks like this:

> We make it the case by Declaration that X has the status Y and thus is able to perform the function F in C.

Where, remember, the function itself will be spelled out as a set of deontic powers. Other forms of implementation will include the constitutive rules and the freestanding Y terms. Let us spell those out. The constitutive rule now looks as follows:

> We make it the case by Declaration that for any x that satisfies condition p, x has the status Y and performs the function F in C.

And this covers everything from presidents of the United States to convicted criminals and base hits in baseball.

The most puzzling case is the case of the freestanding Y terms where we create, for example, a corporation. The law that enables the corporation is itself a Declaration that enables other Declarations to be performed. Let us go through those in order. The law is of the following form:

> We make it the case by Declaration that for any x that satisfies a certain set of conditions p, x can create an entity with Y status function by Declaration in C.

Thus, in the text of the law I quoted, the condition p is being a natural person, a corporation, and so on, and any such an entity can create a corporation by Declaration. So the law is a Declaration that authorizes other Declarations. And then when you actually create a corporation, here is what it looks like:

> We make it the case by Declaration that an entity Y exists that has status function(s) F in C.

We have to put it that way because we need to specify not just that the function exists but that there is an entity Y, the corporation, that has the function, even though the entity is, as they say, a "fictitious" entity. The point is that in such cases there is no independently existing X. There is just a creation of an entity that has the Y status function, so the noun, "corporation," carries both the name of an entity and the existence of the status functions. Not all freestanding Y terms are of this form. When the bank creates money simply by lending money that it does not have, the Declaration looks like this:

> We make it the case by Declaration that a status entity Y exists with the functions F. Thus in lending Jones the money, the bank makes it the case by Declaration that a certain percentage of the money loaned now exists that did not previously exist. (I will say more about the creation of money later.)

What goes for the line of stones, the king, the corporation, and money goes for private property, governmental leaders, universities, public holidays, cocktail parties, licensed drivers, and nation-states, as well as the United States Army, the Mafia, Al Qaeda, and the Squaw Valley Ski Team. In all of these cases, there is a creation of status functions by Declaration. God can create light by saying "Let there be light!" Well, we cannot create light but we have a similar remarkable capacity. We can create boundaries, kings, and corporations by saying something equivalent to "Let this be a boundary!" "Let the oldest son be the king!" "Let there be a corporation!"

III. Speech Acts and Deontic Powers

With these examples in mind we can now state the general principles on which institutional reality is created and maintained in existence. We require exactly three primitive notions: first, collective intentionality; second, the assignment of function; and third, a language rich enough to enable the creation of Status Function Declarations, including constitutive rules. I have explained collective intentionality and said something about the assignment of function in Chapter 3. In Chapter 4 I tried to explain how a language could evolve with a deontology and with speech acts of Declaration.

When I wrote *The Construction*, I thought that this third element in the creation and maintenance of institutional facts simply amounted to the existence of constitutive rules or procedures by which we attach status functions, and these had the form "X counts as Y in C." What I did not ask myself then but am asking myself now is, What exactly is that procedure from the point of view of a theory of speech acts? Well, there are two radically different sorts of cases. The literal utterance of the sentence "Snow is white" counts as the making of a statement that snow is white, simply in virtue of its meaning. No further speech act is necessary. But when we count pieces of paper of a particular sort as twenty-dollar bills we are making them twenty-dollar bills by Declaration. The Declaration makes something the case by *counting it as*, that is, by declaring it to be, the case. It is essential to understand this asymmetry to understand both the nature of language and the nature of institutional reality. I will say more about it later in this chapter.

Not all impositions of status function have this form "X counts as Y in C," because sometimes, as in the case of corporations, or electronic money, we create a status function with deontic power but without attaching it directly to any person or material object. These are cases of what Barry Smith calls "freestanding Y terms."[4] So the formula "X counts as Y in C" is one form, but not the only form, in which we implement what I have called the most general logical form of the creation of institutional reality:

> We (or I) make it the case by Declaration that a Y status function exists in C.

Because the whole point of doing this is to create deontic powers, we need also to specify the creation of those powers within the scope of the Declaration. And here is what that looks like:

> We (or I) make it the case by declaration that a Y status function exists in C and in so doing we (or I) create a relation R between Y and a certain person

---

4. Smith, Barry, "John Searle: From Speech Acts to Social Reality," in Barry Smith (ed.), *John Searle*, Cambridge: Cambridge University Press, 2003, 1–33.

or persons, S, such that in virtue of SRY, S has the power to perform acts (of type) A.

The point of adding this extra clause is to make it clear that we are not just creating Y status functions for their own sake but to assign powers—positive, negative, conditional, and so on—to actual people by *relating them to the Y status functions created*. These relations can vary with the type of status function in question. In the case of the presidency, the person is *identical* with the bearer of the Y status function. In the case of money, the person is the *possessor* of the money. In the case of private property, the person empowered is the *owner* of the private property. In the case of corporations, specific persons have specific powers and obligations. So far then, we have introduced an operator that creates a status function, and then within the scope of that operator, we have introduced powers that attach to the status function. The next step is to show the form in which the recognition of the status function is essential to its operation:

> We collectively recognize (Y exists in C and because (SRY (S has the power (S does A)))).

In order for the collective recognition to enable the functioning of the deontic power, both the existence of the status function and its relation to S must be within the scope of the collective recognition.

IV. The Continued Maintenance of Institutional Reality: More Status Function Declarations

We need both collective intentionality and the assignment of function to enable these operations to work in actual societies. Unless the institutional facts are collectively recognized or accepted and the participants understand the deontology carried by status functions, the institutional facts will not lock into human rationality and will not provide reasons for action. For example, unless there is some form of collective recognition or acceptance of property rights, and unless the participants have the concept of a "right" in the first place, the system of private property will not work, nor will it even be intelligible.

The actual complexities will introduce special features. For example, you do not need a *separate* attitude of recognition or acceptance for institutional facts within a preexisting institutional structure. If, for example, you accept the institution of baseball, then a given home run or base hit requires no separate acceptance. You are already committed to that acceptance by your acceptance of the institution. The only problems are epistemic. Was it really a base hit? Did he really commit the crime? This is why we have baseball umpires and criminal courts. Given the system of constitutive rules, did the act in question actually fall within the rule? The system, once accepted by participants, commits them to the acceptance of facts within the system because the system consists of sets of standing Declarations, and satisfying the conditions set down by these Declarations counts as constituting the institutional facts in question.

In addition to the power creation operator we need a collective recognition or acceptance operator that marks the continued existence and maintenance of the status function:

We collectively recognize or accept (S has power (S does A)).

Just as we had to include both the status function creation and the power relation within the scope of the original Status Function Declaration, so now we have to include both the status function maintenance and the power relation within the scope of the collective recognition. Here is what it looks like:

We collectively recognize or accept (There exists Y in C, and because S R Y (S has power (S does A))).

In plain English, we collectively recognize that a Y status function exists in context C, and because a human subject S stands in certain appropriate relations R to the status function Y in C, we further recognize that S has the power to do A, the acts determined by the Y status function. The intuitive idea is that the point of creating and maintaining institutional facts is power, but the whole apparatus—creation, maintenance, and resulting power—works only because of collective acceptance or recognition.

I think it is reasonably clear that the creation of the status functions is by way of Status Function Declarations. It is less obvious, but I think also true, that the continued existence of the status functions requires representations that work like SF Declarations. Why? The institution and the institutional facts within the institution require continued recognition or acceptance because they exist only as long as they are so recognized or accepted. One mark of recognition or acceptance is continued usage of the institution and institutional facts, and this requires the usage of the corresponding vocabulary. Acceptance need not take the form of an explicit speech act and can range all the way from enthusiastic endorsement to grudging acquiescence. This is why I frequently use the expression "recognition or acceptance" to mark the fact that I do not mean to imply approval by the specification of the attitude that institutions and institutional facts require for their continued existence. Recognition in the form of speech acts functions like Declarations, even when the speech acts are not in the form of a Declaration. By continuing to use the vocabulary of the status functions we reinforce the status functions. Unlike shirts and shoes, institutions do not wear out with continued usage. On the contrary, the continued usage of such institutions as marriage, private property, and money reinforces the institutions, but the "usage" requires talk, and that talk functions to maintain and reinforce both the institution and institutional facts within the institutions.

One sees the role of the vocabulary in the activities of revolutionary and reformist movements. They try to get hold of the vocabulary in order to alter the system of status functions. The feminists were right to see that the vocabulary of "lady" and "gentleman" involves a deontology that they wanted to reject. Again, the Communists in Russia wanted people to address each other as "comrade" as a way of creating new status functions and destroying old ones. The continued use of the vocabulary maintains and reinforces the existing status functions. Another way to see this phenomenon is to see how words that mark status functions can gradually fall into disuse with a corresponding erosion of the status function itself. The word "spinster" figures prominently in older American laws, but it is not a word that you hear in common speech now. When I asked my class, "How many of you are spinsters?" only one fierce middle-aged woman had the courage to raise her hand. A similar decay of the use of the word "bachelor" may be occurring as I write these lines, and with it, a decline in the associated status functions. So the daily use of the vocabulary with the downhill direction of fit already has a cumulative uphill direction of fit in sustaining the existence of the status functions across time.

If this is right, there will be no sharp dividing line between the creation of a status function by gradual verbal acquiescence in its existence and the continued existence of the same status function. There may be no specific point at which we can say, "Now the line of stones has really become a boundary" or "Bill has really become our leader" as distinct from saying "We continue to recognize the line of stones as a boundary" and "We continue to recognize Bill as our leader."

V. Further Questions

Now that we have stated the general theory, we need to answer the following questions:

1. What is the point of doing this? How do we benefit from these institutions and institutional facts?
2. How do we get away with it? It seems that we are inventing a reality out of nothing.
3. How does our account of institutional facts meet our basic requirement, the requirement that the human reality of institutions and institutional facts must not only be consistent with the basic structure of the world but must be a natural outgrowth of that basic structure?
4. Why is language special, and not just one institution among others?
5. What is the special role of *written* language?
6. If institutional facts have to be believed to exist, in order to exist, then how can we discover new and surprising information about them? How are surprising discoveries in the social sciences possible?
7. What is the logical form of statements about institutional facts, and how do we account for their apparent lack of extensionality?
8. What is the role of imagination in creating institutional reality?

I have already answered some of these questions implicitly, but I now want to make the answers explicit.

QUESTION I: STATUS FUNCTIONS AND DEONTIC POWERS

Why do we do this? Why do we create these elaborate institutional structures such as money, government, property, and universities? There is no single purpose served by all human institutions, and indeed, institutional reality is almost as various as human reality itself. But, I have argued, there is a common element that runs through all (or nearly all) institutions, and that is that they are enabling structures that increase human power in many different ways. Think what life would be like if we did not have money, schools, property rights, and above all, language. Some social theorists have seen institutional facts as essentially constraining.[5] That is a very big mistake.

---

5. Durkheim, Émile, *The Rules of Sociological Method*, George E. G. Catlin (ed.), trans. Sarah A. Solovay and John M. Mueller, Glencoe, IL: Free Press, 1938.

There is indeed an element of constraint in social institutions. For example, you cannot be president unless you get elected, you cannot spend money you do not have, and in baseball, you cannot have four strikes. But the very institutions of money and baseball increase our powers. I have claimed that the general form of the power operator is this:

We recognize (S has power (S does A)).

So for example, the president has the power to veto legislation passed by Congress. Congress in turn has the power to override his veto. I claim that all deontic powers created by institutional structures can be treated as exhibiting this structure, as a result of Boolean operations on this basic power creation operator. Thus, if I receive a parking ticket, and I am obligated to pay a fine of $50, I have a negative deontic power, an obligation, that looks like this:

We recognize (not (S has power (not (S pays $50 to the authorities)))).

In ordinary English, I do not have the power to not pay the money I owe. And if I have two strikes on me as a baseball batter, then at least part of my deontic status is conditional: if I get one more strike I am out. I have a conditional negative deontic power.

Let us constantly remind ourselves that the whole point of the creation of institutional reality is not to invest objects or people with some special status valuable in itself but to create and regulate power relationships between people. Human social reality is not just about people and objects, it is about people's activities and about the power relations that not only govern but constitute those activities.

QUESTION 2: HOW DO WE GET AWAY WITH IT?

My main strategy of exposition in this book is to try to make the familiar seem strange and striking. One of the strangest and most striking features of institutional facts is that there is nothing institutional there to the institutional fact prior to its creation. And since its creation is really just words, words, words, we have to ask, How does it get to be so successful? How do we manage to get away with it? Is it not just a sleight of hand? The short answer to the question is that we get away with it to the extent that we can get other people to accept it. As long as there is collective recognition or acceptance of the institutional facts, they will work. They work because they consist of deontic powers, and the deontic powers will function if they are accepted. Sometimes, of course, they have to be backed by police and military force. But police forces and armies are themselves systems of status functions.

But this answer does not answer the question that worries us. It says, we get away with it, when we get away with it, by getting people to accept it. But the question then becomes, *Why do people accept institutions and institutional facts?* The most general answer is that most of the institutions one can think of work for our benefit by increasing our powers. Many institutions like language and money are in pretty much everybody's interest, and it is hard to know how one would go about rationally rejecting them. But beyond such vague remarks about how some institutions tend to be in everybody's interest, there is no general answer to the question of why people accept institutions. Indeed, there are all sorts of institutions where people cheerfully accept what would appear to be unjust arrangements. One thinks of various class structures, the low position of women in many societies, and vastly disproportionate distributions of money, property, and power. But one feature that runs through a large number of cases is that in accepting the institutional facts, people do not typically understand what is going on. They do not think of private property, and the institutions for allocating private property, or human rights, or governments as human creations. They tend to think of them as part of the natural order of things, to be taken for granted in the same way they take for granted the weather or the force of gravity. Sometimes, indeed, they believe institutions to be consequences of a Divine will. Thus, for example, they believe that people are "endowed by their Creator with certain unalienable Rights."[6] I am not at all sure that a general understanding of how institutions are created and function would actually facilitate their functioning. Many of them are based on beliefs, such as beliefs in the supernatural, that I think are almost certainly false; and even those institutions that are not formed on the basis of doubtful beliefs, such as money and government, tend to work best when they are taken for granted and not critically analyzed. As Karl Marx pointed out, "One man is king only because other men stand in the relation of subjects to him. They, on the other hand, imagine that they are subjects because he is king."[7] A related reason that people recognize or accept institutions and institutional facts is that even in cases where they are aware of the arbitrariness or even the injustice of the institutional phenomena, they despair

6. *Declaration of Independence.*
7. Marx, K., *Capital: A Critical Analysis of Capitalist Production,* London: Swan Sonnenschein & Co., 1904, vol. 1, 26n.

of ever being able to change it. Yes, the distribution of property is unjust, and perhaps there is something unjust about the institution of private property itself, but there isn't much that an individual can do about it, so the individual tends to feel helpless in the face of the institution. I will say more about this phenomenon when I talk about political power.

A related and powerful motive for acceptance of institutions and institutional facts is the human urge to conform, to be like other people and to be accepted by them as a member of the group, a sharer of collective intentionality.

Beyond such general reasons as I have been citing—self-interest, increased power, ignorance, apathy, despair, and conformism—there does not seem to be any general answer to the question, What motivates acceptance? There are specific motivations for specific institutions. When the institutions involve power relations that can be threatening, as in the case of governments and political power generally, the question of legitimation becomes crucial. I will say more about this in Chapter 7 on power.

QUESTION 3: HOW IS THIS ACCOUNT CONSISTENT WITH THE BASIC REQUIREMENT?

How can we make the existence of institutional facts that have no physical realization consistent with our basic requirement that everything in the real world should bottom out in the entities of physics and chemistry and the rest of the real world? If we think, as we must, that all institutional facts have to bottom out in brute facts, then how do we deal with these cases that seem to have an abstract or free-floating ontology? On the conception of basic ontology that I have been espousing, it should be impossible for anything in the real world not to be grounded in the basic facts, to be in this way, freestanding. Money, corporations, and blindfold chess cannot just float on thin air.

I have already answered this question implicitly, but let us now make it fully explicit. When we combine the formula that states the creation of the status function in the way that I suggested earlier, it looks like this:

> We make it the case by Declaration that the Y status function exists in C, and in so doing we create a relation R between a person, or persons, S and Y, such that in virtue of SRY (S has power (S does A)).

Seen in this light, it turns out that the freestanding Y terms always bottom out in actual human beings who have the powers in question because they are represented as having them. So it is true that you don't need a physical realization to have money or a corporation, or chess pieces in blindfold chess, but you do have to have *owners* of money and *officers* and *shareholders* of corporations, and the *players* in a game of chess, and the power creation operator operates over them. Institutional facts still bottom out in brute facts, but the brute facts in these cases are actual human beings and the sounds and marks that constitute the linguistic representations.

To put the point succinctly: ontologically speaking, to create a minimal institutional reality you need exactly three things: (1) human beings (or some sort of being with the relevantly similar cognitive capacities) with (2) intentionality, including collective intentionality including the capacity to impose functions on objects and people, and (3) a language capable of Declarational speech acts—that is, speech acts with the double direction of fit. If the freestanding Y status functions are at all complex and are to persist through time, you need a fourth thing: writing. The cases of the freestanding Y terms are always cases in which humans and language are the only two phenomena necessary for the specific form of institutional reality. For other cases such as private real property, licensed drivers, and married couples, you need material objects, or human beings that have specific physical properties, to which the status function can be assigned.

QUESTION 4: WHY IS LANGUAGE SPECIAL? WHY IS IT NOT JUST ONE SOCIAL INSTITUTION AMONG OTHERS?

Intuitively, before we even begin to think about it, it seems that language is the primary social institution. You can imagine a society that has a language but has no government, property, marriage, or money. But you cannot imagine a society that has a government, property, marriage, and money but no language. Intuitively, pretheoretically, we are all aware that somehow language is constitutive of institutional reality. Even the authors whose work I find so inadequate would have accepted the sentence, "Language is constitutive of social reality." Indeed, I think everybody from Aristotle on would have accepted it. The problem is to state exactly how language is constitutive. What *exactly* is the form of the speech act by which institutional reality is created? What *exactly* is the ontological status of the reality so created and, and by what sort of speech act *exactly* is it maintained? These are precisely the questions I am attempting to answer in this book.

I have claimed that all of institutional reality is created by Declarations and is maintained in its continued existence by representations (thoughts as well as speech acts) that function like Declarations. But language itself is not created by Declaration. In this section I am going to ask, Why is there this asymmetry between language and other social institutions? And I am going to attempt to answer that question in a way that will show why language is the foundation of all other institutions.

Let us begin by attempting to minimize the differences between language and other institutions by noticing the apparent similarities between linguistic facts and institutional facts generally. Two points of apparent similarity stand out. First, the "X counts as Y" constitutive rule seems to work the same way for language and for nonlinguistic institutional facts. Thus we count Barack Obama as the president of the United States, and we count the sentence "Snow is white" as a sentence of English. In both cases it seems that some sort of status function is created. Furthermore, we count the utterance of the sentence "Snow is white" as a statement to the effect that snow is white. The second apparent similarity to notice is that performatives seem to work the same way for the creation of speech acts by Declaration as they work for the creation of nonlinguistic institutional facts. Thus utterances of "War is hereby declared," and "The meeting is hereby adjourned" are performative creations of institutional facts, facts about war and adjournment, respectively. I am told that in some Muslim countries a man can divorce his wife with a performative utterance. He need only say "I divorce you" three times while throwing three white pebbles. And similarly, utterances of "I promise to come and see you" and "I request that you leave the room" are also performatives; the first creates a promise, the second creates a request. Notice, however, that in these examples, we have identified two different kinds of performatives, which I will call "linguistic performatives" and "extralinguistic or nonlinguistic performatives." The linguistic performative creates a linguistic act, a speech act such as a promise or a request. The nonlinguistic performative is indeed linguistic (it is, after all, a speech act) but it can create other sorts of institutional facts such as divorces and adjournments.

What is the difference between linguistic and nonlinguistic or extralinguistic institutional facts? The first difference to notice is that the nonlinguistic institutional facts require linguistic representation in order to exist. So Obama can only be president, and I can only be a professor, and this car can only be my property if they are represented as such, and these representations are collectively recognized or accepted. But the sentences of English do not require further linguistic representation to be sentences of English. If they did, it looks like we would get an infinite regress. "Yes," one might say, "But maybe the fact that your view leads to an infinite regress is a refutation of your view, and not a proof of the distinction between language and extra-linguistic institutional facts. You still have not made out that distinction." In order to make out the distinction, I need to introduce the notion of meaning, where meaning consists in the imposition of conditions of satisfaction on signs or marks. And once we introduce that notion, we can see that the way the constitutive formula applies to nonlinguistic institutional facts is really quite different from the way it applies to sentences. So if we count Obama as the president of the United States, that specifies an *operation* of counting. We have to do something in order to count him as such. But when we say that an utterance of the sentence "Snow is white" counts as a statement to the effect that snow is white, the "counts as" does not in this case specify an operation; rather, the fact that the utterance counts as a particular statement is *constitutive* of the meaning of the utterance. The meaning of the sentence is already such that its appropriate utterance, by itself, is constitutive of the making of the corresponding statement. But the utterance of the sentence "Obama is president" by itself is not constitutive of making Obama president or of his being president. The notion of meaning that we are using here is the notion of something having a propositional content in an illocutionary mode. So the sentence "Snow is white" is meaningful because it assertively represents the state of affairs that snow is white. But the president or the item of private property is not in that way meaningful. It doesn't stand for or represent anything. Rather, it has to be represented as having the status function it has; otherwise it cannot have that status function.

The performative creation of linguistic institutional facts is quite different from the performative creation of nonlinguistic institutional facts. Why? Notice that in the case of adjourning the meeting, declaring war, or divorcing, we require something in addition to the *meaning* of the sentence. In addition to the conventions that create meaning, we require a convention or rule to the effect that the utterance of that sentence by the appropriate person counts as adjourning the meeting, declaring war, or divorcing. There must be some outside convention, some extra-linguistic convention beyond the conventions of the language itself. To put this point succinctly, to make a promise or request, all you need is to be a competent speaker of the language, using language in accordance with the conventions. But to declare war, adjourn the meeting, or divorce, you need something more than that: you need to be in a special position where an extra-linguistic convention gives you the power to create the corresponding institutional fact. That special power itself has to be created by language. So the apparent parallel between the nonlinguistic performatives for war, adjournment, and divorce and the linguistic performatives for promising and requesting is illusory. The nonlinguistic cases require Status Function Declarations in order that they can perform their function. But the linguistic cases do not. All that the linguistic cases require is meaning. The meanings of the performative sentences are themselves sufficient to enable a competent speaker to perform the speech act with those sentences. In the creation of nonlinguistic institutional facts by the performance of Status Function Declarations, the creation of the institutional fact goes beyond the meaning of the sentence narrowly construed. In these cases, we use the semantics of language to create a power that goes beyond semantics.

To see these differences, let us contrast the way we count the utterance of "Snow is white" as making the corresponding statement and counting Barack Obama, because he satisfies certain conditions, as the president of the United States. For "Snow is white" all you need to understand in order to understand the way that the utterance constitutes a statement is to understand the meaning of the sentence. But in the case of Barack Obama, there is a set of constitutional provisions. Anybody who gets a majority of votes in the electoral college counts as the president-elect, and when the president-elect is sworn in by the Chief Justice of the United States, he counts as president of the United States. In the case of the sentence "Snow is white," meaning is all you need for the "counting as" to take place. No further operation is necessary. But in the case of the president, the sentence "Obama is president" is not enough. You have to count him as president in accordance with certain procedures, and this is what I am calling an "operation" as opposed to the "constitution" of meaning. In the case of written constitutions, you have to have the extra-linguistic convention prior to its application in actual operations.

In sum, our two apparent parallels were both illusory. The "X counts as Y" formula works differently for language than for nonlinguistic institutional facts. And the role of performatives in creating linguistic institutional facts is different from its role in creating nonlinguistic institutional facts. Both differences have to do with the nature of meaning and the role of meaning in the two cases. In the creation of nonlinguistic institutional facts we use meaning, the semantic powers of language, to create a set of deontic powers that go beyond the semantic powers. Semantic powers are simply the powers to represent in one illocutionary mode or another, and these include the power to create speech acts through performative utterances. But in the case of nonlinguistic institutional facts, when we use language, we do more than represent; we create that which is represented. We create extra-linguistic deontic powers, such as the powers of the presidency or the powers of money and marriage.

We can summarize these differences in the following chart.[8]

	Linguistic Institutional Facts	Nonlinguistic Institutional Facts
Requirements for Creation	Conventions of language.	Conventions of language plus extra-linguistic conventions (themselves created by language).
Constitutive Elements	Utterance constitutes creation.	Utterance in certain special circumstances, and sometimes with accompanying actions, constitutes creation.
Agents	Any competent speaker can create linguistic institutional facts.	Speaker typically requires a special position or special condition to create nonlinguistic institutional facts.

We can now see in a deeper sense why language is the fundamental social institution and why it is not like other institutions. All other institutional facts require linguistic representation because some nonsemantic fact is created by the representation. Thus money, government, and private property are created by semantics but in every case the powers created go beyond semantics. Meanings are used to create powers that go beyond meaning. But language itself does not have powers that go beyond meaning. It says on the twenty-dollar bill, "This note is legal tender for all debts public and private." Now why don't they add a sentence next to it that says, "This is really a sentence of English and it means what it says"? Would we find that reassuring? The sentence on the bill is a Status Function Declaration. It certifies that the note is legal tender. But the sentence I imagined can't add any additional certifi-

8. I am indebted to Asya Passinsky for suggesting the inclusion of this chart.

cation to the effect that the other sentence really is a sentence. The language itself determines that it is a sentence with that meaning.

So if our question was, "Why don't the deontic powers of language have to be represented linguistically in a way that all other deontic powers have to be represented?" The answer is that those deontic powers do have to be represented insofar as they go beyond meaning. Meaning by itself doesn't enable you to divorce somebody or even adjourn a meeting. You have to have some extra-linguistic convention. But the capacity of a sentence to represent linguistically does not require additional powers of linguistic representation. They are already built into the semantics of the sentence.

By itself, the only power that meaning (semantics) has is to represent conditions of satisfaction—truth conditions, fulfillment conditions, obedience conditions, and so on—in one or more of the different illocutionary modes; but in the nonlinguistic Status Function Declaration, we do more than represent: we create. We use the powers of the semantics to create powers that go beyond semantics.

The account so far makes a strong prediction and I need to make it explicit. It would predict that you could not have performative verbs for such things as adjourning a meeting, declaring war, or pronouncing somebody husband and wife where the literal meaning alone was sufficient to guarantee the successful performance, because you need some extra-linguistic convention in order to do these things. Linguistic representation by itself is not enough.

But there is also a deeper point that I want to reemphasize: all of the capacities of language that I have been talking about go beyond semantics as traditionally conceived. In mainstream philosophy of language, there is no account of literal meaning—not in model theory, not in possible worlds semantics, not in truth conditional semantics—that will explain the properties of language that I have been describing as consequences of literal meaning. On my account, meanings are used to create a reality that goes beyond meaning. That is one reason, by the way, why the problems are so fascinating. We are investigating a branch of extra-semantical semantics.

Finally, I want to conclude this section by noting a certain irony. In my earliest account of language, in *Speech Acts*,[9] I tried to use the similarity with

---

9. Searle, John R., *Speech Acts: An Essay in the Philosophy of Language*, Cambridge: Cambridge University Press, 1969.

games and other institutional phenomena to explain language. I tried to explain language by showing how it was like games. Now I am urging that the existence of games and other nonlinguistic institutional phenomena can be explained only in terms of language. You can't use the analogy with games to explain language because you understand games only if you already understand language.

QUESTION 5: WHAT IS THE SPECIAL ROLE OF WRITING?

Once a tribe gets written language, all sorts of other developments become possible. *This stability of written language enables the creation and continued existence of status functions that do not require any physical existence beyond the linguistic representations themselves.* Two striking examples of this are both fairly modern inventions, invented long after the creation of written language: modern forms of money that dispense with actual currency, especially electronic money, and limited liability corporations.

In the case of freestanding Y terms, there is no physical object or person to which the Y status function is assigned, and consequently, written language is in general essential for the creation and maintenance of these status functions. For example, money can exist without any physical realization. The magnetic traces on computer disks in banks that record bank balances are not actually money, but they represent the amount of money you have in your account, which you are able to spend without incurring any indebtedness, even though that money has no physical existence. Limited liability corporations do not have any physical existence (this is why they are called "fictitious persons"). And in a game of blindfold chess, the pieces in the game have no physical existence; they are simply represented by expressions in the standard chess notation. In all these cases there is a physical existence of the representations of institutional objects such as money, corporations, or chess pieces, but there is no physical existence of the institutional objects themselves. All of these are made possible by the existence of writing, for a written record provides an enduring representation of the status functions in question. Another benefit of writing is that written documents endure and thus attest to the existence of the status function in question over long periods of time.

Furthermore, ownership documents acquire a kind of status function life of their own. For example, they enable the owner to borrow money against the property, and they enable the state to tax the owner of the property. Hernando

De Soto regards ownership documents as an important element in the development of prosperity of otherwise poor landholders.[10]

QUESTION 6: IF INSTITUTIONAL FACTS EXIST ONLY BECAUSE THEY ARE BELIEVED TO EXIST, THEN HOW CAN WE DISCOVER SURPRISING NEW FACTS ABOUT THEM? HOW CAN THE SOCIAL SCIENCES TELL US ANYTHING NEW?

Several commentators on the Construction,[11] especially social scientists, pointed out that there can be institutional facts of which the members of the community are unaware, and which can be discovered by social scientists. So, for example, an economy might undergo a recession or go through the phases of the business cycle without the members of the community even having the concept of a recession or business cycle. I have said in my account that institutional facts only exist insofar as they are represented as existing. But in these cases it appears that there are institutional facts that exist independently of anybody's representing them as existing, and can indeed be discovered independently of anybody's opinions.

What shall we say about these cases? Remember that institutional facts are such only under a description, and the primary descriptions, the ones on which the others depend, require recognition or acceptance by the community in question in some form or other. Cases that do not seem to meet this condition are systematic fallouts, or consequences, of ground-floor institutional facts. So the facts that people are engaged in buying, selling, and owning goods, and providing services for money, are ground-floor institutional facts. The totality of such facts will have higher levels of description where they can be described as a part of a business cycle, or a recession, but these fallouts are constituted by the ground floor institutional facts. Åsa Andersson[12] describes these as "macro" institutional facts that are constituted by the "micro" institutional facts. Reflection on these will deepen our understanding of institutional facts.

For the people involved in the institution, the ground floor institutional facts can only exist insofar as they are represented as existing. But that set of

10. De Soto, Hernando, *The Mystery of Capitalism: Why Capitalism Triumphs in the West and Fails Everywhere Else*, New York: Basic Books, 2003.
11. Thomasson, Amie, "Foundations for a Social Ontology," *ProtoSociology* 18–19 (2003): 269–90; Friedman, Jonathan, Comment on Searle's "Social Ontology," in Roy D'Andrade (ed.), *Anthropological Theory* 6 (2006): 70–80.
12. Andersson, Åsa, *Power and Social Ontology*, Malmö: Bokbox Publications, 2007.

institutional facts and the inherent representations will also satisfy other conditions that are not, or need not be, themselves represented. To take a trivial example, it has been discovered in baseball that, statistically, left-handed batters do better against right-handed pitchers, and right-handed batters do better against left-handed pitchers. This is not required by the rules of baseball; it is just something that happens. I propose to call these "third person fallout facts from institutional facts," or more briefly, "fallouts" from institutional facts. They are "third personal," because they need not be known by participants in the institution. They can be stated from a third-person, anthropological, point of view. They carry no additional deontology, so no new power relations are created by fallouts. The term "recession," defined as a fall in Gross Domestic Product for two or more consecutive quarters, was originally introduced to name a systematic fallout and not an institutional status, but it could easily become a status with a status function (and for all I know it may already have become such) if Congress decides to pass a law assigning deontic status to recessions. Thus, for example, Congress might require that the Federal Reserve Board adjust interest rates during a recession. In such a case "recession" would become a status term marking a status function because recessions would then have deontic powers.

There is an interesting logical property of the class of cases where you simply discover systematic fallouts: you can have intentionality-independent facts about intentionality-relative phenomena. In other words, once the intentionality-relative phenomena are created by the participants in the institution, then anybody, participants or others, can discover further intentionality-independent facts about them. And the test, as always, is, If people do not now believe it, and did not in the past believe it, would it still be true? In the case of a recession, if people didn't believe that it was a recession, it would still be a recession. Whereas in the case of the existence of money, or the existence of presidents, if no one had ever believed that money existed or ever believed that presidents existed, under these or some deontically equivalent descriptions, then such institutional phenomena could not exist. So you have the paradox that a phenomenon can be intentionality-relative and yet we can then discover intentionality-independent facts about that phenomenon. Thus, on this account, recessions are mind-dependent but not intentionality-relative.

In economics the ground-floor facts are in general intentionality-relative. For example, so and so bought and sold such and such goods. But the facts reported by economists are typically intentionality-independent. For example, the Great Depression began in 1929.

Another class of phenomena are the cases in which an outsider might choose to describe a system of actual status functions in a way that the members of the community are not themselves aware of and might not even accept. So, for example, we might describe a society as "racist" even though members of that society do not think of themselves as racists or do not even have the concept of racism. Thomasson thinks this is like the phenomenon of the discovery of a recession as a systematic fallout, but I think the two cases are quite different. In this case, if people are genuinely treating people of different skin color as having a different deontic status—as having different rights and responsibilities for that very reason—then they have a system of institutional facts. The fact that they do not think of themselves as racist is irrelevant because they are in fact assigning a deontic status to members of the community based on race. This is the crucial point: as long as the members of the community are assigning a deontic status to people and objects they will have to have some way of representing that deontic status, because the deontic status cannot exist without being represented as such. There will be other descriptions that will have the same extension as those under which the deontic status is assigned, but the members of the community need not be aware of these descriptions or even accept them once presented with them, as long as they continue to recognize the deontology. Thus, to nail this point down to the historical case, they assigned to people of a different race a deontic status that was inferior to the status of the dominant race. In doing so, they created and maintained institutional facts. The fact that we would describe them as "racist" and they might not accept that description themselves is irrelevant to whether they are creating institutional facts.

This raises an interesting question and that is, To what extent can people be mistaken about the Y status function? So, for example, people can believe that it is a marriage only if it is made in heaven, and yet on my account, it is still a marriage even if it is not made in heaven. The crucial question is, What rights and obligations does the couple have? How do people actually treat them and how do they regard themselves? If the members of the community accord the marital status to them, then whether they do that on the basis of false beliefs is really irrelevant. However, more needs to be said about this issue. Suppose a community believes that someone has divine powers, for example, that the pope is infallible. The status function is believed to carry extraordinary powers that may not exist. Is it still a status function? Well, on my definition it is, because the pope still has deontic powers. For example, Catholics are under an obligation to believe him. But the powers are not recognized as status functions. The pope now is believed to have an additional, physical (supernatural) power where the belief goes beyond the fact, and the status function only works as a status function precisely because it is believed not to be a status function but a brute intentionality-independent fact about the universe. The acceptance of an institutional fact, or indeed, of a whole system of status functions, may be based on false beliefs. From the point of institutional analysis, it does not matter whether the beliefs are true or false. It only matters whether the people do in fact collectively recognize or accept the system of status functions. In the extreme case an institutional fact might function only because it is not believed to be an institutional fact. In such cases the collective acceptance is of the deontic powers, but they are accepted only because of some other belief.

QUESTION 7: WHY ARE STATEMENTS OF INSTITUTIONAL FACTS TYPICALLY INTENSIONAL-WITH-AN-S?

Institutional facts consist in power relations created by linguistic representations and partly constituted by those representations. That is why the statements of these facts are not always extensional. They fail such tests as the substitutability of coreferring expressions (Leibniz's Law). For example, the "counts as" creates an intensional context, one that is, in Quine's terms, referentially opaque.

1. As the winner of the 2008 election, Barack Obama counts as the present president of the United States.
2. The present president of the United States is identical with Michelle's husband. 1. and 2. do not entail.
3. As the winner of the 2008 election, Barack Obama counts as Michelle's husband.

Obama is only a president or a husband insofar as he is represented as such, and the conditions for one representation need not carry over to the other.

Indeed, quantificational logic, the philosopher's favorite device for formalizing any topic, is not much help to us in discussing institutional reality. Notice that for some of the cases we have discussed, such as creating a corporation, we cannot have a universally quantified rule that ranges over a domain of preexisting objects. And more interestingly, we cannot even have an existentially quantified form to the effect that there is some x such that x is a corporation, because by hypothesis there is no preexisting x which becomes the corporation. The general form of the rule, as I quoted it, is that such and such a speech act counts as the creation of the corporation. So the logical form of the creation of a particular corporation is not the following:

For some x, x becomes the corporation, Y.

Rather, its form is that of a Declaration:

We make it the case by Declaration that the corporation Y exists.

On the standard accounts of the semantics of quantificational logic, the quantifiers range over a domain of existing objects. But in the case of the creation of entities that have status functions, there is no such domain.

The creation of money without currency by banks has a different logical structure. If we consider banks other than central banks, then typically banks create money by issuing loans of money they do not have. Again these are Declarations. Suppose the Bank of America lends Jones $1,000. The Declaration has this form:

We the Bank of America hereby lend Jones $1,000, and we do that by opening an account under his name with a balance of $1,000.

This is a fascinating case, because as the creation of money is standardly described in economics textbooks, it is in part a systematic fallout of an institutional fact rather than a ground-floor fact. The institutional fact is lending money. The banker may not be aware that by lending money the bank does not have, the bank is actually creating money by adding to the money supply available in the economy.

So the speech act, as X, makes it the case that Jones has the Y status function: possessor of $1,000. But there need be no physical reality to the $1,000; there is just a representation.

To repeat the crucial point, the logical structure of the creation of all institutional reality is the same as the structure of the performative. You make something the case by representing it as being the case. But in this case, the Declaration made it the case that there was a loan. The creation of money was a systematic fallout.

What is the proof that the creation of money is a systematic fallout and not the content of the Declaration? Ask yourself what the bank is trying to do. It is trying to loan Jones some money, not to increase the money supply in the economy. The proof is this. Suppose the Federal Reserve Board decides to keep the amount of money in the economy constant by removing money from the economy whenever a new loan creates new money. All the same, the loan would go through, even if the systematic fallout did not occur.

QUESTION 8: WHAT IS THE ROLE OF IMAGINATION IN CREATING INSTITUTIONAL REALITY?

The status function doesn't really exist except insofar as it is represented as existing. In a sense, there is an element of imagination in the existence of private property, marriage, and government because in each case we have to treat something as something that it is not intrinsically. As far as the ontogenic development of this human capacity is concerned, it is worth pointing out that human children very early on acquire a capacity to do this double level of thinking that is characteristic of the creation and maintenance of institutional reality. Small children can say to each other, "Okay, I'll be Adam, you be Eve, and we'll let this block be the apple." This, if one allows oneself to think about it, is a stunning intellectual feat. It was pointed out to me by Tomasello and Rakozcy[13] and it seems reasonable to suppose that it is the ontogenetic origin of the human capacity to create institutional reality. If in fantasy we can count an X as a Y that it is not really, then with maturity it is not at all hard to see how we can count an X as a Y where the Y has a kind of existence, because it regulates and empowers our social life, even though the Y feature is not an intrinsic feature of nature. Notice that you can't do any of this without language. The children cannot think "I'll be Adam, you be Eve, and we will let this be the apple" unless they have some linguistic vehicle to form the thought and express it. Notice, furthermore, a deep point: that children typically don't think this about the words themselves. In general they don't say, "Let this block be a word, and we will pretend that it means such and such." At an early age a child can think, in fantasy, a double level corresponding to brute facts and institutional facts. But it is very hard to make the same move for language. Adults have a similar blind spot where language is concerned. It is not at all difficult for adults to see the distinction between words and their meanings. But it is very hard for adults to think away language altogether, to imagine what their lives would be like

13. Rakoczy, Hannes, and Michael Tomasello, "The Ontogeny of Social Ontology: Steps to Shared Intentionality and Status Functions," in Savas L. Tsohatzidis (ed.), *Intentional Acts and Institutional Facts*, Dordrecht: Springer, 2007, 113–37.

without language at all. All of the great philosophers that I can think of who philosophized about social reality took language for granted. They all assumed that people had a language and then asked, "How could they form a society?" One of the main themes of this book is that once you have a common language, you already have a society.

VI. Conclusion

In spite of the stunning variety of human forms of institutional social existence, I am convinced that there is a single logical principle that underlies all of the structures and a small set of ways in which the principle is implemented in actual institutions. The basic, and simple, idea is that all nonlinguistic institutional facts are created and maintained in their existence by speech acts that have the same logical form as Declarations.

I have found three ways in which this general principle can be implemented. In the first way, we simply create status functions on an ad hoc basis. The tribe, for example, makes someone their leader simply by treating him or her as their leader. The second form of implementation is to have a standing Declaration, a constitutive rule, and this is perhaps the most common form for advanced complex civilizations. The third way is really a special case of the second, and that is where we have a constitutive rule that does not require any actual person or object over which the rule operates, but it simply creates an entity by Declaration. These constitutive rules of this third type are typically Declarations that empower other Declarations to create institutional facts.

6

FREE WILL, RATIONALITY, AND INSTITUTIONAL FACTS

I. Deontic Power

So far I have described the structure of institutional reality, and now it is time to say more about how these institutions actually function in human life. Of course, human institutions vary enormously, all the way from religions to nation-states to sports teams to corporations, and I will not attempt to make empirical generalizations about them but simply identify some purely *formal* features they have in common that enable them to function in human life in a way that is unlike anything I know of in nonhuman animal life. I have been describing this formal feature by saying that institutional facts provide us with a deontology, with deontic powers. So far I have simply listed examples of deontic powers. It is now time to say something about how they actually function in human behavior. Typical names of deontic powers are "rights," "duties," "authorizations," "requirements," "permissions," and "certifications." These nouns connect with important verbs, especially the modal auxiliary verbs "ought," "should," "can," and "must." Thus, for example, I *must* give a lecture tomorrow morning at 8 A.M. because I am under a firm and binding *obligation* both to my students and to the university to give a lecture at that time.

These are the sorts of things I had in mind when I said that deontic powers give us desire-independent reasons for action. One of the aims of this chapter is to explain how there can be such reasons for action and how institutional facts figure in such reasons. However, if that were the only point of institutional facts, they would give us a rather gloomy life. The main point of institutions is that they create enormous possibilities. So, for example, you cannot desire to make a lot of money, get married, or become president of the United States unless there are the institutions of money, marriage, and the

United States presidency. And this goes also for informal uncodified institutions; you cannot want to have a great love affair or give a great dinner party without the corresponding status functions. The existence of institutions, as I have emphasized over and over, is enormously enabling in human life, and gives us all kinds of possibilities that we could not otherwise conceive of. We have possibilities that are unknown even to the advanced primates of species different from our own.

Human institutional facts lock into human rationality. They figure in our reasons for acting. If I am going to explain how they function, I have to first say a little bit about rationality and about reasons for action. This is a very large subject; I have written a fairly lengthy book about it,[1] and I will not repeat all or even very many of the details here. But I want to give you enough of a picture of rationality so that you can understand how institutional reality relates to rationality.

Consider the old chestnut of an argument:

1. Socrates is a man.
2. All men are mortal.
3. Therefore Socrates is mortal.

As a matter of logic, 1 and 2 imply or entail 3. And what does that mean? Well, in part it means that if they are true, then 3 must be true. So far, all of these points are about the semantics of these three statements. Given the truth of 1 and 2, 3 must be true. Now what does that have to do with human rationality? Well, if you tie these logical points to certain psychological concepts such as belief, inference, knowledge, you get results like the following: If you believe 1 and 2, you are *committed* to believing 3. If you *know* 1 and 2 to be true, you are *justified* in inferring the truth of 3.

All of this is about so-called theoretical reason, reasoning about what to believe, infer, or conclude. But there is another form of rationality called practical reasoning, which is reasoning about what to do or what one ought to do. Let us examine an argument form of practical reason.

Suppose I look out the window and have an experience that I would describe as "I see that it is raining." On the basis of this experience, I come to believe that it is raining. Now let us suppose also that I plan to go outdoors, and I do not want to get wet. Let us suppose also that I believe that I can avoid getting wet only by taking an umbrella. On the basis of these considerations, I

1. Searle, John R., *Rationality in Action*, Cambridge, Mass.: MIT Press, 2002.

conclude that I will carry an umbrella. Leaving out various details, we can put this as a three-step argument:

1. I desire to stay dry.
2. I believe that I will stay dry in this situation only if I carry an umbrella.
3. Therefore, I will carry an umbrella.

In the case of theoretical reason, the conclusion of the argument led to a belief; in the case of practical reason, the conclusion of the argument leads to an intention or, in some cases, an action. Step three in this derivation is the expression of a prior intention, not a prediction.

This is an example of what Aristotle called "the practical syllogism." It is common to sneer at Aristotle for saying that an action itself might be the conclusion of a practical syllogism, but on my account of action there is nothing unreasonable about that conception at all. An action itself has an intentional propositional content, the intention-in-action. And the intention-in-action as well as the prior intention can be the conclusion of a practical syllogism. So one way for me to reason would be simply "I desire to stay dry," "I believe that I will stay dry in this situation only if I carry an umbrella," and then, I simply open an umbrella and go outdoors where the propositional content is manifested by my intention-in-action, the propositional content of the conclusion that I carry an umbrella.

In this example of the practical syllogism, an essential "premise" was my desire to stay dry. This is an example of a desire-dependent reason for action. And such desire-based cases of the practical syllogism are usually thought to divide into two kinds: those where some end is desired for its own sake and those where something is desired as a means to some end, which is desired for its own sake. The latter type of reasoning is called "means-ends" reasoning, and the umbrella case is a textbook example. If, on the other hand, I just want to drink beer, and so I drink beer, the drinking of the beer is not a means to some further end. It is desired for its own sake. But in both cases, carrying the umbrella and drinking the beer, the reasoning that leads to the action is desire-dependent.

Before I go on to examine institutional facts, I want to introduce a terminology to describe what is going on in all of these cases. I apologize that the examples are so boring, but they enable me to introduce some crucial apparatus that we will need in our examination of how institutional facts figure in practical reason. Notice that in both theoretical and practical reason the elements that operated in the reasoning process always had an entire propositional content. For example, I see that it is raining; I desire to stay dry; I believe that in this situation the only way I can stay dry is to carry an umbrella; and so on. All of these elements of the reasoning process—visual experiences, desires, beliefs, and so on—contain whole propositional contents. And this is a general feature of rationality. Rationality and reasoning always have to deal with entities that have entire propositional contents. These can be intentional phenomena such as desires, beliefs, and perceptions. They can be facts in the world such as the fact that it is raining, and they can also be phenomena such as obligations, rights, duties, and responsibilities. I introduce a general name for all of these sorts of entities that have a propositional structure: I call them "factitive entities." The reason for emphasizing this label at this point is that it is going to turn out that all of our desire-independent reasons for action, such as obligations, requirements, duties, and others, are factitive entities, and it is for that reason that they can figure in rationality and the reasoning process.

I want to introduce four other notions that will be crucial for understanding rationality in action. These four are the notions of a *total reason*, a *motivator*, an *effector*, and a *constitutor*. I will explain these by way of examples. If somebody asked me, "Why are you carrying an umbrella?" I can say a variety of different things. I can say, "I want to stay dry." I can say, "It is raining." Or even, "I need the umbrella to stay dry." Each of these states a reason for an action. But such reasons can be reasons only if they are part of a total reason for the action. The total reason for the action in this case consists of a desire and a belief: the desire to stay dry and the belief that the only way I can stay dry is to carry an umbrella. In this case, the total reason includes both (a desire for) the end, that I stay dry, and (a belief about) the means, that I carry an umbrella. Both the belief and the desire are factitive entities, but, as I have remarked earlier, they have different directions of fit. The desire has the upward or world-to-mind direction of fit ↑, the belief has the downward or mind-to-world direction of fit ↓. In this case the desire to stay dry provides the motivation for carrying the umbrella, and I call all such reasons for action, where the factitive entity in question has the upward or world-to-mind direction-of-fit ↑, *motivators*; and I want to make another general claim of which this is an example: all total reasons for action must contain at least one motivator, where the motivator consists of a factitive entity, such as a desire or an obligation, which has the upward direction of fit. I need two other technical notions to complete this brief account: the notion of an *effector* and the notion of a *constitutor*. In typical means-end reasoning, we have the means that brings about the end as an effect. I call such means "effectors." Thus, for example, carrying the umbrella is an effector to the end of staying dry. Effectors are actual or potential causes, but not all cases of practical reason are cases of finding causal processes that will achieve an end as a certain effect. Sometimes the reasoning leads to something that *constitutes* and *does not cause* the end. So, for example, if I desire to utter a French sentence, and I then, in order to satisfy this desire, utter the sentence "Il pleut," my saying "Il pleut" does not *cause* me to utter a French sentence; it *constitutes* uttering a French sentence. I call such factitives "constitutors." Carrying the umbrella is an effector to the end of staying dry. Uttering "Il pleut" is a constitutor to the end of uttering a sentence of French.

I can summarize this brief exposition of the formal apparatus for analyzing practical reason as follows. Every reason is a factitive entity. A factitive entity functions as a reason only if it is part of a total reason; and a total reason must contain at least one motivator. It may also contain constitutors and effectors. Furthermore, if the argument or the reasoning is to be any good, there must be systematic logical relations between the constitutors, effectors, and the motivators.

Many philosophers think that the sort of reasoning I have just described, desire-based reasoning about actions, is the only kind of reasoning about actions that there is; that all rationality is desire based. There is something very appealing about this view because every voluntary action is an expression of a desire to perform that very action then and there. If I go to my dentist to have my tooth drilled, it is not because I find it fun to have my tooth drilled but because the tooth drilling is a means to an end that I desire: having good teeth. But all the same, when I do go to the dentist to have my tooth drilled, that is what I want to do then and there. My *primary* desire to have good teeth leads to a *secondary* desire to go to the dentist and have my tooth drilled.[2] So my desire to have my tooth drilled is a desire-dependent desire. It depends on the primary desire: the desire to have good teeth. But now we come to an interesting class of desires that function differently. These are what I have been calling desire-independent reasons for action, and they include obligations, rights, duties, and so on. What I am going to argue is that it is a peculiarity of human beings that they have the rational capacity to create and

---

2. As far as I know, the terminology of primary and secondary desire was first introduced by Thomas Nagel in his book *The Possibility of Altruism*, Oxford: Clarendon Press, 1970.

act on desire-independent reasons for action. I do not know of any nonhuman animals that have that, and it seems to me unlikely that other animals have it, because it requires language, and indeed a rather specific kind of language in order to create, formulate, and act upon desire-independent reasons for action.

Human institutional reality locks into human rationality. This is what gives it its constitutive power. This is how it creates human society, and this is how it distinguishes humans from many, perhaps all, other animals. Aristotle was wrong to think that man was the *only* rational animal because other animals can, for example, engage in ends-means reasoning. But the extent and scope and power of human rationality vastly exceeds that of other animals because we have a special capacity for language, which is unlike the linguistic capacities of any other animal known to me.

Consider my obligation to give a lecture tomorrow. I am under an obligation whether I want to give the lecture or not. And I have various beliefs about the means necessary for me to give that lecture. For example, I have to drive to the campus and walk to the lecture hall. There are various other things that I have to do such as prepare the lecture. But here the interesting thing is that the obligation to give the lecture is desire-independent. Well, what exactly does that mean? It means that I have a reason for doing it that is independent of what I feel like at the moment. Even if I do not feel like lecturing on this particular day, or I would rather not, all the same, if I recognize that I am under an obligation to do it, then I recognize that I have a reason for doing it that is independent of my desires. My obligation is a motivator and my recognition of the obligation is a recognition of a desire-independent reason for action. On the account that I have been giving, the recognition of something as an obligation requires a representation at a higher level than that of simple inclinations. It is such things as recognitions of obligations that can give us the capacity to reflect on, alter, and override our first-order beliefs and desires. It is this second-level character of the kinds of desire-independent reasons for action that I am talking about that distinguishes language-based rationality from rationality that does not require language.

But now we encounter an apparent paradox. I said that all conscious voluntary actions are expressions then and there of a desire to perform that action. When I am doing something unpleasant, something I otherwise do not want to do, all the same, if I am doing it then and there, intentionally and voluntarily, then that is what I want to do then and there. For example, if I go to the dentist to have my teeth drilled when I otherwise don't want to suffer the pain and discomfort of having my teeth drilled, all the same, that is what I want to do then and there: go to the dentist to have my teeth drilled; but I want to do that as a means to the end of having good teeth. So the desire-dependent reason of having good teeth gives rise to a desire-dependent reason of having my teeth drilled, something I would not otherwise desire. What is paradoxical about the obligation case is that there need not be any independent desire to do the thing that constitutes fulfilling the obligation. So the pattern of reasoning in such a case is that I recognize the validity of the obligation. On the basis of the recognition of the obligation, I then form a desire to do something that constitutes fulfilling the obligation. How then is it possible that the recognition of an obligation can ever motivate me? The answer is that because I recognize the validity of the obligation and I recognize it as giving me a valid reason for doing the thing I am under an obligation to do, the obligation can then be the ground of a desire to do the thing I am under an obligation to do. In short, the desire derives from the obligation, or more strictly, it derives from the recognition of the obligation, and the obligation does not derive from the desire. The obligation can be a *desire-independent* reason for action and nonetheless *motivate* action because it can be the *ground of a desire* to perform the action that constitutes fulfilling the obligation. So I have one motivator—the obligation—that forms the ground of another motivator—the desire—that is then satisfied by the constitutor—giving the lecture.

It is important to keep emphasizing that I say it *can* be the ground of a desire. I do not think it follows as a matter of logical necessity that everybody who recognizes an obligation is inclined to fulfill it. The recognition of a desire-independent reason for doing something is already the recognition of a ground for the desire to do it. But in real life it doesn't always work. There are lots of cases in which people recognize valid obligations but just do not do the thing that they recognize they are under an obligation to do. In this case, the obligation is a motivator that fails to motivate.

So we can now restate the paradox and the resolution of the paradox. The paradox is that there can be desire-independent reasons for action, but at the same time, every action must be the expression of a desire to perform that action. The resolution of the paradox is that the recognition of desire-independent reasons can ground the desire and thus cause the desire, even though it is not logically inevitable that they do and not empirically universal that they do.

The way that the system of deontic powers works, then, is by way of human rationality. This is disguised from us by the fact that in most habitual cases we don't have to think about the matter at all. We simply carry out our daily obligations without reflecting on the underlying logical structure. They become part of our Background dispositions, though they can always be brought into the foreground and reflected on, as I am attempting to do now. I want to emphasize something that I mentioned earlier, and that is that the relation of desire-independent reasons in the functioning of rationality requires that they be represented linguistically in order that they can function as higher level representations that enable us to reflect on our grounds for beliefs and desires. It is this feature that makes language essential to full-blown deontology of the kind that I am trying to describe. One implicit point needs to be made fully explicit. A desire-independent reason can function for an agent only if the agent recognizes it as valid. There is a sense then in which all the desire-independent reasons for an agent are created as such by the agent. I will come back to this point later.

It is important to emphasize that these deontic reasons organize time in a way that is not characteristic of other species. We resemble other conscious animal species in that, for us, time is organized by such things as the cycle of the seasons and the diurnal rising and setting of the sun. But by creating a desire-independent set of reasons, human beings can also organize time in ways that are quite arbitrary. I can arrange to meet you at any time of the day or night that we both find convenient. We are enmeshed in systems of deontic powers.

It has seemed to many people in the history of philosophy that one can never have a motivation for doing something one does not independently desire to do, at least as a means, if not as an end. Famously, Hume argued that "reason is and ought to be the slave of the passions."[3] And Bernard Williams argued that there are no "external" reasons, reasons that do not appeal to a preexisting motivational set.[4] The way to answer this objection is to appeal to the nature of rationality itself, and the best way to see how one can be motivated to act on something one does not otherwise desire is to see how one can be motivated to accept the truth of a proposition that one does not

3. Hume, David, *Treatise of Human Nature,* Book II, Part 3, Section 3, L. A. Selby-Bigge (ed.), New York: Oxford University Press, 1978.
4. Williams, Bernard, "Internal and External Reasons," *Moral Luck: Philosophical Papers 1973–1980,* Cambridge: Cambridge University Press, 1981, 101–13.

otherwise want to believe. If I have a medical test that delivers very unpleasant results—let us suppose I am told I have a terminal ailment and less than two months to live—I do not wish to believe that. All the same, rationality requires me to accept it. In this case, I have a desire-independent reason for accepting it. In answer to this you might say, "Well, it is only because you desire to believe the truth." Yes, but the requirement that I believe the truth is built into the concept of belief. You cannot have a belief without wanting to have a true one rather than a false one, because a belief is a kind of commitment to truth. In this case, as in the case of the desire-independent reasons for action, *the reason is the ground of the desire, rather than the desire being the ground of the reason.* To take a famous example, if I recognize that I have made a promise, then I have a desire-independent reason for keeping the promise; and it is no good to say to that, "Yes, but it is only because you want to keep your promises." I do indeed want to keep my promises, but the desire to keep my promises comes from the nature of promising rather than the nature of promising coming from the desire to keep them.

The truth behind the mistaken conception of rationality in both Hume and Williams is this: an external motivator such as a fact in the world or an obligation I am under can only actually motivate me, can only succeed in affecting my behavior through the exercise of rationality if I internalize the external motivator in the form of some intentional state. Thus, a fact in the world, such as the fact it is raining, can affect my behavior only if I, for example, *perceive* it, and thereby come to *believe* it. Similarly, an obligation that I am under can affect my behavior only if I *recognize* the obligation and on the basis of that recognition form a desire to do the thing I am under an obligation to do.

In order to be rationally binding on an agent, desire-independent reasons for action contained in institutional facts must be, explicitly or implicitly, created as such by that agent. Such a reason is explicitly created when an agent overtly commits himself or herself to a course of action by, for example, buying and selling, getting married, or making a promise. It is implicitly created when an agent recognizes the binding force of some situation in which she finds herself, such as being a member of a family, a citizen of a country, or a good friend. To fully develop the argument for this would be a complex task that goes beyond the scope of this book, but the basic intuitive idea can be stated simply: take any statement asserting the existence of a desire-independent reason for action for a specific agent. Now ask yourself, What fact reported by this statement constitutes a valid claim against that agent? Suppose, for example, a group of people in Australia get together and decide that I am under an obligation to pay them $1,000. "X counts as Y in C," they assure me, "and we are counting you as someone who owes us money in this context." Unless I have in fact undertaken such an obligation, or unless for some other reason they have a valid claim on me, their claim has no force and the alleged obligation does not exist. Now contrast this case with the sort of case where I really have created such a reason by explicitly making a promise or by recognizing the obligations implicit in the situation in which I find myself, for example as a member of my family. Many people simply go along, unreflectively, with social situations in which they find themselves. But this can amount to a form of inauthenticity or even bad faith, because they are creating desire independent reasons which are rationally binding on them but which they might not have created if they had thought about the question.

II. Why Should Society Have This Structure and Not Some Other?

So far I have given an account of institutional reality and tried to explain how institutional facts can motivate behavior. Let us suppose for the sake of this discussion that my account is, broadly speaking, correct. That is, let us suppose that institutional structures are matters of collective intentionality typically in the form of collective recognition, that these consist of the assignment and maintenance of status functions, are created and maintained by types of representations that have the logical form of Declarations, and that the functions are such that they can only be performed given collective acceptance or recognition.

The question naturally arises, "Why should it be like that?" That is, one can imagine all sorts of other ways of organizing society—so why should human society have evolved these particular forms? We are certain sorts of biological beasts, and we have certain sorts of institutional structures. Why do the sorts of beasts that we are have the sorts of institutions that we have?

As usual, "why?" questions are ambiguous in several different ways. One of the questions we are asking is, What are the advantages to having institutional reality? I think that question has a rather easy answer, but more difficult questions are, Given the obvious advantages to having institutional structures, what are the advantages of having the particular logical form of the structures we have? And furthermore, Is there any *necessity* to having these structures? Would other structures do just as well in giving us the advantages?

I do not know the answers to all of these questions, but one of the purposes of this chapter is to explore some of them. The answers I am going to suggest center around the following fact: we have a special kind of consciousness in which we have a sense of making decisions that are not forced, the kind of consciousness where we choose one thing but we have a sense that we could have chosen something else. In such cases we sense a *causal gap* between the reasons for our decisions and actions and the actual decisions and actions. Though we do act on reasons, the reasons do not normally set causally sufficient conditions for our decisions and actions, and in that sense there is a gap between the causes and the effects. For example, though I voted for a particular candidate in the last presidential election, I could equally well have voted for the other candidate. The reasons I had inclined me to vote one way rather than another, but they did not force me. To use Leibniz's famous slogan (with a sense he did not intend) the reasons "incline without necessitating." The traditional name of this gap in philosophy is "the freedom of the will." I am very reluctant to use that expression because it has such a sordid history. So, for the most part, I will continue to use the expression "the gap" to name the experienced gap between the causes of our decisions and actions, in the form of reasons, and the actual decisions and actions that we make and perform. The thesis I will present and explore is this. The possibilities of life are increased enormously if you have the sorts of institutional structures I have described; but more important, *given our conscious experience of the gap, other sorts of structures that one can imagine will not do the job.* I will argue that without the gap—that is, without the consciousness of freedom—institutional structures are meaningless; but with the gap, they are essential. It is quite possible that the gap is an illusion, but that doesn't matter for this argument. We have to presuppose the gap when we make decisions, so even if the gap is an illusion it is one we cannot shake off.

III. The Construction of Society as an Engineering Problem

In addressing these questions I will continue my strategy of treating certain philosophical problems as if they were engineering problems. In this case, I will imagine the construction of society as an engineering problem. How would you design a society if you were, so to speak, working from scratch? My project in describing the construction of society might seem to bear certain affinities with traditional political philosophy. Both utopian theorists and social contract theorists had variations on the engineering approach. For the utopians, How would you design the ideal society? For the social contract theories, What sort of a society would you contract into? But the interesting thing from our present point of view is how much of a rich apparatus of preexisting social and institutional structures they had to presuppose. The worst problem is that in theorizing about the state of nature, the theorists took it for granted that humans in the state of nature had language. But, as I have repeated perhaps too often, to have language is already to have a rich structure of institutions. Statement making and promising are human institutions as much as property or marriage. Furthermore, once the creatures in question have a full-blown human language, certain other institutions are going to be inevitable. Once people can say of objects, "This is mine," they are already laying claim to property. To put this point very briefly, I will repeat a claim made in earlier chapters. If by "the state of nature" we mean a state in which humans live like other animals without any institutional structures, then *for language-using human beings there can be no such thing as the state of nature.*

To state the historical situation briefly, we can say: the utopians took institutions for granted and asked what the ideal ones would be. The contract theorists took some institutions for granted and asked how we might explain the creation of government and the obligations of citizens to the government. Contemporary updates of the social contract theory, such as Rawls's,[5] take institutions for granted and ask how we might distinguish just from unjust institutions. I am engaged in none of these investigations. My question in this chapter is, Granted that institutions have a certain logical structure, why should they have that and not some other structure?

I am going to continue the thought experiments of earlier chapters of imagining the design of society as an engineering problem that we start from scratch. In those chapters, we imagined that first we evolve a language, and once it has evolved, all sorts of other interesting conclusions about society will follow. In this chapter, I want to continue the thought experiment, but this time in light of different conceptions of human nature.

If we are examining the relations between institutional structures and human nature, there are, formally speaking, at least two possibilities. We can

---

5. Rawls, John, *A Theory of Justice,* Cambridge, Mass.: Harvard University Press, 1971.

assume a certain conception of human nature and then see what sorts of institutional structures will fit, or we can assume a certain conception of institutions and then see what sorts of beings will fit those institutions. Let us start with the first possibility and begin with a currently influential conception of human nature. Let us take seriously the idea that human cognition operates according to standard cognitive science computational models. We will assume that cognition is computational and algorithmic, and that in consequence consciousness does not really matter. Either consciousness is epiphenomenal, or it is itself simply another computational mechanism. If this sounds like a far-fetched fantasy to you, it is worth reminding yourself that this is in fact the conception of human cognition and human rationality that was once dominant, and may still be quite common, in cognitive science. So let us attempt to imagine that we construct society according to this computational cognitive science model. We have a set of conscious robots and we give them programs that will respond to stimulus inputs with the appropriate motor outputs. The systems are completely deterministic. So now we have a society of perfectly "rational" robots, and it does not really matter to their behavior whether they are conscious or not. All of the causal work in determining their behavior is done by the implemented computer programs.

IV. Could Unconscious Robots Have Institutions?

Now let us suppose we give them institutional reality of the sort that I have described, starting with language. We will give them a set of symbolic mechanisms for representing time and space so they can communicate about times and places other than those immediately experienced. This increases their cognitive powers enormously. For example, now they can linguistically represent not only what they want and believe about the immediate present but also about the future and about other places. We will also give them a set of linguistic mechanisms for representing actually existing states of affairs (e.g., Assertives such as statements) and mechanisms for representing states of affairs that other robots are to bring into existence (e.g., Directives, such as orders and commands). Let us suppose we also give them mechanisms for representing certain courses of action that they are to perform (e.g., Commissives, such as promises). But now a serious difficulty appears. In what sense exactly could we say these robots are making statements, giving orders, or making and keeping promises? Let us suppose that robot A is so programmed that when it cognizes a future need on the part of robot B, A makes a "promise" to render B the appropriate assistance in the future. Given the way I have described the case, it is not clear what these words could mean. A is in a certain program state that matches certain future states of B. Notice that we cannot even say that A's states *represent* B's future states, because we have given no sense to the concept of representation in this case. We can just say there is a matching relation. A sends a signal to B, which is systematically related to A's subsequent behavior. But what I cannot find in this situation is the deontology that is essential to institutional reality in its human form. The notion of making and keeping promises presupposes the gap. It presupposes that the promise is not an unconscious, determined mechanical emission from the mouth of the promissor, and it presupposes that the keeping of the promise is also not an unconscious, determined, mechanical operation on the part of the promissor. To put the point bluntly, making and keeping promises requires consciousness and a sense of freedom on the part of the promise-making and promise-keeping agent. Furthermore, once the agent has conscious intentional promise-making in the literal sense in which I intend these words, then it already has the double level of intentionality that goes with the deontology that I described earlier. That is, in addition to having beliefs and inclinations, it must have a set of ways of appraising its beliefs and inclinations in light of its creation of commitments, in light of its creation of desire-independent reasons for action.

What goes for promising goes for institutional reality generally. Consider property. We might program robots so that for each robot there is a set of objects to which it stands in a special relation. It interacts with its objects in a way that it does not interact with the objects of other robots, and the other robots are programmed to respond similarly in ways that distinguish between their objects and objects of the other robots. Does this ersatz give us private property? I don't think so. What we have left out is any sense of property *rights*. The robots respond to objects as they might respond to rain. They are programmed to respond in certain ways and that's that. Similar remarks could be made about money. The robots, we will suppose, are given a set of counters that they can use to satisfy their needs. When they run short of fuel, they go to the fuel provider and exchange counters for fuel. But the difficulty in the way that I have described it is that the features do not yet have the structure of a genuine exchange. There is no buying or selling, because there is no sense of property *rights, duties,* or *obligations* involved. In a completely mechanistic universe, buying and selling would be exactly like the operation of a machine that spits out four quarters when a dollar bill is inserted.

Institutional reality of the sort we are familiar with essentially contains deontic powers. Think, for example, of eating in a restaurant. There the menu and the price list constitute *offers* by the establishment and my *ordering and consuming the ordered product* constitute *undertaking an obligation* to pay. But the notion of a deontic power makes no sense unless you presuppose consciousness and the gap. Once you regard the creatures as like the computational models common in cognitive science, then, it seems to me, you cannot have institutional reality in our sense. You might program the machinery to resemble some of the forms of institutional reality, but the substance would be removed. If we program the machines so that in certain circumstances they print out "I promise" and subsequently behave in such a way that we could describe as if it were the keeping of a promise, then we could simply skip the promising stage. The state of the program that produced the promise is already sufficient to produce the "keeping of the promise." So in a sense we have already skipped the promising stage because it made no special difference. It is just one state of the machine table, like any other. The machine is just programmed to produce a particular sequence.

If this argument is going in the right direction, it suggests that the concept of freedom is essential to our notion of institutional reality.

V. Could We Be Programmed to Behave Like Robots?

So far, I have tried the thought experiment of holding institutional reality constant and then imagining that we construct a different human nature, the one that is, in fact, or was until recently—I have been attacking it for decades[6]—postulated by much of contemporary cognitive science. But now let us try to reverse the thought experiment. Let us suppose that we have normal existing thought processes and that we make our decisions and act on them in the gap. Could we imagine a completely different sort of institutional reality? Could we imagine an institutional reality that did not allow us the

6. For example, in *Minds, Brains and Science,* Cambridge, Mass.: Harvard University Press, 1984. Also, "Minds, Brains, and Programs," *The Behavioral and Brain Sciences* 3 (1980): 417–57. Also, *The Rediscovery of the Mind,* Cambridge, Mass.; MIT Press, A Bradford Book, 1992.

types of free choices that we currently have, but was mechanical and algorithmic? Well, this seems much more promising. In fact, some kinds of institutional reality seem to fit this model. For example, when you read these sentences, your brain automatically parses them and you automatically understand them as having a certain semantic content. There is no question of any free choice. The processing is all done by the brain automatically. Now, why couldn't all institutional reality be like that? Imagine that appropriate behavior in institutional reality was, so to speak, preprogrammed, that you automatically kept your promises, respected property rights, and spoke the truth in the same way that you automatically parse sentences when you hear them. But the difficulty with this hypothesis is that it runs dead counter to the assumption that we made about ordinary human consciousness and decision making. If we laid down a set of rules for how people were supposed to behave, so that they did not have status functions and deontic powers and all the rest of it, but just a set of precise rules of how to respond to such and such a situation, there would be an immediate problem. People might just disobey the rules. They might just say, "To hell with the rules," and do what they felt like doing. The cases where the algorithmic style of rules works are cases where there is no gap, where there are, for example, perceptual processes but no voluntary actions involved. In the first thought experiment we imagined a society of robots operating within a system that requires the gap, that requires free will, and we found that the system loses its meaning in such a society. In the second thought experiment, we imagined a set of rules appropriate for robots being imposed on people like us, and we find that the system will not work because the people have no independent motivation for following the rules. Even if we program them to follow the rules, if they are free agents they can violate the program. Following the rules would not be like unconsciously following the rules of English in parsing the sentences that you are now reading. We are supposing the agents are operating freely in time, so they have the option of obeying or disobeying the rules; you, however, do not have any conscious option of obeying or disobeying the rules for parsing the sentences that you are now reading.

So far I have argued that our system of deontic powers makes sense only for beings who have a sense of the gap, who have, in traditional terminology, a sense of "free will." But conversely, once they have a sense of freedom, they cannot be programmed to follow the rules. It will always be up to them to break the rules of the program. You can have consciousness and the gap without having institutional reality. (That is exactly the situation that the higher nonhuman animals are in.) But you cannot have institutional reality in our sense without consciousness and the gap, because in such a case the institutions would be without a function, and once you have consciousness and the gap, a system of rules will work only if it comes with some motivational structure. Just having rules that prescribe behavior won't work because for free agents, it will always be up to the agent to violate the rules.

VI. The Connections between Deontology, Rationality, and Freedom

I have been insisting that institutional reality of the sort that is characteristic of human societies necessarily contains a deontology. But that claim presents us with the following question: Why is this deontology so important for institutional reality? Specifically, how does the deontology relate to the essential character of humans in their preinstitutional state? There are two parts to the answer. The first part is that if we are assuming that there is a deontology in the society we are creating, then the creatures for whom we are designing a society will only lock into the institutional structures if they experience the gap. Without free will the structures of private property, voting in elections, going to cocktail parties, and giving lectures in a university are meaningless. That was the point of imagining the deterministic computational models. Without free will the structures do not have a point. The second part of the answer is this: because the creatures in question have free will and rationality, the structures in question will be effective on them only if the structures have some influence on their conscious rational behavior. Participation in the institutional structures has to be capable of motivating the agents who are participating. But the only way that this system can provide the motivations in question is by giving the agents reasons for action. The immediate inclinations of the agent are not going to be enough. So the system has to be able to create desire-independent reasons for acting. In a restaurant, I have a desire-independent reason to pay the bill. In making any statement, I have a desire-independent reason for speaking the truth. And this is characteristic of the deontology. To recognize the deontology is to recognize desire-independent or inclination-independent reasons for acting. And the institutions in question—statement making, property, and so on—cannot survive and function in a society of free agents unless they can provide such reasons. So there is a double relation between the deontology and the society of conscious free agents. The first is that the gap gives substance to the deontology. If there are no conscious free agents then there is no substantial deontology, only a formal shell. But, second, the deontology makes it possible for rational and conscious agents to use the institutions without destroying them. Unless conscious agents recognize, for example, a reason for paying their restaurant bills, for not stealing the items in the museum, and for speaking the truth, restaurants, museums, and statements will all be out of business.

This is why, where institutional reality is concerned, the acceptance of the institution—what Max Weber called the problem of "legitimation"—is so crucial. I have been emphasizing throughout this book that institutions work only to the extent that they are recognized or accepted. But that recognition or acceptance, especially in the case of political institutions, often requires some sort of justification. In such cases people have to think that there is some ground for the acceptance of the institution. Typically, institutions work best when they are simply taken for granted and no justification is ever demanded or offered, as, for example, we take language and money for granted. But any institution can be challenged. And social change often occurs when institutions are no longer accepted, when the system of status functions simply collapses. An obvious case in point is the collapse of the Soviet system in 1989.

I asked earlier why we couldn't just give the creatures a biological inclination to respect property rights or speak the truth. But now we see the answer. If they also have free will, these inclinations will be inadequate when it comes to the crunch. If the inclinations are all they have, if the only motivation is inclination, then the strongest inclination will always prevail.

I also asked, Why couldn't we all just decide to behave like the computational models? And once again, the answer is that if we have free will the decision will not be binding on us unless we *already have a deontology that is not part of the computational ontology.* Without the deontology we will do what we feel like doing regardless of the model.

For beings such as us, who act under the presupposition of freedom and the constraints of rationality, our sorts of institutional structures can both facilitate behavior that could not exist without the institutional structures and do that in a way that is systematically related to freedom and rationality. The human engaged in the institutional structure does indeed act under the presupposition of freedom. The institution as such does not force the behavior. It simply creates possibilities, but the possibilities are constrained by the way the system of constitutive rules enables the agent to create reasons for action that are independent of the inclinations that the agent may otherwise have. This is true in general of institutions. When I recognize something as your property, when I recognize something as my government, when I recognize something as a promise made by me, when I recognize something as my statement, I am in each case recognizing not just the possibilities of behavior that could not exist without these institutions, but I also recognize restrictions on my behavior as an agent operating within these institutions. It is this combination that is special to our form of institutional reality. For conscious beings like ourselves, the augmentation of our powers by the creation of new enabling systems is not enough. The enabling systems have to coordinate with our rationality; that is, they have to coordinate with our ability to act on reasons. The special feature of reasons in institutional reality is that many of these reasons are desire-independent. You will be operating within marriage, money, private property, or government only if you recognize that in operating within these institutions you have reasons for doing things regardless of whether or not you are otherwise inclined to do them. Institutional structures enable us to do all sorts of things that we could not do without those structures; but this enabling function can be performed only if it is, at least in part, constituted by a deontic system, a system of desire-independent reasons for action.

Furthermore, participation in human institutions reinforces the deontology. Cars and shirts wear out after much usage. Universities, ski teams, and governments do not wear out. The more they are used, the stronger they get.

VII. Institutions and Brute Force

But if the institutional structure provides reasons for action, why does it so often have to be backed by the threat of force? Why is it necessary to have police and various other coercive mechanisms within the system of institutions? What is the relation between the deontic powers and the coercive powers? Given the gap, it is always possible to violate the rules when using the institution. And of course, many people lie, steal, and cheat in various ways. What is special about our institutional structures is that participation in them gives the rational agent a reason for not cheating, and for not doing something he wants to do, as well for doing something even when he does not feel like doing it then and there. People have strong motivations to break the rules, and the rules are not self-enforcing. Sometimes you have to call the police or use other coercive measures. But the necessity of the police is not inconsistent with the power of the deontology. The police powers presuppose the deontology rather than being inconsistent with it, because the content of the police powers must be mirrored in the deontology. For example, the criminal law and the police enforcement of the law function to protect personal and property rights. Organized coercion is indeed necessary to sustain certain systems of status functions, but police forces, armies, and other forms of organized coercion are themselves systems of status functions.

Suppose that the only reasons for action within institutional structures were prudential reasons. Suppose that the only rational question to ask myself before making a statement is not, "Is it true?" but "What are the advantages for me to say it?" Suppose I had no conception of property "rights" but was simply concerned with the question, "What are the prudential advantages for me of treating material objects and real property in one way rather than in another?" And suppose that in making promises I had no reason whatever to regard them as undertakings of obligations. I consider them as simply noises, referring to my future behavior. But when the time comes to "keep the promise," my only rational consideration is prudential: What are the advantages for me in doing what I "promised" to do? Now in fact, some philosophers have suggested that that is the situation we are already in. On one standard interpretation, Hume thinks the only reasons for keeping promises are prudential reasons. And Richard Rorty claimed (though frankly I cannot imagine that he or anyone else actually believed it) that truth as a commitment to correspondence to the facts is not an inner constraint on statement making. It seems to me that in a situation as I have described it, if there were no deontic reasons at all, no desire-independent reasons for action whatever, then the corresponding institutions would simply collapse. The systems of statement making, ownership of property, and promising function only on the presuppositions that, other things being equal, one can reasonably assume that one's own utterances and the utterances of other people are attempts at stating the truth; that property ownership confers rights and duties on the owner; that the making of a promise, other things being equal, creates a reason for the agent to keep the promise.

So there is a double aspect to the relation between freedom and constitutive rules. Only to the free agent do such systems make any sense, but precisely for free agents such systems are necessary. A system that did not have this capacity to create desire-independent reasons for action would collapse.

VIII. Conclusion

I can summarize the general line of argument in this chapter as follows:

1. Human institutions are, above all, enabling, and human institutional facts give us enormous sets of powers that we would not otherwise have.

2. The system functions by enabling agents to create desire-independent reasons for acting. These reasons are capable of motivating behavior because although they are desire-independent, they can rationally provide the basis for desires.

3. If you ask, "Why have institutional reality at all?" the answer can be stated bluntly: we are better off than animals in countless ways by living a civilized life.

4. If you ask, "Why should we have the sorts of structures we do?" then the question is more interesting. The answer has to do with the connections between consciousness, freedom, and rationality. The experience of freedom is peculiar to a certain sort of consciousness, the consciousness of deciding and acting in the gap. The concept of rationality is not the same concept as the concept of freedom, but their area of application is coextensive. The concept of rationality only applies to free actions because otherwise rationality would make no difference. Our institutional structures—property, universities, government, money, and so on—have evolved precisely under the presupposition of the gap, and institutional facts within those structures provide rational grounds for free actions.

5. Without the gap, our deontic structures are meaningless. There is no point to a deontology in a universe that is totally mechanical.

6. Given creatures operating in the gap, that is, capable of thinking and acting under the presupposition of freedom, a system of rules will work only if there is some reason to obey the rules. Rules, however strict, would simply be ignored if the agent had no motivation for following the rules.

7. Given the gap, our deontic structures make sense, but the fact that they enable us to create desire-independent reasons for action is essential to the survival of the structures. There are two levels of description of our institutions. There is the level at which the system as a system of constitutive rules makes possible forms of behavior that could not otherwise exist—rules of money, private property, and games, for

example. But, at a second level, within the system, human agents are enabled to create facts that also constrain. The institutions enable free agents to do things they could not otherwise do, but in so enabling they constrain the agents in ways that make the continued functioning of the institutions possible at all.

7

POWER: DEONTIC, BACKGROUND, POLITICAL, AND OTHER

I. The Concept of Power

Throughout this book I have been using the concept of power without explanation, and I have identified a specific form of power that goes with human social and institutional reality. I have called it "deontic power." I have identified this power by listing names of general types, such as obligations, authorizations, permissions, and requirements. In Chapter 6 I showed how such deontic factitives can function in rational behavior. In this chapter I will explain how deontic power relates to power in general and to political power in particular. It is not my aim to offer a general theory of power, but we cannot understand deontic power without saying some things about power relations among human beings in general.[1]

The first thing to notice about the concept of power is that it is not confined to relationships between human beings. In the same literal sense in which the president of the United States has certain powers defined by the Constitution, my car engine has a certain amount of power measured as horsepower. There is no pun involved here. The notion of power is the notion of a *capacity*, and for that reason, a power may exist without ever being used or exercised. I have never used the full horsepower of my car engine, and several of the powers of the president are seldom, if ever, exercised. For example, no American president, while president, has ever commanded the U.S. Army in

---

1. There is a sizable amount of interesting current work on the subject of power. Four books that are relevant to the issues discussed in this chapter are Andersson, Åsa, *Power and Social Ontology*, Malmö: Bokbox Publications, 2007; Foucault, Michel, *Power*, James B. Faubion (ed.), trans. Robert Hurley et al., New York: New Press, 1994/2000; Ledyaev, Valeri G., *Power: A Conceptual Analysis*, New York: Nova Science, 1998; Lukes, Steven, *Power: A Radical View*, 2nd ed., New York: Palgrave Macmillan, 2005.

the field, though he has the power to do so. So power has to be distinguished from its exercise. Power, in short, does not name an event but names a capacity, or ability. Because power is manifest in its exercise, we will in this chapter analyze not only sentences ascribing power but sentences about its exercise.

We begin with paradigmatic power-ascribing sentences. If you make a list of the president's powers, or the powers of a university department chair, or the powers of the Berkeley police force, the sentences on your list have something like the following syntax:

X has the power (is able, has the capacity) to do A;

where doing A relates to other people

X has power over Y with respect to action A.

A clue that deontology can be a form of power is provided by the fact that the deontic vocabulary is typically used to specify political powers: the California governor has the *right* to veto legislation, and he has the *obligation* to submit a budget. A common way, but not the only way, to exercise power is to give people reasons for actions that they would not otherwise have.[2] An order given by someone in a position of authority, for example, is such a reason. And threats of violence create prudential reasons. The source of the power, in the case of the threat, is the potential violence, but not all sources of power are based on the possibility or threat of violence, as we will see.

In this investigation, I will be concentrating on certain paradigmatic usages, where power involves a relationship between people or institutions and is always with respect to certain things and not others. So, for example, the president has power over Congress to veto congressional legislation. But Congress has power over the president to override his veto by a two-thirds majority vote in both houses. This is characteristic of social power ascriptions: they describe relations between people and institutions and describe the power holders as having certain powers and not others.

So far we have just analyzed the syntax and not the concept itself. What sort of power over other people or institutions is it to have political power, or police power, or military power? The simplest paradigmatic idea in the notion of power, the core notion of power concerning the power of some people over

2. I am indebted to Cyrus Siavoshy for reminding me of this point.

others (and this has been remarked on by several authors),[3] is that it involves the ability of an agent of power to get subjects to do what the agent wants them to do whether the subjects want to do so or not. In general, the *agent* of power can get what he or she wants, regardless of whether the *subject* of power wants the same thing. One way, therefore, to exercise power is to get the subject to want what the agent wants him or her to want. And thus, a special case of this would be instances in which someone gets others to *want* something they would not otherwise have wanted. Another type of case, discussed by Lukes,[4] occurs when the agent of the power gets the subjects to perceive only certain courses of action as open, so the subjects come to want what the agent wants them to want, even though they would not have wanted it if they had seen all the available courses of actions. To a general characterization of power as the ability to get people to do something whether they want to or not, we have to add two special cases. First, the agent of power can exercise power by getting the subjects to want to do something they would not otherwise have wanted to do. Second, the agent can exercise power by presenting the options he or she wants as the only options available, thus leading subjects to want something they would not have wanted had they known other options were available. There is thus a counterfactual element in the notion of power exercise: it is an exercise of power if agent A gets subject S to do act B even when S does not want to do B, would not have wanted to do B without A's getting him or her to want to do B, or would not have wanted to do B if A had not made S unaware of the available alternative options.

It is important to emphasize that power can exist even when it is never exercised and even when the subject, over whom power could be exercised, wants to do the action anyway. Power does not, in short, necessarily involve getting people to act against their desires and inclinations, but rather is the *ability* to get them to do so. It is only an *exercise* of power if the agent gets the subject to do something whether or not the subject wants to do it. But if the subject is doing what he wants to do anyway, then the agent is not in such a case *exercising* power over the subject, even though he could.

In simple paradigmatic cases of getting someone to do something, the power wielder does not necessarily have to use force. Indeed, this is a characteristic feature of deontic powers. They involve getting people to do things without using force. The fact that "deontic powers" are still powers but

3. For example, Ledyaev, *Power: A Conceptual Analysis.*
4. Lukes, *Power: A Radical View.*

not characteristically cases where someone is forcing somebody to do something shows that we need an expanded version of power beyond paradigms of simple brute physical force or the threat of force. So, if I make a promise to you, then you do indeed have a deontic power over me, because I have created a binding reason on myself for doing what I promised to do. I think this is a case of a power relation, but deontic powers are typically cases in which the power consists of *reasons for action*. If I have a negative deontic power such as an obligation to pay you the money I owe you, then I have a reason for doing something and you have a reason to expect me to do it. And if I have a positive deontic power, such as that I am authorized to go fishing on your property, then I have a power over you in that I can go fishing on your property and you have a reason for not interfering whether you want me to fish there or not. So *deontic* power is legitimately described as *power* even though typically it is not a case of the use or threat of force. When we turn to talking of governmental political power, we will see that typically it is backed by force. The subjects of power can be arrested, shot, deported, or otherwise dealt with. As I suggested earlier, the vocabulary in which we describe political power is typically deontic: the president has the *right* to veto legislation; he has the *obligation* to deliver the State of the Union address.

Something has to be added to our core concept of power, and that is the notion of its *intentional* exercise. So, for example, if someone smells so bad that whenever he enters a room, everyone gets up and leaves, his entering the room smelling bad is not an exercise of power. But it can become an exercise of power if he does so intentionally to get them to leave. So we have to revise our formulation to say "X has power over Y if and only if X is able *intentionally* to get Y to behave in a certain way with respect to action A whether or not Y wants to behave that way." Power is an ability or capacity, but the exercise of power, as power, is always an intentional act.

Influence is generally regarded as a species of power and indeed it often is a kind of power. But not all cases of exerting influence are necessarily cases of exercising power. For example, John Dewey had a huge influence on education in the United States, but most of the actual power was exercised by school boards and local governments, who changed educational requirements because they were *influenced* by Dewey. The exercise of influence may be an exercise of power if the influential agent is able to change people's behavior by intentionally getting them to do something that they would not otherwise have done. This, I take it, is part of what is referred to by the concept of the "power of persuasion."

The exercise of power may vary in its degree of overtness. The massing of Russian troops on the Czech border at the time of the Communist coup in 1948 was an exercise of power though they did not actually invade Czechoslovakia. They were present there intentionally to get the Czechs to behave in a certain way as opposed to behaving in some other way. The threat to use force may itself be an exercise of power, though no force is used. Historically, it is said that the mere appearance of British ships in the harbor of a colonial city could put an end to an uprising.

Power also has to be distinguished from leadership, and leadership is not coextensive with being a leader. Many leaders lack leadership, and many people who have leadership are not actually leaders, because they are "out of power." So, for example, when Jimmy Carter was constitutionally the leader of the American republic, he lacked the leadership abilities to exercise his constitutional powers effectively. Most of the actual day-to-day decisions of government are made by bureaucrats, often no higher than the level of GS 13. A common complaint among government people against Carter was that he did not express a clarity of vision so that they could know what they were supposed to do on a day-to-day basis. With an effective leader, for example, Ronald Reagan, the GS 13 knows what he is supposed to do in specific decision-making situations. Franklin Roosevelt, in contrast to Carter, had both power and leadership. One of the marks of a political leader is the ability to remain powerful and influential even when "out of power." De Gaulle and Churchill are good examples of this.

As I mentioned earlier, another type of power, discussed by Lukes,[5] is the power to set the agenda of human action in certain ways. For example, power can be exercised by restricting the range of apparent choices available to the agent over whom the power is being exercised. If the subject perceives a small range of choices open, when others are in fact also possible, then the agent who can create this perception has exercised a very strong form of power, the power of manipulating the subject's perception of available options. To take a real-life example, when in 2003 President George W. Bush convinced a large number of people that the only options for the United States were to go to war with Iraq or risk being the target of Iraqi weapons of mass destruction, then, assuming he did this intentionally, he exercised a strong form of power—the power to set the agenda of possible courses of action. This agenda may have reflected Bush's own perception of the available options. This is a

5. Lukes, *Power: A Radical View.*

special case of our core concept, but it is still an exercise of power. The power wielder gets people to see only certain options as available and gets them to want things they would not otherwise have wanted if they had been aware of other options. This is a special case of getting subjects to do something whether the subjects want to do it or not, by getting them to want to do something they would not otherwise have wanted to do.

It is important, however, to see that the person who can set the agenda in this way will be exercising power only if this is done intentionally. All kinds of things happen that affect people's Background sensibilities and ways of perceiving things that may not be actual exercises of power because they are not done intentionally. For example, people who designed and marketed professional football on national television in the United States had effects on all sorts of American practices, but for the most part, these were achieved unintentionally. Their only intention was to make money by having a large viewership and thus being able to charge a lot of money for television commercials. But such results as increasing the sales of beer and potato chips for consumption on Sunday afternoons in front of the television set was not one of their intentions, unless they happened to be advertising beer and potato chips. Consequently, it was not an exercise of power on their part, though they were unintentionally influential in this regard. On the account that I am presenting here, unintentional influence is very common, but the unintentional exercise of power typically occurs when the intentional exercise of power has unintended consequences. For example, when the United States Congress passed the alternative minimum tax in the 1980s, they did so with the intention of forcing a rich portion of the population to pay what Congress thought was their fair share of taxes. Due to inflation, however, the long-term consequence has been that Congress unintentionally raised taxes on a lot of less-rich people whom Congress had not intended to target with the alternative minimum tax. This was an unintentional exercise of power over a class of people against whom the original legislation was not intended. In general, one can say that an unintentional exercise of power is an intentional exercise of power described in terms of its unintended effects and consequences.

The unintentional exercise of influence is very common. For example, any professor unintentionally influences his students in various ways. Often he may not even know that the students are attracted or repelled by his style of speaking, that they attempt to imitate or reject his mode of speaking, style of dress, and so on. All of these are cases of influence, but they are not cases of the exercise of power. I am not exercising power over my students if they imitate (or try to avoid) my style of speaking because I am not intentionally trying to influence their behavior.

The issues discussed so far have been rather miscellaneous, but there are certain principles that emerge implicitly from this discussion, and I want to make them fully explicit.

1. The core notion of power is that A has power over S with respect to action B if and only if A can intentionally get S to do what A wants regarding B, whether S wants to do it or not. Special cases of this are cases in which A gets S to want to do B when he would otherwise not have wanted to do it and where S wants to do B because he has been prevented by A from seeing all the available options.

2. Power between human beings is normally exercised through the performance of speech acts. These typically have the illocutionary force of Directives. Sometimes these are standing Directives, in the sense that a general Directive is issued that then operates over an indefinite number of future cases. An obvious example is the criminal law, which is a set of standing Directives that prohibit, and provide specific punishments for, certain forms of behavior. Just as we saw that typically constitutive rules of the form "X counts as Y in C" function as standing Status Function Declarations, so statements of the criminal law function as standing Directives.

3. The concept of power is logically tied to the concept of the intentional exercise of power. "S has power to do B" implies "other things equal, S is able to intentionally exercise the power to do B." (We have to say "other things equal" because S, might, for some irrelevant reason, be unable to exercise the power he has. He might, for example, be sound asleep at the relevant moment.) The specification of the exercise of power therefore requires a specification of the intentional content of that exercise. No intentionality, no exercise of power. The intentional exercise of power may have unintended consequences and the intention may be unconscious, but all the same all exercises of power have intentional contents. Let us call this the "intentionality constraint."[6]

---

6. Direct attributions of power are extensional, but attributions of the intentional exercise of power are not extensional. In the arguments below, continued in the note on the next page, (a) and (b) imply (c). But (d) and (b) do not imply (e).

(a) X has power over Y to get Y to do A.
(b) A = B

imply

(c) X has power over Y to get Y to do B.

4. It is a constraint on any satisfactory discussion of power that whenever one talks about power one should be able to say, who exactly has power over exactly whom to get them to do exactly what? For future reference, let us call this "the exactness constraint." This constraint applies even when both the agent and the patient of power are unknown to each other. For example, Congress as a body exerts power over millions of citizens, who are unknown to the members of Congress, to get them to pay taxes. For the most part, the members of Congress and the taxpayers involved in this exercise are unknown to each other, but all the same, the attribution satisfies the exactness constraint.

5. The threat, or even the known option, of exercising power can in certain circumstances be an exercise of power. So the policeman who is present and visibly armed can exercise a kind of a power even though he needs to do nothing to enforce the law. The specification of the intentional content in such cases would include not only the actual intentional content but also the counterfactual specification of the sanctions that would be imposed if that intentional content is not fulfilled. Specifically in this case, the intentional content is "You must obey the law," and the implicit sanctions are "If you don't obey the law, I have the power to arrest you." In such cases, the visible appurtenances of power are sufficient for its exercise. Similarly, the Soviet Army massing on the Czech border in 1948 was a threat to exercise power, and that threat was itself an exercise of power.

II. Foucault and Bio-Power

Foucault's discussions of bio-power have been so influential that I want to say at least something about them. His views are not entirely clear, and he insists that they are not supposed to constitute a theory. Nonetheless, there are certain themes in his account that are relevant to our investigation. He introduces the notion of "bio-power." On his view, bio-power is pervasive throughout society. He gives a historical, or as he would prefer to say in

---

But the following derivation is not valid.

    (d) X intentionally exercised power over Y to get Y to perform A,
    (b) A = B
    (e) X intentionally exercised power over Y to get Y to perform B.

Nietzschean style, a "genealogical," account of the development of bio-power. It is a matter of the achievement of control over the bodies of human beings by subjecting them to the *normalizing* practices of society. Educational institutions, parents, prisons, hospitals and health care techniques, the practices of the religious confessional, and psychoanalysis—along with lots of other practices and institutions—all have the effect of producing a certain kind of normalization that creates human subjects who can be administered.

It is important on Foucault's account that some things that appear to be liberating are in fact further expressions of bio-power. For example, the sexual liberation movements of the middle decades of the twentieth century were thought by many of their participants to be liberating from repression; but according to Foucault, these participants were exchanging one kind of control for another. The public moved from "control by repression" to control by "stimulation."[7] We are normalized to the idea that we should be good looking and sexually active, and this is as much a power relation as was the repression that preceded it.

Foucault's favorite example of the operation of bio-power is Bentham's panopticon. In the panopticon the prison guard sits in the central tower and observes all of the inmates who are in cells surrounding the tower through windows that enable the observer to perceive each inmate, but the inmate cannot observe the observer and can never know whether he is then and there being observed. One feature of the panopticon is that the inmate becomes his own observer and will police himself because he does not know whether he is being observed by the authorities at any given moment. His behavior is perfectly normalized by the epistemic situation in which he has been placed. Foucault takes this as a model of the connection between knowledge and power. The perfect knowledge of the observer gives him complete power. Like the panopticon, bio-power is pervasive, anonymous, and constant. Foucault takes many of the ordinary bureaucratic, disciplinary, educational, and therapeutic techniques that have developed over the past two centuries as examples of this connection of power/knowledge. One immediate objection is that the panopticon works as a vehicle of power only because the observer already has power independent of his epistemic status. He is not just a voyeur or Peeping Tom. He has power over the inmates regardless of his observations. Knowledge, in such cases, does not create power but only enables the more efficient and effective use of power that is already there. One way to see this is

---

7. Cited in Lukes, *Power: A Radical View,* 94.

to reverse the epistemic roles. Suppose all of the prisoners can see the guard, but he can't see them. As long as they remain locked up, this does not reverse the power relationships. Foucault sees society as pervaded by these invisible anonymous normalizing practices that constitute the subjects and their subjection.

What are we to make of the concept of bio-power? On the face of it, not all of Foucault's examples seem to be able to satisfy our constraints of exactness and intentionality. We cannot say who exactly is exercising power over whom exactly and what exactly is the intentional content of the exercise. Health care professionals, teachers, social workers, and government employees will strive to create what they consider healthy normal human beings. But who exactly is exerting power over whom exactly with respect to what actions exactly? And what exactly was the intentional content of the intentional exercise of power? If the net result was to produce human beings who are more manageable by bureaucratic authorities, it does not follow that that is a form of exercise of power. Foucault says that people know what they do, but they don't know what, what they do, does. But if that is right, and it certainly seems plausible, then producing the effects (what, what they do, does) is not an exercise of power because it satisfies neither the exactness constraint nor the intentionality constraint. Oddly enough, Foucault seems to recognize these constraints. He says, "Power exists only as exercised by some on others, only when it is put into action, even though, of course, it is inscribed in a field of sparse available possibilities underpinned by permanent structures."[8]

Lukes criticizes Foucault because, according to Lukes, Foucault is presenting "sociological commonplaces" as if they constituted a new and radical theory: "Individuals are socialized: they are oriented to roles and practices that are culturally and socially given; they internalize these and may experience them as freely chosen; indeed their freedom may, as Durkheim liked to say, be the fruit of regulation—the outcome of disciplines and controls."[9]

I will not be much concerned with the extent to which Foucault was original or radical, but I want to explore the question of whether such "sociological commonplaces" can state cases of power relationships. My aim in what follows is emphatically not to discuss Foucault's work either by way of commentary, explication, or criticism, but the following pages were in part provoked by reflection on whether conceptions like his can be made intellec-

---

8. Foucault, *Power*, 340.
9. Lukes, *Power: A Radical View*, 97.

tually respectable to the extent that they can conform to the exactness constraint and intentionality constraint.

III. Background Practices and the Exercise of Power

The exactness constraint says that any legitimate attribution of power will have to say exactly who has power over exactly whom, and the intentionality constraint says that any attribution of the intentional exercise of power must specify the intentional content of the exercise.

With these principles in mind, I want to explore the idea that there is a type of power in society that is not codified, is seldom explicit, and may even be largely unconscious. Just to have a word for this, I am going to call it "Background/Network power," or simply "Background power" for short. (In Chapter 2, in the discussion of intentionality, I introduce these two notions. Roughly, the Background consists of the set of capacities, dispositions, tendencies, practices, and so on that enable the intentionality to function, and the Network of intentionality consists of the set of beliefs, attitudes, desires, and so on that enable specific intentional states to function, that is, to determine their conditions of satisfaction. For brevity, in this discussion, I will use "Background" as short for both Network and Background.) My discussion bears certain affinities with and was partly inspired by Foucault's discussion of bio-power and Åsa Andersen's discussion of what she calls "telic power." The sorts of things I have in mind are the various typically uncodified sorts of Background and Network constraints on social, sexual, verbal, and other forms of behavior. So what is regarded as an appropriate thing to say in a conversation, what is regarded as appropriate dress, what is regarded as permissible sexual behavior, what is regarded as permissible political and moral opinions are all cases of Network and Background as I have been describing them. So far it does not seem like there is much by way of power involved in these things, though certain constraints are imposed. I, for example, feel constrained in the sort of clothing that I wear by the practices of my community. But so far, such things would not satisfy our two constraints of exactness and intentionality. We would still have to specify who has power over whom with respect to what exactly and what is the intentional content of the exercise of power. If I hold political opinions that are regarded as immoral or outrageous, or if I am known to engage in sexual practices that are regarded as impermissible, then society will impose certain sanctions on me, and the threat of those sanctions, I want to argue, is, or can be, an exercise of power. I will try to make some sense of the notion that society can exercise power over its members.

But let us go back and look at the last two sentences more closely. Famously, Margaret Thatcher said society does not exist; only people and their families exist. I reject that claim in light of the arguments that I have advanced in this book, and I claim that there is a social ontology to any group that shares collective intentionality. A social fact, as I define it, is any fact that contains a collective intentionality of two or more human or animal agents. Society consists not just of people and their families but includes ski clubs, nation-states, corporations, and other social entities. However, there is something right about what she is saying, and that is that "society" does not name a form of collective intentionality. On this definition, the existence of a society need not be a social fact; it is only a social fact if there is a collective intentionality shared by the members of the society. There are particular societies in which there is a pervasive collective intentionality, and the nation-state is perhaps the most famous form of political collective intentionality.[10] There is also a deeper point that I want to expound here and it is this: though "society" does not name a form of collective intentionality, there are Background practices, presuppositions, and so on that are typically shared by the members of a society. Indeed, without some degree of shared Background, it is hard to see how a society could function. I will argue that some (not all) of the Background practices and presuppositions can constitute sets of power relations. But to show that, I first have to show how such attributions satisfy the intentionality constraint and the exactness constraint. My problem is this: I think any serious discussion of power should satisfy the constraints that I specified, but at the same time I feel that society is capable of exercising power. Social pressures can be a form of power. Can we capture that intuition consistently with the constraints? I will argue that we can.

The Background and Network, as I have defined them, contain among other things, a set of norms of behavior. If someone violates the norms of the community, various sorts of sanctions can be imposed on the violator. Those

10. It is common, by the way, in American journalism, to talk of something called the "black community." I doubt if there is such a community, but one thing I am certain of is that there is no such thing as "the white community" simply because there is no collective intentionality that pervades all or even most of the people of the so-called white race.

may vary from simple expressions of disapproval to strong forms of ostracism, contempt, hatred, derogation, and even violence. To bring this down to historical examples, consider the treatment of homosexuals before the recent so-called gay liberation movement. In such a case, who is exercising power over whom? I think the answer in such cases is that, provided that there is indeed a set of shared Background norms, *anybody* can exercise power over *anybody* else. So if you share the Background assumptions of your society, then you are capable of exercising the power that goes with those shared assumptions. Your treatment of people who hold forbidden opinions or engage in impermissible behavior is a form of exercise of power, and indeed the mere threat, or even the perceived option of the exercise of power, can be itself an exercise of power. I am not talking here about legal sanctions, but about social pressures.

For example, all of us in various ways are constrained by the dressing practices of our culture. A woman professor in my university, for example, though she cannot give her lectures naked, can choose to give her lectures in a dress and high heels or she can give her lectures in blue jeans and a T-shirt. This is a change in the Background possibilities. Fifty years ago, blue jeans and a T-shirt would have been out of the question for both men and women. In my case, the Background practices still constrain me in ways she is not constrained. I cannot give a lecture wearing a dress and high heels. This is, indeed, a Background constraint. Is it a question of the exercise of power? Is my inability to give a lecture wearing a miniskirt, stockings, and high heels a form of power that is enforced on me? In fact, I don't want to dress in that way, and it seems odd to say that it is an exercise of power on me that I am unable to do so. Who is exercising this power over me and how do they exercise it?

My knowledge that sanctions can be imposed upon me and that I would find those sanctions unacceptable places me in a power relation with those who have the perceived option of imposing the sanctions. That is, they are able intentionally to get me to do something, whether I want to do it or not, and that satisfies our initial core definition of power. This is also a case in which the known option or threat of exercising power can itself be an exercise of power. We have to state these relations exactly: As long as I don't want to dress in the impermissible way, no power is being *exercised* over me. But the moment that I do want to dress in an impermissible way, and am constrained not to do so by the perceived threat of the other members of the society, then power is being exercised over me. Let's see how we can satisfy our constraints:

First, the core concept of power: members of my society have power over me, though they are unconscious of having it, because they are able to get me to do something whether or not I want to do it.

Second, this power will be exercised only in cases in which I am constrained from doing something that I would otherwise do. Where the social Background and Network norms function as power mechanisms, they function as *standing Directives*. They tell each member of the society what is and what is not acceptable behavior. What exactly is their intentional content? Well, because we are talking about the Background, we are not talking about something members of society are consciously thinking. But if it came to the point where they did impose sanctions, where I was treated with derision, hostility, contempt, boycott, and other negative utilities, they would presumably say something like "That is an outrageous way to dress," "You just cannot dress like that," "You look absolutely ridiculous," and so on. That is, having the known option to impose sanctions can itself be an exercise of power, if the knowledge that the sanctions can be imposed can get the subject of power to behave in a certain way, even in cases where he or she does not want to behave that way. The certainty of the sanctions can constitute an unconscious exercise of power when the intentional content is implicit. The intentional content in its most general form is "Conform!" The argument that this content is implicitly present in the situation is that the predictable sanctions make sense only if you suppose that they are imposed because of a failure to conform. The subject conforms because a failure to conform elicits the expected sanctions. Of course, it is always possible for one to ignore or be indifferent to social sanctions. But this form of indifference is rare. Most people are acutely sensitive to the approval and disapproval of others.

The exercise of Background power, like the criminal law, extends the intentionality constraint from events to standing Directives. The simplest forms of the intentionality constraint, the paradigmatic cases, are events— the president issues a directive, the general orders his troops to advance—but in the case of Background power, like the criminal law, we have a standing power and a standing intentional content. The intentional content is not just "Conform on this occasion"; it is "Conform!"

But what about the exactness constraint? Who exactly is exercising power over whom exactly? The answer I am suggesting is that in these cases *anybody* can exercise power over *anybody*. If you are a member of the society, and as such you know that you share the norms of that society, then you are in a position to exercise power because of your capacity for imposing informal sanctions against those who violate the norms, in the knowledge that your sanctions will be supported by others. But you are also a subject of power, because anybody can impose those sanctions against you for any of your violations. Heidegger says, "Das Man never dies." And he should have added, "You are das Man."

I am trying to make sense of the idea that societies can exert power over their members. I think that we feel there must be something to this idea because we are all subject to "social pressures." The problem is to give a coherent statement of this sort of power that does not violate the intentionality constraint or the exactness constraint. But one might think, What difference does it make? After all, "power" is just a word and what does it matter whether we apply or withhold the word to cases of socially imposed pressures to conform? I think it matters if we are trying to get an understanding of social mechanisms and how they operate. You will understand the functioning of the Network and the Background better if you see that at least in part they function as power mechanisms. And the exercise of power occurs when the members of the society impose conformity on the other members of the society.[11]

Our whole mode of sensibility is shaped by forces and influences that are, for the most part, invisible to us—what it is to be male, what it is to be female, what is involved in being a citizen, what is involved in being a professor. Though sometimes these points are made explicit—citizens, for example, are authorized to vote in elections—there are all sorts of ways in which they are inexplicit. For example, what is regarded as a civilized form in which citizens disagree with each other about political issues varies enormously from one culture to another. What are appropriate topics in a conversation? What is appropriate courtship behavior? What sorts of social relations can one have with friends, colleagues, and family members? Indeed, the very concepts of what constitutes a friend, a colleague, or a family member are heavily shaped by the Background.

11. In my experience, an extremely conformist social group is American academics. American professors are conditioned even as graduate students to accept a certain set of Background assumptions and presuppositions about what sort of taste it is proper to have, what sorts of friends one can be seen with, what the acceptable political views are, what sorts of cultural artifacts one can admire, and so on. Pressure to conform is, for many, overwhelming, and independence is rare. Tenure is supposed to provide intellectual independence for all sorts of nonconformist thought and behavior. But if so, it is an independence that is seldom exercised.

The basic concept of Background power is that there is a set of Background presuppositions, attitudes, dispositions, capacities, and practices of any community that set *normative* constraints on the members of that community in such a way that violations of those constraints are subject to the negative imposition of sanctions by *any member* of the community. So if I walk down the street in Berkeley carrying a racist sign, I will be subject to the Background power of just about anyone in the community. Who exercises power over whom? The answer is *anybody* who accepts the Background presuppositions and knows that these presuppositions are widely shared in the community can exercise power over *anybody* who violates those presuppositions. The form in which these powers are exercised, or attempted to be exercised, ranges all the way from expressions of disapproval, contempt, ridicule, shock, and horror to physical violence and even murder.

Not all Background capacities are matters of power. For example, how far apart people are disposed to stand from each other in elevators or when they are carrying on a conversation is, I take it, a Background disposition, but it is not a power relationship.

Background power has to be distinguished from its exercise, like all other forms of power. As long as one is not constrained from doing what one wants to do, and as long as one is not constrained to do something one does not want to do, then no power has been exercised. But Background power is exercised when it actually affects people's behavior. Given our earlier discussion of the counterfactual component in the concept of power, power is exercised when the agent makes the subject want something he or she would not otherwise have wanted or limits the subject's perception of the available options; should we then not say that the Background power is exercised when the Background shapes my wants or limits my perception of the available options? To take the case of the Background construction of sexual desire, is the fact that one's desires are shaped by one's society, and one's perceptions of the available options are similarly shaped, cases of the exercise of power? I think not, because in these cases one cannot answer the question: who exactly is exercising power over whom exactly?

IV. The Paradox of Political Power: Government and Violence

So far the account is fairly neutral about the distinctions between different sorts of institutional structures, and it might seem from such an account that there is nothing special about government, that it is just one institutional structure among others, along with families, marriages, churches, universities, and so forth. But in fact it is not just another instititition. There is a sense in which in most organized societies *the government is the ultimate institutional structure.*[12] Of course, the power of governments varies enormously from liberal democracies to totalitarian states; but all the same, governments have the power to regulate other institutional structures such as family, education, money, the economy generally, private property, and even the church. Economics affects everybody's life, and in the present era important economic issues are automatically regarded as political issues, subject to governmental action. In stable societies, governments tend to be the most highly accepted system of status functions, rivaled only by the family and the church. Indeed, one of the most stunning cultural developments of the past few centuries was the rise of the nation-state as the ultimate focus of collective loyalty in a society. People have, for example, been willing to fight and die for the United States, or Germany, or France, or Japan in a way that they would not be willing to fight and die for Kansas City, Vitry-le-François, or Alameda County. It is no mean achievement to get the boundaries of the nation and the boundaries of the state to coincide. The nation is a cultural entity; the state is a governmental entity. There is no a priori guarantee that in any historical situation the boundaries of the nation and the boundaries of the state will coincide. Much of the history of the past two centuries is about such boundary inconsistencies. In the nineteenth century, Germany and Italy each formed a national state out of what had been collections of small principalities. At the end of the twentieth century, Yugoslavia and the Soviet Union ceased to be states, as many of the nations that they contained became nation-states of their own.

As I write these lines a number of Muslim extremists regard religion as more important than government and believe that governments should be controlled by fundamentalist Muslim clerics. The separation of church and state is so widely accepted in the Western democracies that it is hard for us to

12. For these purposes I would use "government" and "state" equivalently. Sometimes "government" is used to refer to the set of people and political organizations that hold power at any given time. I am using it to refer to the institutional structure itself. In the United States, "state" is typically used to refer to the state government as opposed to the national government.

understand the truly radical conception of the relation of the religion to the state that is held by a sizable number of Muslim fundamentalists.

These two historical developments, the rise of the nation-state and the separation of church and state, are both fairly recent historical developments. Neither is inevitable, and indeed we should allow ourselves to be struck by how counterintuitive they are. If government is the repository of ultimate power and religion the source of ultimate values, then it would seem natural to conclude that government should use its power to enforce the values of religion. To a lot of people, that seems a natural conclusion. In actual practice, it is almost invariably disastrous, for reasons I will shortly explain. Over a very long period, Western democracy evolved in a way that allows governments to be independent of ecclesiastical control.

The bad consequences of not separating church and state are not just an empirical result of specific historical circumstances; there is a philosophical inconsistency in trying to unite the two. Why? Politics, as I will argue shortly, is by definition about conflict and its peaceful resolution. But for dogmatic religions of the sorts we are familiar with, conflict is an abnormal situation. For such faiths, if church and state are united, then criticism of the government, even criticism of the people who happen to be in control of the government, is a form of blasphemy, and attempts to change the government are heresy. For such a system, any attack on the government is an attack on God. Some of the essential characteristics of democratic governments, such as the free discussion of all issues, the temporary character of the distribution of power, and systematic verbal attacks on those in power, are profoundly inconsistent with the Background presuppositions of dogmatic religions. I cannot exaggerate the importance of this distinction. Democratic governments are by their very definition committed to the permanent acceptance of disagreements and inconsistencies. It is not a flaw of democratic governments that rival political parties have different sets of values and different fundamental beliefs. But where revealed religion is concerned, all of this is at best blasphemy and at worst worthy of extermination. The whole idea of revealed religions is that there is only one truth, only one right way, only one correct way of doing things in the light of God's law. There is no way that democratic government can be made consistent with revealed religion. In the recognition of this fact, we have evolved—and it was a very painful evolution—a set of mechanisms for separating church and state, for preventing religious institutions from having complete control of government policies.

Governments can vary in their degree of control, ranging all the way from near anarchy to totalitarian states, where life for ordinary citizens is highly restricted. At the ultimate extreme of "government" control, a concentration camp allows no freedom at all. But whatever its degree of control, the powers exercised in governmental operations exceed those of other institutional structures. Because governments typically have a monopoly on armed violence, it is difficult to make a clear distinction between voluntary acceptance of governmental power and just passively going along with it.

How do governments, so to speak, get away with it? That is, how does the government manage to be accepted as a system of status function superior to other status functions? Typically governments have two special, connected features: a monopoly on organized violence and control of a territory. The combination of control of the land with a monopoly on organized violence guarantees governments the ultimate power role within competing systems of status functions. In cases in which the government fails to have a monopoly of organized violence over certain parts of its territory, then it ceases to function as a government in that part of the territory. This is currently the case in some African states, and it has been the case in southern Italy and Sicily when the Mafia, the Commora, and other criminal organizations functioned as de facto governments over certain parts of the state territory. The paradox of government could be put as follows: governmental power is a system of status functions and thus rests on collective recognition or acceptance, but the collective recognition or acceptance, though typically not itself based on violence, can continue to function only if there is a permanent threat of violence in the form of the military and the police. Legitimation is crucial for the functioning of government because political power requires some degree of acceptance. But where government is concerned, legitimation by itself is never enough. Though military and police power are different from political power, in general there is no such thing as government, no such thing as political power, without police power and military power (more about this later).

The sense in which the government is the ultimate system of status functions is the sense that traditional political philosophers were trying to get at when they talked about sovereignty. I think the notion of sovereignty is a somewhat confused notion because it implies transitivity. But most systems of sovereignty, at least in democratic societies, are not transitive. In a dictatorship, if A has power over B and B has power over C, then A has power over C, but that is not typically true in a democracy. In the United States, there is a complex series of interlocking constitutional arrangements among the three branches of government and between them and the citizenry. So the traditional notion of sovereignty may not be as useful as the traditional political philosophers had hoped it would be. Nonetheless, I think we will need a notion of the ultimate status function power in order to explain government.

Because governments are the ultimate repository of deontic powers in a society, the question of legitimacy becomes crucial for government in a way that it is hardly a problem for institutions that are in everybody's interest, such as language or money. I am going to summarize some of the essential points about political power as a set of numbered propositions.

I. ALL POLITICAL POWER IS A MATTER OF STATUS FUNCTIONS, AND FOR THAT REASON ALL POLITICAL POWER IS DEONTIC POWER.

Deontic powers are rights, duties, obligations, authorizations, permissions, privileges, authority, and the like. The power of the local party bosses and the village council as well as the power of such grander figures as presidents, prime ministers, the U.S. Congress, and the Supreme Court are all derived from the possession by these entities of recognized status functions. And these status functions assign deontic powers. Political power thus differs from military power, police power, and the brute physical power that the strong have over the weak. An army that occupies a foreign country has power over its citizens, but such power is based on brute physical force. Among the invaders there is a recognized system of status functions and thus there can be political relations within the army, but the relation of the occupiers to the occupied is not political unless the occupied come to accept and recognize at least some degree of validity to the status functions. To the extent that the occupied accept the orders of the occupiers, without accepting any validity of the status functions, they act from fear and prudence. They act on reasons that are desire dependent.

I realize, of course, that all of these different forms of power— political, military, police, economic, and so on—interact and overlap in all sorts of ways. I do not suppose for a moment that there is a sharp dividing line, and I am not much concerned with the ordinary use of the word "political" as distinct from "economic" or "military." The point I am making, however, is that the logical structure of the ontology where the power is deontic differs from the cases where it is, for example, based on brute force or self-interest.

The form of motivation that goes with a system of accepted status functions is essential to our concept of the political, and I will say more about it shortly. Historically, the awareness of its centrality was the underlying intuition that motivated the old Social Contract theorists. They thought that there is no way that we could have a system of political obligations, and indeed, no way we could have a political society, without something like a promise, an original "contract" that would create the deontic system necessary to maintain political reality.

2. BECAUSE ALL POLITICAL POWER IS A MATTER OF STATUS FUNCTIONS, ALL POLITICAL POWER, THOUGH EXERCISED FROM ABOVE, COMES FROM BELOW.

Because the system of status functions requires collective recognition or acceptance, all genuine political power comes from the bottom up. This is as much true in dictatorships as it is in democracies. Hitler and Stalin, for example, were both constantly obsessed by the need for security. They could never take the acceptance of their system of status functions for granted, as a given part of reality. It had to be constantly maintained by a massive system of rewards and punishments and by terror.

Lenin's greatest invention, imitated by both Mussolini and Hitler, was the Party—not a traditional political party, but an elite organization of disciplined, committed fanatics who could work for the overthrow of the old system of status functions and take power once they had overthrown it and then create a new system of status functions. The "October Revolution" was not a revolution; it was a classic coup d'état carried out because Lenin had complete control of the Party and the Party was easily able to overthrow the Provisional Government. The Bolsheviks did in fact bring about revolutionary changes, but the use of the expression "October Revolution" falsely implies that there was a massive uprising from below. That was not the case. In Germany, Weimar politicians were astounded at the speed and completeness with which the Nazis gained control of the state once Hitler became chancellor. It was as if the NSDAP had a script. Everybody knew in advance what they were supposed to do. In both these cases the Party became an intermediate set of status functions between the leadership and the general populace. Party loyalty was essential to the functioning of the leadership and was ensured by a combination of incentives and terror.

The single most stunning political event of the second half of the twentieth century was the collapse of communism. The question of exactly how it collapsed is a matter for historical research, and I have not seen a definitive historical work that analyzes that collapse. But as far as the logical structure is concerned, we can say it collapsed when the structure of collective intentionality was no longer able to maintain the system of status functions. The structure that Lenin had created required systems of interlocking elites, especially and above all the Party. Once the head of the elite, in the person of Gorbachev himself, lost confidence in the acceptability of the then-present system, it began, simply, to unravel. Apparently Gorbachev thought he could reform communism, but the attempted reform destroyed the system. It is absolutely essential to understand the structure of this. The person on top, the dictator, has to have acceptance by the immediate Party and other sorts of elite structures. They in turn operate because they can control the populace with a mixture of acceptance and terror. But the whole structure begins to unravel when the people at the top lose confidence and the people lower down cease to accept or recognize the legitimacy of the people on top and the structures they control. Similar transformations occurred when the Shah abandoned Iran, and the Marcos family fled the Philippines.

3. EVEN THOUGH THE INDIVIDUAL IS THE SOURCE OF ALL POLITICAL POWER, BY HIS OR HER ABILITY TO ENGAGE IN COLLECTIVE INTENTIONALITY, THE INDIVIDUAL, TYPICALLY, FEELS POWERLESS.

The individual typically feels that the powers that be are not in any way dependent on him or her. This is why it is so important for revolutionaries to develop some kind of collective intentionality: class consciousness, identification with the proletariat, student solidarity, consciousness raising among women, or some such identification with a distinct group that will make them feel empowered and will in fact empower the group. Because the entire structure of the existing society rests on collective intentionality, its destruction can be attained by creating an alternative and inconsistent form of collective intentionality.

I have so far been emphasizing the role of status functions and consequently of deontic powers in the constitution of social and political reality. But that naturally forces a question on us: How does it work? How does all this stuff about status functions and deontic powers work when it comes to voting in an election or paying income taxes? How does it work in such a way as to provide motivations for actual human behavior? It is a unique characteristic of human beings that they can create and act on desire-independent reasons for action. As far as we know, not even the higher primates have this ability. This I believe is one of the keys to understanding political ontology. This leads to point number 4.

4. THE SYSTEM OF POLITICAL STATUS FUNCTIONS WORKS AT LEAST IN PART BECAUSE RECOGNIZED DEONTIC POWERS PROVIDE DESIRE-INDEPENDENT REASONS FOR ACTION.

Typically we think of desire-independent reasons for action as intentionally created by the agent, and promising is simply the most famous case of this. But one of the keys to understanding political ontology and political power is to see that the entire system of status functions is a system of providing desire-independent reasons for action. The recognition by the agent, that is to say by the citizen of a political community, of a status function as valid gives the agent a desire-independent reason for action. Without such a recognition, there is no such thing as organized political or institutional reality.

Part of what we are trying to explain is the difference between humans and animals who lack institutional structures. The first step in explaining the difference is to identify the features of institutional reality. Institutional reality is a system of status functions, and those status functions always involve deontic powers. For example, the person who occupies an office near mine in Berkeley is the chair of the philosophy department. The status function of being chair of the department imposes rights and obligations that the occupant did not otherwise have. In such ways there is an essential connection between status function and deontic power. But, and this is the next key step, the recognition of a status function by a conscious agent—such as I am—can give me reasons for acting, which are independent of my desires. If my chairman asks me to serve on a committee, and if I recognize his position as chairman, I have a reason for doing so, even if committees are boring and there are no penalties for refusal.

More generally, if I have an obligation, for example, to meet someone at 9:00 A.M., I have a reason to do so, even if in the morning I do not feel like it. The fact that the obligation requires it gives me a reason to want to do it. Thus, in the case of human society, unlike other animal societies known to me, reasons can motivate desires instead of being motivated by desires. The most obvious example of this is promising. I promise something to you and thus create a desire-independent reason for doing it. But it is important to see that where political reality is concerned, we do not need to make or create desire-independent reasons for action explicitly, as when we make promises or undertake various other commitments. The simple recognition of a set of institutional facts as valid, as binding on us, creates desire-independent reasons for action. To take an important recent example, after the year 2000 elections, many Americans thought George W. Bush got the status function of president in an illegitimate fashion. But the important thing for the structure of deontic power in the United States is that with very few exceptions they continued to recognize his deontic powers. Anyone interested in how Background presuppositions enable democracy to function should look closely at the year 2000 elections. Normally, in an election, there is a margin of error. And normally, the margin of victory vastly exceeds the margin of error, so the error does not matter. But in the 2000 elections, the margin of error vastly exceeded the margin of victory. This meant, in a word, there was no winner. The election ended in a tie. But elections cannot end in a tie. So what is one to do? Americans have a Background presupposition that is nowhere stated in the Constitution that all hard cases are to be decided by the Supreme Court, and this one was. I will not say whether their decision was intelligent or unintelligent, justified or not justified, but the remarkable thing was that it was accepted by the populace at large. Various European commentators suggested that the election of 2000 showed the weakness of American democracy. I believe it showed its strength. Though the election ended in a tie, and the ultimate decision to award the victory to George W. Bush had inconclusive justification, it was almost universally accepted by the population at large. There was no rioting in the streets; no tanks were called out. I saw a few bumper stickers in Berkeley saying "He is not my president." But I do not think the president or anybody else worried about them. The point I am making now is that democracies work not just on rules, but on Background presuppositions, on practices, and modes of sensibility.

It is a consequence of what I am saying that, if I am right, not all political motivation is self-interested or prudential. You can see this by contrasting political and economic motivation. The logical relations between political and economic power are extremely complex: both the economic and the political systems are systems of status functions. The political system consists of the machinery of government, together with the attendant apparatus of political parties, interest groups, and the like. The economic system consists of the economic apparatus for creating and distributing goods and services. Though the logical structures are similar, the systems of rational motivations are interestingly different. Economic power is mostly a matter of being able to offer economic rewards, incentives, and penalties. The rich have more power than the poor because the poor want what the rich can pay them and thus will do what the rich want. Political power is often like that, but not always. It is like that when the political leaders can exercise power only as long as they offer greater rewards. This has led to any number of confused theories that try to treat political relations as having the same logical structure as economic relations. But such desire-based reasons for action, even when they are in a deontic system, are not deontological. The important point to emphasize is that the essence of political power is deontic power.

5. IT IS A CONSEQUENCE OF THE ANALYSIS SO FAR THAT THERE IS A DISTINCTION BETWEEN POLITICAL POWER IN GENERAL AND POLITICAL LEADERSHIP AS A SPECIAL ABILITY.

Roughly speaking, power is the ability to get people to do something whether they want to do it or not. Leadership is a special case of power, the ability to get them to want to do something they would not otherwise have wanted to do. Leadership is a form of power and can thus be exercised intentionally. Thus, different people occupying the same position of political power with the same official status functions may differ in their effectiveness because one is an effective leader and the other is not. They have the same *official* position of deontic power, but different *effective* positions of deontic power. For example, both Roosevelt and Carter had the same official deontic powers—both were presidents of the United States and leaders of the Democratic Party—but Roosevelt was far more effective because he maintained deontic powers in excess of his constitutionally assigned powers. The ability to do that is part of what constitutes political leadership. Furthermore, the effective leader can continue to exercise power and to maintain an informal status function even when he or she is out office.

6. BECAUSE POLITICAL POWERS ARE MATTERS OF STATUS FUNCTIONS, THEY ARE, IN LARGE PART, LINGUISTICALLY CONSTITUTED.

I have said that political power is in general deontic power. It is a matter of rights, duties, obligations, authorizations, permissions, and the like. Such powers have a special ontology. The fact that Barack Obama is president has a different logical structure altogether from the fact that it is raining. The fact that it is raining consists of water drops falling out of the sky, together with facts about their meteorological history, but the fact that Barack Obama is president is not in that way a natural phenomenon. That fact is constituted by an extremely complex set of explicitly verbal phenomena. There is no way that fact can exist without language. The essential component of that fact is that people regard him and accept him as president, and consequently they accept a whole system of deontic powers that go with that original acceptance. Status functions can exist only as long as they are represented as existing, and for them to be represented as existing there needs to be some means of representation, and that means is typically linguistic. Where political status functions are concerned it is almost invariably linguistic. It is important to emphasize that the content of the representation does not need to match the actual content of the logical structure of the deontic power. For example, in order for Obama to be president people do not have to think "We have imposed on him a status function using Status Function Declarations, according to the formula X counts as Y in C," even though that is exactly what they have done. But they do have to be able to think something. For example, they typically think "He is president," and such thoughts are sufficient to maintain the status function because they have the logical form of Status Function Declarations, and thus have the double direction of fit characteristic of all Declarations.

7. IN ORDER FOR A SOCIETY TO HAVE A POLITICAL REALITY IN OUR SENSE, IT NEEDS SEVERAL OTHER DISTINGUISHING FEATURES: FIRST, A DISTINCTION BETWEEN THE PUBLIC AND THE PRIVATE SPHERE WITH THE POLITICAL AS PART OF THE PUBLIC SPHERE; SECOND, THE EXISTENCE OF NONVIOLENT GROUP CONFLICTS; AND THIRD, THE GROUP CONFLICTS MUST BE OVER SOCIAL GOODS WITHIN A STRUCTURE OF DEONTOLOGY.

I said I would suggest some of the differentia that distinguish political facts from other sorts of social and institutional facts. But, with the important exceptions of the point about violence and control of a territory, the ontology I have given so far might also fit nonpolitical structures such as religions, corporations, universities, or organized sports. They too involve collective forms of status functions and consequently collective forms of deontic powers.

What is special about the concept of *the political* within these sorts of systems of deontic powers?

I am not endorsing any kind of essentialism, and the concept of the political is clearly a family resemblance concept. There is no set of necessary and sufficient conditions that define the essence of the political. But there are, I believe, a number of typical distinguishing features. First, our concept of the political requires a distinction between the public and private spheres, with politics as the paradigm public activity. Second, the concept of the political requires a concept of group conflict. But not just any group conflict is political. Organized sports involve group conflict, but typically they are not political. An important feature of political conflict is that it is a conflict over social goods, and many of these social goods include deontic powers. So, for example, the right to abortion is a political issue because it involves a deontic power—the legal right of women to have their fetuses killed.

8. A MONOPOLY ON ARMED VIOLENCE IS AN ESSENTIAL PRESUPPOSITION OF GOVERNMENT.

As I suggested earlier, the paradox of the political is this: for the political system to function there has to be recognition or acceptance of a set of status functions by a sufficient number of members of the group sharing collective intentionality. But, in general, in the political system that set of status functions can work only if it is backed by the threat of armed violence. This feature distinguishes governments from churches, universities, ski clubs, and marching bands. The reason that the government can sustain itself as the ultimate system of status functions is that it maintains a constant threat of physical force. The miracle, so to speak, of democratic societies is that the system of status functions that constitutes the government has been able to exercise control through deontic powers over the systems of status functions that constitute the military and the police. In societies where that collective acceptance ceases to work—for example, in the German Democratic Republic in 1989—the government, as they say, collapses.

9. SOME SPECIAL FEATURES OF DEMOCRACIES

Carl Schmitt[13] says correctly that all politics involves a distinction between friend and enemy. But he then says—incorrectly, as far as democracies are

13. Schmitt, Carl, *The Concept of the Political,* trans. George D. Schwab, Chicago: University of Chicago Press, 1996.

concerned—that it is part of the concept of the political that each side wants to kill the other. This is definitely not true of successful democracies. Stable democracies like the United States or the countries of Western Europe are based on a Background presupposition of tolerance of disagreement. It is not just that in fact rival political parties typically do not kill their political opponents; it appears that they do not even want to kill their political opponents. They want to beat them in the next election, they want to be in power and have the opponents out of power, but typically they do this without wanting to murder anybody. Another near miraculous feature of stable, healthy democracies is that political conflicts are remarkably subdued. The competing politicians may hate each other with a passion, but the Background is such that they had better conceal that hatred or it will cost them votes. When in American history the conflict became so extreme that it could not be resolved by the normal constitutional methods, we had the Civil War.

If we assume that democracies are defined in part by majority rule as expressed in elections, then another feature of successful stable democracies is that few, if any, of the important problems of life are determined by elections. Such questions as who will live and who will die, who will be rich and who will be poor, cannot be decided by elections if the country is to be stable. Why not? Elections are too unpredictable for people to be able to plan their lives based on the outcome of elections. If you knew that if your opponents won the next election, you were likely be thrown into a concentration camp, or executed, or have all of your property confiscated, you could not make stable and enduring life plans. In successful democracies it does not and should not much matter who gets elected. Traditionally in the United States, the parties are competing for the middle range of voters, and consequently, if anything, they try to look more like each other than they really are. There are interesting differences that come out of elections, but I have noticed that life pretty much goes on after the election as it did before, regardless of who gets elected. This is a sign of a healthy democracy. How then do we decide life and death issues in a democracy? Well, ideally, most of them never come into the political arena. Whether you are rich or poor, alive or dead, living on the East Coast or the West Coast, educated or uneducated is for the most part not a function of who gets elected. Sometimes a really important issue comes up that arouses so much passion that the politically active elements of the population would prefer not to deal with it. In such a case in the United States, the matter is usually settled by the Supreme Court. Two famous cases in the past hundred years have been racial equality and abortion.

The intellectual gyrations that the Supreme Court had to engage in to settle the abortion issue are truly Byzantine, but no one seems to mind. The deontic power of females to have their unborn fetuses killed is treated as a question concerning the *right to privacy*, as guaranteed by the Fourth Amendment. However, there are constant attempts to reopen the issue.

V. Conclusion

This chapter has two sets of aims. The first set concerns the concept of power. There I try to describe some general features of power and then introduce the concept of Background power, where the collectively accepted Background and Network in a society can result in power relations over its members. I argue that these are properly construed as power relations because they satisfy the constraint that the members of the society can force other members to behave in certain ways whether they want to or not.

In the last part of the chapter I try to describe the distinguishing features of the political, within the system of desire-independent reasons for action, showing that the concept of the political requires a distinction between the public and the private spheres, with the political as the preeminent public sphere; it requires the existence of group conflicts settled by nonviolent means, and it requires that the group conflict be over social goods. And the whole system has to be backed by a credible threat of armed violence. Governmental power is not the same as police power and military power, but with few exceptions, if no police and no army, then no government.

8

HUMAN RIGHTS

This book is mostly about the nature of and the relations among institutions, institutional facts, status functions, and deontic powers. Prominent among the nouns in English that name these deontic powers is "right," along with others such as "obligation," "duty," "entitlement," and "authorization." Most of the rights that one can think of exist within institutions: the rights of property owners and university students, for example.

But now we reach a peculiar apparent anomaly. It is generally agreed that there are such things as *human* rights, even *universal* human rights that I do not have in virtue of my institutional memberships, such as the rights of a citizen, a professor, or a husband; but rights that I have solely in virtue of being a human being. How can there be such things? Does it really make sense to talk about human rights as distinct from the rights of husbands, professors, and citizens? People talk comfortably about universal human rights, but I have not heard much, nor indeed any, talk about universal human obligations. As we will see later in this chapter, if there are such things as universal human rights, it follows logically that there are universal human obligations. But if you pose the question, "Are there universal human obligations?" it certainly sounds different from the question, "Are there universal human rights?"

There is a peculiar intellectual hole in current discussions of human rights. Most philosophers, and indeed most people, seem to find nothing problematic in the notion of universal human rights. Indeed, Bernard Williams tells us that there is no problem with the existence of human rights, only with their implementation and enforcement. He writes, "We have a good idea of what human rights are. The most important problem is not that of identifying them but that of getting them enforced."[1] But

---

1. Williams, Bernard, *In the Beginning Was the Deed: Realism and Moralism in Political Argument*, Geoffrey Hawthorne (ed.), Princeton, N.J.: Princeton University Press, 2005, 62.

there is a skeptical tradition founded by Jeremy Bentham and continued by Alasdair MacIntyre that finds the whole idea of universal human rights absurd. If we are going to make sense of the notion of rights we have to answer the question, What exactly is their ontological status? The ontological status of property rights and citizenship rights is much less problematic, and indeed one of the aims of this book is to lay out the logical structure of such status functions. Can we do a similar analysis on universal human rights?

Let us start with the skeptical argument. Jeremy Bentham thought that the idea that there could be rights that you have apart from legal recognition, but just in virtue of being human, "simple nonsense." In a wonderful article,[2] written after the French Revolution and opposing the revolutionary claims of the "Rights of Man," he writes:

> Natural rights is simple nonsense: natural and imprescriptible rights, rhetorical nonsense—nonsense upon stilts. But this rhetorical nonsense ends in the old strain of mischievous nonsense: for immediately a list of these pretended natural rights is given, and those are so expressed as to present to view legal rights. And of these rights, whatever they are, there is not, it seems, any one of which any government can, upon any occasion whatever, abrogate the smallest particle. (line 230 ff)

Bentham thought that all rights, what he called the "substantive rights," are created by laws. Again, the passage is worth quoting:

> Right, the substantive right, is the child of law: from real laws come real rights; but from imaginary laws, from laws of nature, fancied and invented by poets, rhetoricians, and dealers in moral and intellectual poisons, come imaginary rights, a bastard brood of monsters, "gorgons and chimaeras dire." And thus it is that from legal rights, the offspring of law, and friends of peace, come anti-legal rights, the mortal enemies of law, the subverters of government, and the assassins of security. (line 730 ff)

More recent but equally enthusiastic skepticism is expressed by Alasdair MacIntyre:

---

2. Bentham, Jeremy, "Anarchical Fallacies; Being an Examination of the Declaration of Rights Issued during the French Revolution," in John Bowring (ed.), *The Works of Jeremy Bentham*, vol. 2, Edinburgh: William Tait, 1843. Accessed from http://oll. libertyfund.org/title/1921/114226 on Feb. 12, 2009.

There are no such things as rights, and belief in them is one with belief in witches and in unicorns.... The best reason for asserting so bluntly that there are no such things as rights is indeed of precisely the same type as the best reason which we possess for asserting that there are no witches and ... unicorns: Every attempt to give good reasons for believing that there are such rights has failed. The eighteenth-century philosophical defenders of natural rights sometimes suggest that the assertions which state that men possess them are self-evident truths; but we know there are no self-evident truths.[3]

I. Rights as Deontic Powers Deriving from Status Functions

Can we answer the Bentham-MacIntyre style of skepticism? I think we can, but to do so we have to recognize universal human rights as status functions; they are deontic powers deriving from an assigned status. The truth in the skepticism is that we do not *discover* that people have universal human rights the way we discover that they have noses on their faces. The existence of such rights is intentionality-relative because they are human creations. But once we get clear about their ontological status, the existence of rights is no more mysterious than the existence of money, private property, or friendship. Nobody says the belief in money, private property, or friendship is nonsense.

I hope it is obvious that in general, rights, such as property rights and marital rights, are status functions; that is, they are deontic powers deriving from collectively recognized statuses. They are deontic powers that are imposed on people and can function only by collective recognition or acceptance. That is why it is pointless, perhaps even nonsense, to say of Robinson Crusoe, alone on his island, that he has any human rights. If we say he has human rights (e.g., a right to be searched for by people who know he is lost), we are thinking of him as a member of a human society.

Because rights are status functions, it follows immediately that they are intentionality-relative. They are always created and imposed by collective intentionality. They are not discovered in nature in the way we might discover photosynthesis or hydrogen ions. Because of the logical structure of the creation and maintenance of human rights, the following two statements

3. MacIntyre, Alasdair, *After Virtue: A Study in Moral Theory*, Notre Dame, Ind.: University of Notre Dame Press, 1981, 69–71.

can be interpreted in a way that renders them consistent even though they look logically inconsistent:

1. The universal right to free speech did not exist before the European Enlightenment, at which time it came into existence.
2. The universal right to free speech has always existed, but this right was recognized only at the time of the European Enlightenment.

If every expression is interpreted univocally, these two statements would be inconsistent, but there is a way of interpreting them that renders them consistent. One of the aims of this chapter is to show how they can be consistent, in spite of the surface appearance of differences. In order to resolve the apparent inconsistency and answer the skeptical doubts we will have to explain both the nature of the creation of universal human rights and the justification for their existence.

II. All Rights Imply Obligations

The logical form of statements of rights always implies a correlative obligation on the part of others. Thus, in a typical sort of case, where X has a right of easement to walk across Y's property (A),

X has a right (X does A)
implies
Y has an obligation (Y does not interfere (X does A))

The important thing to emphasize is that rights are always rights *against* somebody. If, as in this example, I have a right of easement to cross your property, then that is a right against you. And you have an obligation not to interfere with my crossing your property. Rights and obligations are thus logically related to each other. If X has a right against Y, Y has an obligation to X. And what we think of in the United States as basic rights, such as the right of free speech, are usually rights against the government. The actual First Amendment text, which guarantees us our right to free speech, simply says, "Congress shall make no law . . . abridging the freedom of speech, or of the press." Literally speaking, our constitutionally guaranteed right to free speech is a right we have against Congress.

In standard deontic logics, it is possible to define all the deontic notions in terms of one. Thus, for example, if we take obligation as the basic primitive, then I am permitted to do act A if and only if I am not obligated not to do act A. I am not entirely satisfied with the deontic logics that I have seen, but on my account there has to be something right about the enterprise. I try to define all status functions in terms of one deontic power so it seems a strict logical consequence of what I am committed to that we should be able to give a complete analysis of deontology in terms of one deontic primitive.

There are apparent counterexamples to the claim that there is a perfect match of this sort between rights and obligations. These are cases in which the right gives the possessor a certain power, so, for example, the president of the United States has the right to veto congressional legislation. But against whom does he have this right? He has it against Congress. One of their obligations is to accept presidential vetoes and to recognize that they need a two-thirds majority to override a presidential veto.

So far it looks like we have the following:

1. For all x, x has a right R (x does A)
   implies
2. There is some y such that x has R against y.
   And that implies
3. y has an obligation to x to allow [not to interfere with, etc.] (x does A).

Is there anything to having a right that is not captured by this pattern? All rights imply obligations, because *all rights are rights against someone,* and the people they are rights against have a corresponding obligation. But do all obligations imply rights? I think if we are speaking carefully, there are a lot of informal social obligations—for example, obligations to invite people to a party—for which there are no corresponding rights. I agree that sometimes people speak loosely and talk about their right to be invited to somebody else's party, but I think that for our purposes, we should pursue the hypothesis that all rights are status functions. To have a right is to have those people, against whom you have the right, obligated to you, and the obligations derive from some status you have. So, at least for this class of cases, where X has a right, deriving from a status function, against Y to do something, we can provisionally characterize the relations between a certain class of rights (what I will later call "negative rights") and obligations as follows:

(X has a right against Y (X does A)) → (X has a status S (S places Y under an obligation (Y not interfere with (X does A)))).

In plain English: to say that X has a negative right against Y to perform act A implies that X has a certain status S, which places Y under an obligation not to interfere with X's doing A. This does not cover all cases of rights, as we will see, but it states an important feature of negative rights.

The first implication is that if there are such things as universal human rights it follows immediately that there are universal human obligations. To say that there is a universal right to free speech implies that it is a right one has against everybody, and consequently, everybody is under an obligation to allow everyone else to express himself or herself freely. This is an important point, and I will come back to it later. For the present just let me emphasize: we need not insist that a statement of rights is equivalent in meaning to the statement of the corresponding obligation on the part of those whom the right is against, but we do need to insist that for every right there is a corresponding obligation not to interfere with the exercise of the right, and consequently if there are universal human rights it follows immediately that there must be universal human obligations.

III. How Can There Be Universal Human Rights?

I have said that the easiest rights to understand are those tied to institutions. Because of your position in an institution, whether it is family, private property, citizenship, or membership in an organization, you have rights, as well as duties and obligations, that are attached to the position you are in. But now we come to an interesting historical development: in addition to the idea that there are rights of property owners, citizens, and kings, someone got the brilliant idea that there are rights that one has just in virtue of being a human being. Being human is a status to which functions can be assigned that fit our definition of status functions. In addition to property rights and citizenship rights there are *human* rights. When and how exactly did this occur? I am not sure, but the best I can come up with at the moment is this: the notion of a natural human right is a corollary of the notion of natural law. If you think that the law maker or law giver in the ideal state should formulate laws in accordance with natural laws, laws of the natural order, then it is a very short step to say that human rights are also a form of natural law. The theory of natural law is the theory that man-made human laws should be consistent with, and indeed follow from, nature—specifically human nature. The assumption is that human nature is universal and consequently there can be universal laws following from human nature. As far as I can tell, Hugo Grotius (1583–1645) was one of the first, and perhaps the first, major modern philosopher to have this idea. Josef Moural tells me that the idea is also in the Stoic philosophers. And Marga Vega tells me that Spanish theologians developed the idea of universal human rights when they encountered the Indians of the New World and thought that these people had rights given by God solely by virtue of being human beings. I am skeptical of both these claims, because I think that the peculiar aura that surrounds the notion of human rights, as we now understand them, is very much a product of the European Enlightenment. It would be a fascinating project to try to discover who first formulated the idea of human rights and how the idea evolved.[4]

One can, of course, interpret the Bible as implying the existence of universal human rights. For example, one can interpret the Ten Commandments as establishing the right of everyone not to be killed, and the rights of fathers and mothers to be "honored." Though I am not going to belabor the point here, I think the modern conception of human rights is a long way from the Bible and indeed from the Stoic philosophers and the Spanish Conquistadores. The modern conception of universal human rights, to put the point somewhat vaguely, is that it is by virtue of our dignity as human beings that we have these rights. Even though bestowed by God, they are bestowed by virtue of our very nature. The biblical conception is simply that there is a series of commandments laid down by God on an unworthy humanity. In any case, as far as I can tell, the terminology of "human rights," and especially universal human rights, is fairly recent and did not exist before the Enlightenment. Our modern conception of universal human rights requires that they be universal in the sense that everyone has human rights, that humans are equal, that everyone has equal rights with everyone else, and that the rights in some sense follow from our nature. *They are natural, universal, and equal.* I do not believe this particular conception was widespread before the European Enlightenment.[5]

But if rights in general are status functions, and the existence of status functions is a matter of institutional facts, then isn't there something puzzling about human rights? Isn't the idea logically absurd? There is no logical

4. For a good historical survey, see Hunt, Lynn, *Inventing Human Rights: A History*, New York: W.W. Norton, 2007.
5. For discussion of the importance of these three features, see Hunt, *Inventing Human Rights: A History*.

absurdity in the idea of there being human rights, because the assignment of rights to humans, logically speaking, is like any other assignment of deontic powers coming from an assigned status. The puzzling feature derives from the fact that in complex social systems rights typically accrue from several layers of *already* assigned status functions such as property, the army, courts of law, government bureaucracy, business enterprise, or marriage. But it is no more logically absurd to assign a status function of a right directly to humans than it is to assign a status function of being money to a piece of paper or a piece of gold. The logical structure is that we must treat being human as a status, like being private property, being a secretary of state, or being married. In the formula X counts as Y in context C, the Y term is "human being"; so if you qualify as a human being, you are automatically guaranteed human rights. However, human rights are puzzling in at least two respects. First, in the case of institutional rights the justification of the right derives from the purpose of the institution. The purposes of property, government, and marriage require rights and responsibilities. In what sense does being a human require rights? The first step in answering the question is to see that we are asking whether being human, by itself, can be a status that imposes desire-independent reasons for action on other humans. The common mistake is to suppose that if something is intentionality-relative, then it is completely arbitrary, that the assignment of rights is totally arbitrary and unjustified from a rational point of view. But that is a mistake. If we are going to have any use for the notion at all, we should be able to give a justification of human rights.

Second, there seems to be an asymmetry between human rights and other institutional status functions because we sometimes want to claim that human rights continue to exist even when they are not recognized. Actually, on closer examination there is a fairly close parallel in this respect between human rights and certain other status functions. In typical institutional facts there are three elements: the X term, the Y term, and the status functions (deontic powers) attaching to the Y status. The status functions only work, they only function, to the extent that they are recognized. For someone who accepts the system, satisfying the X term automatically qualifies as satisfying the Y term and thus as having the Y status functions. But what about cases in which something satisfies the X term but is denied the recognition that goes with the Y term and correspondingly denied the functions that go with the Y status? So, for example, it has sometimes occurred in American history that somebody who was born in the United States and thus automatically qualified as an

American citizen was denied the rights of citizenship and perhaps some would deny that he was a citizen. We can say either he lost his citizenship rights or that he kept his citizenship rights but they were not recognized. We can also say either he was really a citizen but no one recognized him as a citizen, or he lost his citizenship because no one recognized it. The situation with human rights is exactly parallel to this with one important exception: the term "human" has a usage that is prior to humanness being recognized as a special status. It does not carry with it by definition a status function in the way that "marriage," "private property," and "president" do. When someone is denied his human rights he is typically not denied his humanity, just the function that is supposed to go with that status for those who accept the deontology of human rights. This will become clearer if we ask, What is the X term in the creation of human rights? The answer to that depends on your theory of human rights. If you think they are given by God, the X term may be something like the following: "Created by God in His own image." Anyone so created counts as a human being and a bearer of human rights. But for some others, including me, the X term is simply a set of biological facts that constitute being a member of our species. To satisfy those conditions is to count as a human being or a human person, and as a human person the bearer of rights. The situation is parallel to that of money, private property, and citizenship with the important exception that in the existence of human rights there is no preexisting institution that defines the rights.

In some cases, especially where moral issues are involved, we treat entitlement to the status functions as a form of possession of the status functions. And thus we can say, without self-contradiction, that it is consistent to claim both that people have lost their rights when the rights are not recognized, and that they did not lose their rights but rather, they retained their rights, but the rights were no longer recognized. The apparent contradiction is removed by seeing that in the first sentence, we are identifying the satisfaction of the X condition as sufficient for the possession of the Y status function; in the second utterance we are recognizing that the functioning of the Y status function requires recognition, and hence, in the absence of that recognition we can deny that it exists. There is a sense, then, in which the concept of "human right" is ambiguous, but it is an ambiguity shared by lots of other status function concepts.

It seems to me that we can now resolve the tension between the claims of Bentham and MacIntyre, who think of themselves as stating obvious commonsense facts when they say there are no such things as universal human rights, and most of the rest of us, who think there are indeed universal human rights. We can say with Bentham and MacIntyre that rights, like other status functions, function only to the extent that they are recognized. No recognition, no deontic powers. At the same time, it seems that we can share the commonsense assumption that you do not lose your rights in cases where they are denied or not recognized. The existence of the ground of the status function in the satisfaction of the X term—you were born in the United States, you are a biological human—is taken as ground for the satisfaction of the Y term. You are entitled to the rights of citizenship, you are entitled to human rights. But one way to read this last sentence is not as saying you are entitled to the existence of the rights, but rather, you are entitled to the recognition of rights that already exist.

As so often happens in philosophy, the appearance of a deep disagreement dissolves under careful analysis. The skeptics think they are stating an obvious truth that ought to be plain to anybody who thinks about it carefully, and the commonsense believers in human rights think they are simply claiming something that ought to be "self-evident" to everybody else. I have tried to make clear what is true in both accounts.

Many people, especially in the United States, suppose that all human rights must come from God; that unless God endowed us with these "inalienable" rights, they would have no basis and we would not be justified in claiming them. For various reasons, this is unsatisfactory. Even if we assume the existence of God, it seems that in giving us rights, God keeps changing His mind because the list of fundamental human rights keeps changing. For example, those who think that the U.S. Constitution is divinely inspired should be worried by the fact that when God gave us these rights, He allowed slavery until 1865. And women had no right to vote until 1920. So there is both a theoretical and a practical defect in trying to derive rights from God. If God does not exist, as I fear is almost certainly the case, then nobody has any rights. And second, there is a problem in trying to figure out what rights God gave us, assuming he gave us a definite list. The list keeps changing. Unlike the Ten Commandments, the Seven Deadly Sins, and the Seven Cardinal Virtues, there is no general agreement on what the human rights are. For example, the United Nations Universal Declaration of Human Rights, Article 15, says, "Everyone has the right to a nationality." Why? Why should the nation be assumed to be a fundamental form of social organization, such that without a nationality you have lost a fundamental human right? In the passage I quoted earlier, Bernard Williams says that the problem with human rights is not that we don't know what they are, but that we are having difficulty implementing them.[6] I think that is mistaken. Our problem is that we don't know what the rights are. One of my aims in this chapter is to provide us with certain principles for settling the claims about what they are. But it is important to emphasize that there is no general agreement on the basic list of human rights.

IV. Negative and Positive Rights

Furthermore, there has been a subtle shift since the eighteenth century. At the time the American Declaration of Independence and Bill of Rights were written, the rights that were supposedly self-evident were all negative rights. That is, they did not require any positive action on the part of the state or anybody else. They simply required that the state not interfere in such things as free expression or the keeping and bearing of arms. But the gradual expansion of the notion of human rights has led to the idea that there are positive rights, such as the right to an adequate standard of living, or the right to education, including higher education—rights that by their very definition impose obligations on other people. So, for example, Article 25 of the Universal Declaration of Human Rights says, "Everyone has the right to a standard of living adequate for the health and well-being for himself and his family including food, clothing, housing, medical care, and necessary social services, and the right to security in the event of unemployment, sickness, disability, widowhood, old age or other lack of livelihood in circumstances beyond his control." The difficulty with such a statement is that in order for the statement to be meaningful there would have to be a specification of who is obligated to pay for all of these "rights." Against whom exactly does one have all these rights? This is an important logical point. We saw earlier that the notion of rights implies obligations. A right is always a right against someone, and the person against whom one has a right is thereby under an obligation. No obligations, no rights. So, if everyone has a right to adequate housing, a good standard of living, and higher education, then, for example, you and I are under an obligation to pay for everyone else having adequate housing, standard of living, and education. It seems to me it would take a very strong argument to establish such a claim. In many discussions of human rights it

6. Williams, *In the Beginning Was the Deed.*

sounds like the authors are simply saying, "It would be a good idea if," and then they supply a statement of desirable "rights." One might agree that it would be a good idea for everyone to have adequate housing, standard of living, and education. But it is another thing to say that you and I and everybody else are under an obligation to provide all of these things for all other people. I believe that the Universal Declaration of Human Rights is a profoundly irresponsible document because its authors did not reflect on the logical connection between universal rights and universal obligations, and they mistook socially desirable policies for basic and universal human rights.

For the universal right to free speech one can give a simple statement of the right and of the corresponding obligation. Thus,

X has a right (X speaks freely)
implies
Y has an obligation not to interfere with (X speaks freely)

How do we give an analogous logical implication for positive rights? It would not be enough to say,

X has a right (X has an adequate standard of living)
implies
Y has an obligation (Y does not interfere (X has an adequate
standard of living)).

That would not be adequate because such a condition would not be sufficient for X to enjoy the standard of living to which he has a right. Such an obligation would give someone only the right to *try to attain* an adequate standard of living. But positive rights require more than noninterference.

We ought never to allow ourselves to speak of human rights unless we are prepared to state (1) whom the right is against, (2) what exactly is the content of their obligations to the right bearer, and (3) exactly why the person against whom the right exists is under those obligations. It seems to me I can make a case for the following as a minimal list of human rights: the right to life, including the right to personal safety, the right to own personal private property (such as clothing), the right to free speech, the right to associate freely with other people and to choose with whom one associates, the right to believe what one wants to believe, including religious beliefs as well as atheism, the right to travel, and the right to privacy.

If the existence of rights implies the existence of obligations, as I think is certainly the case, then where human rights are concerned, we need to make a fundamental distinction between negative and positive rights. I do not think we can make this distinction with absolute precision, but the intuitive idea is clear enough: negative rights such as the right to free speech obligate others to leave one alone. If I have the right to free speech, then you are under an obligation, as is everybody else, to let me exercise my free speech. Positive human rights such as, for example, the alleged right to adequate housing, impose an obligation on everybody else to provide everybody with adequate housing. The sorts of justifications that one could give for positive human rights seems to me quite different from that for negative rights. I think negative rights are fairly easy to justify. It is much harder to justify positive rights.

The United Nations Declaration of Human Rights, if we attempt to take it literally and seriously, has to be construed as an attempt to impose an obligation on every human being in the world, and I do not think that in the case of all the positive rights they have given us grounds for doing that. I need to make two clarifications immediately. First, it is important to distinguish between a decision by an actual government, let us say the State of California, to guarantee every citizen of the state a right to adequate housing, and to tax and spend so as to implement that right. Such a case is not a case of universal human rights but the rights of the citizens of a particular state as enacted by the legislative power of that state. The United Nations Declaration of Human Rights, on the other hand, is not the imposition of a state authority but rather an attempted imposition of a negative deontic power on every human being in the world. So interpreted, it would be outrageous. But it is so unintelligent that I do not suppose many people take it seriously. I do not think that the United Nations, nor anyone else, has done anything like justifying the claims made in the Declaration of Human Rights.

Second, it needs to be emphasized in the case of the positive rights that many of the "rights" in question would be perfectly legitimate if stated not as positive rights but simply negative rights entitling one to pursue the various aims that the positive rights purport to guarantee. Thus, I do not believe that everyone has a universal human right to adequate housing, but I think that everyone has a right to attempt to get adequate housing for themselves and their families. And that actually is a meaningful right because it means governments are under an obligation not to interfere with that right. And similarly with private property, when I say that everyone has a right to private property, I do not mean they have a right to specific objects, but rather they have a right to try to acquire and maintain possessions. How far one goes with that is, I think, a matter of considerable dispute. But that I am entitled to have property rights to the clothing I wear, the house I live in, and the car that I drive seems to me a legitimate claim of a negative right.

V. The Right to Free Speech

I said earlier that I thought one could make a case for a minimal list of absolute negative rights. In order to lead into that discussion, I want to examine a fundamental negative right, one which seems to be generally agreed on by just about every theory of human rights: the right to free speech and free expression. This discussion will also enable me to clarify the distinction between negative rights and positive rights. Why should society grant free speech? It seems to me that the actual arguments one sees for the right of free speech are notoriously weak. There are two types of argument. One is that the right to free speech was granted to us by God and is therefore necessarily valid. Another argument is that free speech is justified on utilitarian grounds. The most famous document presenting this position is Mill's "On Liberty."[7]

It is, by the way, an oddity of the United States that discussions of rights are often simply cut short by citing the constitutional provision in question. Thus, for many Americans the justification for the right to free speech is simply that it is guaranteed by the First Amendment of the Constitution. End of discussion. On this view the only thing wrong with slavery is that it violates the Thirteenth Amendment. I am assuming for the purpose of this discussion that neither of these is an adequate justification for the rights in question. It may be politically useful to be able to short-circuit discussions about rights in the United States, but it is not philosophically satisfactory. Similarly with appeals to God: if rights are a form of imposed status functions, then they have to be justified on rational grounds. I now propose to examine the justifications for the right to free speech.

Utilitarian justifications of rights are notoriously inadequate, and nowhere more inadequate than in the case of free speech. If my right to free speech derives from the fact that the exercise of my free speech conduces to the

7. Mill, John Stuart, *On Liberty and Other Essays,* New York: Oxford University Press, 1998.

greatest happiness of the greatest number, then the existence and exercise of that right are entirely dependent on certain facts about the greatest happiness of the greatest number. In cases in which I manifestly do not produce the greatest happiness of the greatest number by exercising free speech—for example, by saying things that are revolting and outrageous to the members of my community—I would lose the right to free speech. And that is an absurd result, so there must be something wrong with the theory. Furthermore, one cannot rescue the theory by appealing to rule utilitarianism. You can see this if you consider the standard cases of rules that have a utilitarian justification. I follow the rule of brushing my teeth twice a day on general utilitarian or consequentialist grounds. I am better off if I brush my teeth twice a day. But if for some special reason, brushing my teeth would have catastrophic consequences (suppose my teeth have suddenly become radioactively charged so that if I brush them today the city will blow up), then there is no *independent* force at all to the rule that I should brush my teeth. The question is simply one of weighing two sets of utilitarian considerations: my dental hygiene against the survival of the city. The rule has no *independent* force. It is simply a summary of a pattern of habitual utilitarian advantages.

Standardly, utilitarians have two answers to these sorts of objections. First they say, you cannot know what the consequences of violating the rule are; therefore, there has to be a presumption of keeping any rule that overall has a utilitarian justification. Even if it seems that the exercise of free speech in this case has bad utilitarian consequences, you can't really be sure. I will call this the epistemic argument. A second argument the utilitarians use is what I will call the trust argument. A rule such as the rule that gives people the right to free speech will function only if people can trust that such a rule will be respected. It will weaken trust in the rule if we fail to follow the rule granting free speech in cases where it seems repulsive to do so. The utilitarian advantages of the trust in the rule have to be added to the considerations concerning whether the rule should be overridden in a particular case.

Neither of these arguments is adequate. To answer the epistemic argument, simply imagine a case in which my epistemic situation is perfect, an occasion in which I know what the consequences will be. Such a case simply blocks the epistemic argument by fiat. The inadequacy of the epistemic argument is demonstrated by the thought experiment of imagining a case in which there is no epistemic difficulty, in which I have epistemically perfect knowledge. In such a case, my right to free speech is unaffected one way or another. The point about free speech is not an epistemic point. The argument from trust is also weak. The claim is that my right to free speech, in cases where my exercise of that right would give offense, is sustained by the fact that an abrogation of the right would weaken trust in the principle. But that makes the right contingent on a doubtful empirical hypothesis: that allowing the principle to be overridden would weaken it. But what about cases where it does not weaken it? As in the epistemic argument, we can simply, by fiat, consider such cases. The weakness in both of these arguments is the same: they fail to come to terms with the fact that the very existence of the right is a desire-independent reason for action, and the features that make it desire-independent also make it utilitarian-independent or consequence-independent. They fail, in short, to give any independent status to the right, and in failing to do so, they fail to grant that the right is a right.

So rule utilitarianism seems to me an inadequate effort to rescue utilitarianism from its obvious weaknesses.

Let us now turn to the actual justification of free speech. The first step is quite simple. We are speech-act performing animals. We are as much speech-act performing animals as we are animals that move about on two legs, or consume food and water, or inhale the earth's atmosphere. The right to free speech is a natural consequence of the fact that human beings are speech-act performing animals and the characteristic capacity of self-expression is innate to us as a species. Recognition of the right to free speech is in part a recognition of the centrality of this feature of our lives.

I said that this is the initial justification for free speech, but I do not think it is a sufficient justification. There are many other natural inclinations to which we do not accord rights. For example, adolescent human males apparently have a natural inclination to beat on other adolescent human males, presumably in their competition for females. But there is no right to beat each other up. What is special about free speech? I think the example of violence to others is not difficult to deal with, because the notion of such violence involves doing harm to others, and there is no way that one could have a right to do that without violating the rights of others. The concept of equality of rights forbids the notion of a right to do violence to others. However, we are still not out of the woods with this issue because there are lots of inclinations we have that do not harm others. An inclination, let us suppose, to take, enjoy, and become addicted to drugs. Do we have a right to do that? I am not going to try to settle the issue here, and I do not think it is a simple one. But the mere fact that we have a natural inclination to do something that does not harm others is not by itself a sufficient guarantee of a universal human right to do the thing in question.

But what then is special about free speech? I think the second feature that we need in our discussion of free speech is that we attach a special importance to our rational speech-act performing capacities. It is not just that we have an inclination to free speech, as we might have an inclination to suck our thumbs. But rather there is something that we think is especially valuable, something essential to our achieving our full potential as human beings, in the exercise of free speech. So we have to recognize at least two features in the right to free speech. The first is that we are speech-act performing animals, and the second is that there is something especially important or valuable about our speech-act performing capacities. There is an important implication of what I just said that I want to make completely clear: *the justification for human rights cannot be ethically neutral. It involves more than just a biological conception of what sorts of beings we are; it also involves a conception of what is valuable, actually or potentially, about our very existence.* I will come back to this point later.

The best way to argue in favor of the right to free speech as following from our nature as speech-act performing animals is to consider various arguments against the right to free speech. A currently fashionable argument goes as follows: according to the best theory of language, language is a form of action. Speech *acts*. But actions in speech, like any other actions, can be hurtful to other people, and therefore we have as much right to regulate speech acts as we do any other sorts of acts. Because my speech acts are capable of harming you, capable of harming others in general, society has a right, indeed an obligation, to place various restrictions on my right to free speech.

Speech acts are indeed a form of action; nonetheless, this argument is fallacious. Why? If I say something to you that you find hurtful, you may be just as much hurt as if I had hurt you physically by hitting you. All the same, there is an enormous difference. The crucial difference is that in the case of speech acts, the perlocutionary effects are psychological states of the hearer and not forms of physical damage. I may be annoyed, exasperated, infuriated, or simply hurt by what you say, but all the same, I am not bleeding and no bones are broken. This is the origin of the old children's adage about sticks and stones.

Furthermore, and this is equally important, the perlocutionary effects on the hearer are in large part up to the hearer. If I am annoyed, exasperated, infuriated, or simply hurt by what you say, there nonetheless is a gap between the reasons for my being annoyed, infuriated, exasperated, or hurt and the actual affective state that I feel. The special feature of speech acts, indeed, is that we are not only speech-act performing animals, but we are thereby rational animals. However offensive speech acts may be, one has the option of rational assessment of the speech acts in determining their perlocutionary effects. I can decide to ignore the speech act and not get upset. Again, speech, however offensive, is quite different from acts by which one is hit or tied up or otherwise physically impacted.

The cases in which it is not true that the perlocutionary effect is up to the hearer—that is, the cases in which there is no scope for rational operation—are precisely the sorts of cases for which lawyers, judges, and legislatures have tried to work out reasonable restrictions on free speech. These fall into two kinds. First, there are the cases where the perlocutionary effect could be catastrophic without any possibility of rational consideration. The standard clichéd example is shouting "Fire!" in a crowded theater. The second sort of case rests on the distinction between the perlocutionary effect on the actual target of the speech and the perlocutionary effects on other hearers and the effect that those may have on a particular individual. It is this feature of perlocutionary effects that leads to the laws of libel and slander. If you say something hostile *to* me it is in an important sense up to me how much I am hurt by this. But if you say something *about* me, which is entirely false and deliberately and maliciously false, to other people, this can do great damage to me in a way that is totally out of my control. This is the basis for laws against libel and slander. It seems to me that the laws of libel and slander, if anything, should be stronger in the United States than they are.

VI. Human Rights and Human Nature

Earlier I started to give a minimal list of negative universal human rights. So far I have listed the following: the right to life, including the right to personal safety; the right to own personal private property; the right to free speech; the right to associate freely with other people and to choose with whom one associates; the right to believe what one wants to believe, including religious beliefs as well as atheism; the right to travel; and the right to privacy. Are there any others? I think the list could be continued, and in an increasingly noisy world I would suggest the right to silence as a strong candidate for inclusion. Any theory of human rights must rest on a prior theory of human nature. The existence of a right is a matter of an imposition of a status function. But since the status functions in these cases do not derive from some other institution—such as property or money or marriage, where the purpose of the institution will automatically dictate the sorts of rights that are inherent in the institution—the justification for any rights that are assigned to beings solely in virtue of being human will have to depend on our conception of what a human being is. For this reason, I doubt that there will be a definite list of human rights that every reasonable person can ascribe to, any more than there would be a list of the definite goals of human life that every reasonable person can ascribe to.

For decades now it has been unfashionable to appeal to "human nature" in discussions of political and social philosophy. I think this is a very serious mistake. In this book, it is a requirement stemming from our acceptance of the basic facts, and indeed it follows from our conception of the basic requirement, that we should at every point try to consider the biological basis of what we are discussing. I do not think you can have an intelligent discussion about human rights without discussing certain biological characteristics of human beings, and the list that I have given is based on a combination of a certain conception of human nature and a certain conception about what is valuable in human life. I think I can justify my conception of human nature biologically, and I can at least argue for my conception of what I think is valuable in human life. These arguments, as is typical in ethics, are not demonstrative, in the sense that any rational person is bound to accept them on pain of irrationality. But from the fact that they have an element of epistemic subjectivity, it does not follow that they are arbitrary or beyond the scope of argument.

How do we now answer Bentham's claim that any genuine right has to be backed by a law? I think that argument can be refuted independently of any discussion of human rights. Law is itself a system of status functions and often provides sanctions for other status functions. But the validity of the status functions is not universally dependent on legal sanctions. There are lots of informal rights that one has that are not legally sanctioned. For example, on the conception of marriage that I and a large number of other people accept, in a marriage each spouse has a right to be consulted beforehand about any life-changing decisions on the part of the other spouse. If, for example, I am considering changing my profession or way of life, my spouse has a right to be consulted before I make any such decision and put it into effect. This is a perfectly valid right, even though there is no law that guarantees it.

VII. Are There Any Positive Rights?

I want to end this part of the discussion by considering a hypothesis that is not generally accepted in present debates. The hypothesis is that there are very few, if any, positive universal human rights. In the way that the right to life and the right to free speech are absolute universal human rights, there are very few such positive rights. And the reason for this is that the existence of a universal human right imposes an obligation on all human beings. It is one thing to impose the obligation on all human beings to leave other people alone with respect to certain actions, such as exercising their right to free speech, but quite another thing to impose an obligation on everyone, for example, to provide a good standard of living for everybody else. All that can mean, as I suggested earlier, is that it would be desirable if, or would be nice if, we could bring it about, but the notion of a universal human right involves a certain sort of deontic claim: an obligation on all human beings. Consequently, in the way that there is an inventory of absolute negative rights—the right to freedom of speech, the right to freedom of religion, the right to free movement, the right to life—there are in that way no such positive rights as the right to a comfortable standard of living, the right to higher education, and the right to free medical care. I want to make absolutely clear what I am maintaining. If the State of California or any other political entity wants to guarantee all of its citizens the right to free medical care and the right to good housing, that seems to me a legitimate exercise of state power. Rights and obligations become matters of statutory law. But the claim we are considering is different. It is that there are universal human rights imposing obligations on all human beings, that such and such positive actions have to be performed. And I am saying there are very few such positive rights. As a matter of fact, prosperous countries send huge amounts of aid to undeveloped countries, but those are gifts rather than obligations due to human rights.

The only examples of absolute, universal human positive rights I can think of would involve situations in which the humans in question are unable to fend for themselves. Thus infants and small children have a right to care, feeding, housing, and so on, and similarly, people who are incapacitated due to injury, senility, illness, or other causes also have absolute rights to care. The principle that makes these different from other putative positive absolute rights is that in each of these cases, the right in question is necessary for the maintenance of any form of human life at all, unlike the right to higher education or decent living accommodations. The suggestion I am making here is that there is indeed a universal obligation to help other people when their very survival is at stake and they have no way of helping themselves. But even this obligation exists only relative to specific situational features. So, for example, if a child is injured in front of my house and will die unless I help her, the child does indeed have a universal right and I have an obligation to help her. But sitting in Berkeley, I have no such obligation to help all injured children in the world. So a formulation of this as an absolute universal human right would have to be something like the following: there is a universal human right to be helped by others in desperate situations when one is unable to help oneself and when others are so situated as to be able to help one.

An objection that some people make to my account is the following: you cannot make a clear distinction between negative and positive rights because sometimes the implementation of the negative right requires enormous and costly positive efforts on the part of the community. Thus, for example, in a famous case in Skokie, Illinois, the implementation of free speech rights for a fascist-style demonstration required enormous cost to the state in the expenses for police and National Guard to protect the demonstrators. Public opposition was so great that it took considerable police and National Guard forces to guarantee the right of free expression. I appreciate the force of this objection, but I think there is a response to it. There will indeed be cases when the exercise of the negative right is expensive for the community, and one may have to decide what sorts of considerations will restrict the *implementation* of the negative right. But there is nothing in the very content of the right itself that requires a positive effort on the part of the community, only the requirement that the exercisers of the right be left alone to exercise their right. In the case of positive rights, however, it is part of the very essence of the right, part of the very content of the right, that it requires costly efforts from all the members of humanity. That is where it seems to me the big difference lies.

Before concluding I need to make a number of important philosophical points and clarifications.

VIII. Pragmatic Considerations of the Formulation of Rights

On my account we will be inclined to specify certain features of human life as rights even though they are no more central to human life than certain other things that we do not think are worth bothering to specify as rights. So, for example, the right to move my arms about as I like, and to move my body into any positions I like, to breathe as deeply or as shallowly as I like, and walk about as I like are, I think, fundamental to human life. They are probably less important than speaking, but still very important. Why then do we think that freedom of bodily movement and position is less likely to be listed on an inventory of human rights than the right to free speech? The answer I think is that the position of my body does not affect other people and is not as potentially offensive as the exercise of my free speech, and is therefore less likely to be interfered with, and so is less in need of explicit protection.

We have practical or pragmatic reasons for listing such things as the freedom of travel across national borders, or the freedom to express opinions, as basic human rights, because they are more likely to need protection, whereas such things as the freedom to eat the food one wants, or the freedom to sit in the posture one wants, or to walk about in the way that one wants need not be listed as human rights, though they are just as fundamental. The point I am making, in short, is that the inventory of human rights will tend to be shaped by practical or pragmatic considerations. The things that are likely to be challenged by us are more likely to be listed as human rights than things that do not bother anybody. Freedom of speech is rightly listed in the Constitution. Freedom of walking is hardly worth bothering to list.[8] Given the general noisiness of contemporary life, I have suggested that we might recognize a universal right to silence. In tacit recognition, many cities already have laws that prohibit loud noise after a certain time of night. I like the idea, but the point for the present discussion is that it illustrates the historically contingent, pragmatic character of what we count as a basic human right.

IX. Five Common Logical Mistakes about Rights: Absolute Rights versus Conditional Rights versus Prima Facie Rights

There are a number of logical and conceptual confusions that infect discussions of human rights, both among philosophers and among the public at large.

---

8. Of course, if such simple things are regulated by, for instance, religious edicts, one might insist on a right to travel on the Sabbath, the right to eat meat, the right not to wear the burka, and the right not to pray.

Typically, these confusions stem from a misunderstanding of the logical nature of a *conflict* of rights. Rights in their exercise typically involve possible conflicts with other considerations of human values—indeed, with other considerations of life. So, for example, I have a right to free speech, but famously, this right does not entitle me to shout "Fire!" in a crowded theater. In this case my right to free speech comes in conflict with other rights, such as other people's right to safety. Legislatures and constitutional lawyers and judges have spent a lot of time working out some sort of practical basis for making decisions as to when one's right may justifiably be overridden by other considerations. It is a natural feature of any sets of values, especially moral values, that they are inherently subject to the possibility of conflict, and in consequence, any theory of values must allow for the possibility of conflict. In philosophy there are several famous sorts of mistakes that people make about these conflicts.

First, some people think that if the right in question can be overridden by utilitarian considerations then it follows that the basis of the right was utilitarian in the first place. That is a mistake. The right is in no way a utilitarian right simply because it might be overridden by utilitarian considerations. The deontology of the right may come in conflict with nondeontic values, but that does not show that the deontology was itself nondeontic. One's right to free speech may be restricted if it presents certain sorts of clear and present dangers, and these considerations may be entirely utilitarian. But it does not follow from the possibility of these restrictions that the right to free speech was a utilitarian and not a deontic right.

A second, deeper, but equally common mistake is to suppose that when a right is overridden by some other consideration, this shows that somehow the right in question was not *absolute*, but merely *prima facie*. That conclusion does not follow. Two absolute rights may easily conflict with each other. My right to free speech and your right to privacy may come in conflict, and the fact that we have to adjudicate these in favor of one side or the other does not show that the rights were not absolute, but merely prima facie. One of the most confused notions in philosophy is the notion of prima facie rights, obligations, and so on.[9] "Prima facie" is an epistemic sentence modifier used in the law. It means, "on the face of it there is evidence to suggest that..."

9. For further discussion of this point, see Searle, John R., "Prima Facie Obligations," in Joseph Raz (ed.), *Practical Reasoning,* Oxford: Oxford University Press, 1978, 81–90.

Thus, if you have a prima facie case, on the face of it the evidence suggests that you have a valid case. But "prima facie" does not name a type of right, obligation, or anything else.

It makes no sense to oppose absolute rights to prima facie rights, but it does make sense to oppose absolute rights to conditional rights, and the confusion between them is a third sort of mistake commonly made in discussions of rights. For example, the right to free speech is absolute, but the right to cross-examine witnesses is conditional. I have the right to cross-examine witnesses against me but only on the condition that I am in a trial, civil or criminal, in which I am the defendant. I do not have the right to cross-examine people who say bad things about me by way of gossiping on the plaza. My right to cross-examine witnesses is literally a conditional right, conditional on my being in certain sorts of institutional structures, but my right to free speech and my right to life are not in that way conditional. They are absolute rights even though they may on occasion conflict with other rights and other values, both conditional and unconditional.

It is very important to emphasize this point. In the great debates about free speech that occurred in the 1960s, the authorities were frequently anxious to insist that the right to free speech was "not absolute." What they meant was that you can override the right to free speech on various utilitarian grounds. But the right to free speech is indeed absolute. You cannot get more absolute rights than free speech and the right to life. The point, however, is that they can conflict with other considerations, including the exercise of other rights. This does not make them any less absolute, nor does it make them conditional.

A fourth common mistake about rights is to suppose that if you have a right to do something, then it must be something that is all right to do, that the existence of a right means that the act performed under that right is thereby valid. But this is a gross mistake. For reasons of the practical organization of human society, it is necessary to give people a wider scope of rights than it would be acceptable for them to actually exercise. A common form of this mistake during the periods of university unrest in the United States was that professors would sometimes say that it was all right for them to use their classroom as a political organizing forum because academic freedom gave them the right to do it. Academic freedom gave them the right to a great deal of autonomy concerning what goes on in the classroom, but the fact that they had that autonomy does not mean that anything they do is thereby acceptable. The fact that something is done under a right does not imply that it is all right to do it.

There is a fifth common mistake about rights that is also worth mention-ing. Some people suppose that when some right or obligation is in conflict with some other value and is overridden by this other value, that somehow or other the recognition of this overriding value brings about a change in the conception of the original right or obligation. Even such a good philosopher as Rawls made this mistake when he said the fact that we recognize that the obligation to keep a promise can be overridden shows that we are changing the rules of promising when we make the recognition.[10] We are not. The fact that there is a ceteris paribus condition in the application of all of these deontic powers does not show that when we make explicit the other-things-being-equal considerations we are changing the constitutive rules that give rise to the deontic power in the first place.

X. Conclusion

My conclusion of this all too brief discussion is that it makes perfectly good sense to speak of universal human rights, and that there is no logical obstacle to treating the fact of being human as a status to which status functions can be attached. Among these status functions are the deontic powers named by human rights. A completely naturalistic conception of human life and society is consistent with a belief in the existence of universal human rights, in the same way that it is consistent with a belief in the existence of money, private property, and governments. I further claim that any attempt to justify human rights and to create a specific list of human rights will require both a conception of human nature and a certain set of values. Discussions of human rights cannot, on my account, be ethically neutral. This does not mean that they are arbitrary, or that anything goes. I think that I can provide reasons for supposing that the right to free speech should be recognized as a valid universal human right, even though in fact it is only cherished in certain very special sorts of communities and cultures. The fact that its justification will be relative to a set of criteria that are not universally shared does not make those criteria arbitrary or invalid.

10. Rawls, John, "Two Concepts of Rules," *Philosophical Review* 64 (1955): 3–32.

APPENDIX

For those who like their logical relations spelled out in quantificational form, I enclose a brief summary. Each formula is accompanied by a paraphrase in ordinary English.

Universal Human Rights

($\forall$x) (biologically human x $\rightarrow$ x has status S (because of S, x has UHR (x does A))

Anything that is biologically human thereby has a human status and because of that status has a universal right to perform a certain sort of action.

Negative Universal Human Rights

($\forall$x) (x has NegUHR (x does A) $\rightarrow$ ($\forall$y) (y is under an obligation (y does not interfere with (x does A))))

If anyone has a negative universal right to perform a certain sort of act then everyone else is under an obligation not to interfere with the performance of that act.

Positive Universal Human Rights

($\forall$x) (x has PosUHR (x does A) $\rightarrow$ ($\forall$y) (y is under an obligation (y takes action to guarantee (x does A))))

If anyone has a positive universal human right to perform a certain sort of act then every other human being is under an obligation to take action to guarantee that the person performs that sort of act.

CONCLUDING REMARKS:
THE ONTOLOGICAL FOUNDATIONS
OF THE SOCIAL SCIENCES

Suppose I am right that human society is largely constituted by distinctive institutional structures that create and distribute deontic power relationships by assigning status functions, and with those status functions differing social roles, in the society. What implications, if any, does that account have for actual research in the social sciences? I guess the short answer is that I don't really know. It is impossible to tell in advance what is going to be useful for actual research. It seems that there are many areas of social science research in which, at least in principle, it is not necessary to understand the foundational issues. So, for example, when I lectured on these subjects at the Memorial for Pierre Bourdieu in Paris, one of the other participants, an American sociologist specializing in the sociology of labor unions, told me that his work began where mine ended. And I take it he meant that it is not necessary for him to know the ontological foundations of trade unionism. All he has to understand is the actual operations of particular historically situated organizations. The picture I think he had was that, just as a geologist might study the movements of tectonic plates without understanding the details of atomic physics, so he might study the movements of trade unions without understanding the details of social ontology. He may be right about that. My instinct, though, is to think that it is always a good idea to understand the foundational issues. It is much more plausible to me to think that an understanding of the basic ontology of any discipline will deepen the understanding of issues within that discipline. In any case, I am not in this book attempting to provide a philosophy of existing social sciences but to offer a logical analysis of the fundamental ontology of the entities studied by the social sciences. This may—or may not—prove useful to the social sciences of the future.

When I studied economics as an undergraduate at Oxford, none of my teachers worried about the ontological presuppositions of the investigation. We were taught that Savings equals Investment (S = I) in the same tone of voice that in physics one would be taught that Force equals Mass times Acceleration (F = MA). We discovered that marginal cost equals marginal revenue in the same way that one might discover that water is composed of hydrogen and oxygen. Economic realities were treated as part of the realities of the scientifically investigatable world. Earlier, when I took a course in sociology at Wisconsin, there was no mention of the foundational ontological issues. As I said earlier, I think it is sometimes possible to do good research without worrying about the ontological issues, but the whole investigation gets a greater depth if one is acutely conscious of the ontology of the phenomena being investigated. It is, for example, a mistake to treat money and other such instruments as if they were natural phenomena like the phenomena studied in physics, chemistry, and biology. The recent economic crisis makes it clear that they are products of massive fantasy. As long as everyone shares the fantasy and has confidence in it, the system will work just fine. But when some of the fantasies cease to be believable, as happened with the subprime mortgage instruments, then the whole system begins to unravel. I welcome the recent revival of interest in institutional economics.[1]

This book makes (at least) three very strong claims. It is important to state them in as strong a version as possible because that makes them easier to refute. The three claims are first, all of human institutional reality, and in that sense nearly all of human civilization, is created in its initial existence and maintained in its continued existence by a single, logico-linguistic operation. Second, we can state exactly what that operation is. It is a Status Function Declaration. And third, the enormous diversity and complexity of human civilization is explained by the fact that that operation is not restricted in subject matter and can be applied over and over in a recursive fashion, is often applied to the outcomes of earlier applications and with various and interlocking subject matters, to create all of the complex structures of actual human societies.

A consequence of the investigation is that all of human social–institutional reality has a common underlying structure. Now if this is right, it is a mistake

---

1. Lawson, Tony, *Economics and Reality*, New York: Routledge, 1997.

to treat different branches of the social sciences, such as sociology and economics, for example, as if they dealt with fundamentally different subject matters. The different social sciences ought to be completely transparent to each other. All the strange and wonderful diverse human institutions are cases of shaping and reshaping the distribution of power by repeated applications of specific forms of linguistic representation, Status Function Declarations. I considered earlier the possibility that maybe one does not have to know much atomic physics to be a good geologist. All the same, in all natural sciences you have to understand that everything has an atomic structure. I am suggesting that a full understanding of the ontology of the subjects studied by the social sciences requires an understanding of the structure I have tried to describe.

I would not wish to overdraw the analogy between the social sciences and the natural sciences; there is nothing reductionist about my account. But if the account is correct, then all of the different social sciences are dealing with a power structure common to all of social reality, and I have tried to describe the basic mechanisms by which that power structure is created and maintained.

SUBJECT INDEX

NAME INDEX

Andersson, A., 21–22, 116n12, 145n, 155
Andrade, R., 21n, 22n11, 116n11
Aristotle, 62, 109, 135
Austin, J., 6, 16

Bentham, J., 153, 175, 175n, 182, 183, 192
Bratman, M., 46, 46n3
Bourdieu, P., 62

Carnap, R., 6
Chomsky, N., 65

Danto, A., 37n7
Davidson, D., 61
DeSoto, H., 116n
Dummett, M., 61
Durkheim, É., 62, 105n, 154

Eccles, J. C., 4n

Feinberg, J., 37n7
Fitch, T., 65
Frege, G., 5, 6, 77
Friedman, J., 21
Foucault, M., 62, 145n, 152–54, 155

Gilbert, M., 45n
Grice, P., 75, 75n, 83, 83n11
Grotius, H., 180

Habermas, J., 62
Hauser, M., 65
Heidegger, M., 159
Hempel, P., 5
Hudin, J., 8, 57n11, 58nn12–13
Hume, D., 130, 130n3, 131, 142
Hunt, L., 180nn4–5

Kant, I., 5

Lawson, T., 201n
Ledayev, V. G., 145n, 147n3
Leibniz, G., 133
Lewis, D., 83, 83n12
Lukes, S., 145n, 147n4, 149, 149n5, 153n, 154n9

MacIntyre, A., 175, 176n, 182, 183
Marx, K., 107, 107n7
Mill, J. S., 187n
Miller, S., 46, 46n, 81
Moural, J., 180

Nagel, T., 127n

Passinsky, A., 58n12, 113n

Quine, W.V.O., 119

Rakoczy, H., 121
Rawls, J., 134, 134n, 198, 198n